The Bible and Christianity in the Scientific Perspective

Compliments of the Author

The Bible and Christianity in the Scientific Perspective

BYUNG KOOK HWANG

Forewords by Wolf-Dieter Ibenthal and Hyun Chul Paul Kim

RESOURCE *Publications* · Eugene, Oregon

THE BIBLE AND CHRISTIANITY IN THE SCIENTIFIC PERSPECTIVE

Copyright © 2025 Byung Kook Hwang. All rights reserved. Except for brief quotations in critical publications or reviews, no part of this book may be reproduced in any manner without prior written permission from the publisher. Write: Permissions, Wipf and Stock Publishers, 199 W. 8th Ave., Suite 3, Eugene, OR 97401.

Resource Publications
An Imprint of Wipf and Stock Publishers
199 W. 8th Ave., Suite 3
Eugene, OR 97401

www.wipfandstock.com

PAPERBACK ISBN: 979-8-3852-5346-3
HARDCOVER ISBN: 979-8-3852-5347-0
EBOOK ISBN: 979-8-3852-5348-7
VERSION NUMBER 08/28/25

Originally published by Tangerine Tree Publishers in 2021. Published in German by Bernardus-Verlag in 2023.

Contents

About the Author | vii
Author's Words | ix
Foreword by Wolf-Dieter Ibenthal | xiii
Foreword by Hyun Chul Paul Kim | xv
Prologue: Let's Get to Know the Bible and Christianity Properly and Anew | xvii

Part I: Understanding the Bible

1. The Meaning and Origin of the Bible | 3
2. The Structure of the Bible | 6
3. Scientific Understanding of the Essence of God | 14
4. God and the Kingdom of God | 20
5. Jesus Is the Messiah and the Life | 29
6. What Is Faith | 40
7. What Is Sin | 51
8. Harmony of Law and Grace | 58
9. What Is the Gospel | 68
10. What Is Salvation | 82

Part II: Understanding Christianity

1. The Origins and History of Christianity | 97
2. Christian Thought: God, Jesus, and the Holy Spirit | 106
3. The Main Points of the Christian Faith | 114
4. The Bible, Christianity, and Science | 134
5. Guidelines for the Christian Life | 147

Epilogue: The Bible and Christianity Make Our Lives Peaceful and Prosperous | 154

About the Author

BORN IN 1947, HWANG grew up in the countryside. He studied at Seoul National University, where he received his bachelor's and master's degrees, and then went to Germany to earn his PhD at the University of Göttingen in 1981. He is currently an emeritus professor in the College of Life Sciences and Technology at Korea University, a member of the National Academy of Sciences of the Republic of Korea, a life member of the Korean Academy of Sciences and Technology, and a fellow of the American Phytopathological Society.

Since 1982, he has been attending church and practicing as a Christian layman. Since 2008, he has been immersed in the Bible and Christianity and has been engaged in biblical and theological research. Based on his youthful experience of the biblical and Christian life of the German people in Germany, his lifelong interaction with the German people, and his life as a life scientist, he spent a decade writing *The Bible and Christianity in the Scientific Perspective* (알기 쉬운 성경과 기독교의 이해) in Korean. This book provides an easy-to-understand explanation of what a practical life of faith according to the Bible is and the way forward for Korean Christianity to be reborn in this era.

About the Author

He has been a professor in the College of Life Sciences and Technology at Korea University for thirty-one years, and from 1988–89, he was a visiting professor at the University of Göttingen, Germany, as a Humboldt Foundation scholar. He has served as president of the Korean Society of Plant Pathology and director of the Institute of Life Sciences and Resources at Korea University. His books include *Phytomedicine* and *Plant Health*. He has published 191 research papers in international journals in the field of phytomedicine in the life sciences and obtained fifty-seven domestic and foreign patents. In 2007, he received the Samil (3.1) Culture Research Award in Korea. He is currently an editor of the international journals *Planta* and *Journal of Phytopathology*.

Author's Words

RELIGION PROVIDES COMFORT AND peace to people in the modern world who are mentally exhausted. For this reason, modern people seek religion. The Bible and Christianity can bring peace and enrichment to our lives. If we truly believe in the God and Jesus Christ of the Bible and live according to the Bible, our lives will be filled with joy and gratitude. I don't have a deep faith in Christianity. However, while learning the Bible deeply, as a life scientist, I wanted to write a book about the Bible and Christianity in a way that would be understandable to the general public. This desire led me to immerse myself in the Bible for more than a decade, to study and reflect on it, and to write this book. In this book, I tried to analyze logically and scientifically the profound revelation and true meaning of God hidden in the word of God in the Bible. I hope that this humble book will help Christians, people of other religions, and even non-religious people to correctly and newly understand the Bible and Christianity. Moreover, it would be great if Christians, who are living under the grace of God, read this book more than non-Christians.

I was born in a traditional, strict Confucian family and grew up in the countryside with mountains, fields, and nature. After being an atheist, I have been attending church since the age of 35, encountering Christianity, reading the Bible, and deepening my understanding of the Bible and Christianity. I went to Germany in 1976 and studied abroad as a single student in the field of life sciences at the University of Göttingen in Germany until 1981. During this time, I was able to live with Germans and immerse myself in the Christian culture of Europe. Later, I continued my research at the University of Göttingen as a visiting professor of the Humboldt Foundation in Germany from 1988–89. Even today, I continue to experience the Christian life of the German people through my interactions with them. After

Author's Words

completing my PhD, I returned to Korea from Germany, met my current wife of maternal faith, married her in 1982, and started attending church as a promise to my wife. As a life scientist, I have served as a professor at Korea University since 1981, faithfully conducting research and teaching in the field of plant immunology in the molecular life sciences. After retiring from the university in 2012, I continue to work with junior professors as an emeritus professor at Korea University, studying the Bible diligently, attending church, and living a life of faith.

The Bible is a testimony about Jesus Christ, and we study the Bible diligently because we believe that we can obtain eternal life from it (John 5:39). By God's grace we receive the gift of eternal life, and grace comes through the Lord Jesus Christ. The Bible contains God's word of truth. It gives us wisdom for salvation through faith that is in Christ Jesus (2 Tim 3:15). When we listen to, obey, and follow the words of God and Jesus Christ in the Bible, we begin to resemble Jesus, and God's love and grace are poured into our lives. The most valuable thing you can get from the Christian faith is the peace of mind you get through faith in God and Jesus Christ. God is the God of peace (1 Thess 5:23). Jesus said, "Behold, I stand at the door and knock; if anyone hears my voice and opens the door, I will come in to him and eat with him, and he with me" (Rev 3:20). "Peace I leave with you. My peace I give unto you: not as the world gives, give I unto you. Let not your heart be troubled, neither let it be afraid" (John 14:27). Christians who believe in Jesus Christ and live a life of grace are free from anxiety and worry and are always at peace.

The Bible contains the words of God and Jesus Christ, written between 3,500 years ago (Old Testament) and 2,000 years ago (New Testament). As such, the Bible is a complete book with a long history and no revisions. The Bible is not a philosophy book, but it is very logical, and it is not a science book, but it is very scientific. The Bible also contains the truth and wisdom needed for human life based on the laws of the universe, making it the best guide for humanity to read. Good Christian books about the Bible contain theological reflection, civilizational history, and scientific understanding based on biblical arguments.

Christianity is a religion of love, life, and grace, based on faith in God and Jesus Christ, with practice. The Bible says, "For just as the body without the spirit is dead, so also faith without works is dead" (Jas 2:26). You can't say you believe in God without doing something. Faith without works is vain and pretentious. "I will show you my faith by my works" (Jas 2:18).

Author's Words

Works are the evidence of true faith. What are works? True works are living righteously and well, according to the will and word of God and Jesus Christ. A true Christian believes the words and gospel of God and Jesus in the Bible and puts it into practice. By God's grace, true believers love their neighbors and live in peace, always with joy and gratitude.

The Korean version of the Bible read today is often mistranslated and written in a way that makes it difficult for the ordinary person to understand what the Bible says. Many church (cathedral) pastors tell Christian believers, "Don't read the Bible critically, but if you obey God and believe well, you will be saved and go to the kingdom of God." In other words, believers must believe blindly. For this reason, laypeople often go to church or cathedral to listen to pastors' sermons and try to understand the Bible literally, rather than reading the Bible correctly. As a result, even devout Christians often misunderstand the meaning of God's words in the Bible and have many questions about their faith. In light of this, more accessible translations of the Bible should be widely available to make it easier for laypeople to read the Bible. Furthermore, I hope that many books on the Bible and Christian doctrine will be published so that people can easily understand the Bible and Christianity and have a correct Christian view. Knowing exactly who God is and who Jesus is, understanding the Bible and Christianity correctly, and believing in them correctly will change your life. Moreover, a true Christian culture can be established in Korea only if there are many true Christians who live a practical life according to God's word.

The Bible and Christianity have developed Western civilization and made European countries advanced welfare states, bringing peace and happiness. As a young man, I lived in Germany, a developed welfare state with a truly biblical and Christian way of life. I could not have written this book without deepening my experience of European Christian culture by living with Germans. German life in all areas of education, society, politics, economy, culture, and science is based on the Bible and Christianity. Germans living in a Christian culture are honest, rational, practical, accurate, sincere, thrifty, and promise-keeping. This practical German character is shaped by the fact that Germans live according to God's word and the Bible. Also, I could not have written this book from a scientific point of view without my entire life as a life scientist. The Bible speaks deeply about the universe, nature, and life phenomena related to human life. The profound spiritual meaning of the Bible, which is difficult to find in a literal reading, is interpreted scientifically in this book to make it for the general public easier to understand.

Author's Words

I am not a church pastor or theologian. However, I studied in Germany, the home of the Reformation of the Christian faith, and interacted with scientists living in Germany. While reading, comparing, and analyzing the Korean and English versions of the Bible, I have written the book *Understanding the Bible and Christianity* (알기 쉬운 성경과 기독교의 이해) over the course of a decade. While writing this book, I listened to the GOOD TV video sermons from various pastors, read many Bibles and Christian books, and spent much time in theological reflection. The fundamental purpose of writing this book is to help Christians and the general publics understand the Bible and Christianity in a way that makes sense. However, I do not intend this book to criticize the Bible or Christianity itself. Through this book, I hope that Christians will understand the Bible and Christianity correctly and anew, so that they can live a truly Christian life with true faith, and that the Christianity of love, life, and grace will spread to the ends of the earth.

As I close this book, I sincerely repent that I have neglected to attend church and practice a faith based on the word of God and the Bible. With the motto "believing right makes a difference to my life," I will live the rest of my life with a true faith that resembles Jesus Christ. First, I would like to express my gratitude to my eternal life partner, Professor Jae-Young Yoon, who allowed me to stay in a world of solitary theological contemplation about the Bible and Christianity until this book came out. She is married to me and has been patiently waiting and watching to help me grow closer to God and Jesus Christ. I would also like to pass this book on to my eternal friend Dr. Wolf-Dieter Ibenthal, who now lives in Germany. Dr. Ibenthal studied with me at the University of Göttingen and has been a constant in my life for more than forty years, showing me an unchanging picture of the true German life. Dr. Ibenthal served as translator for the German edition of my book *The Bibel und das Christentum aus wissenschaftlicher Sicht* (Bernardus-Verlag, 2023). I also thank Dr. Ibenthal and Dr. Hyun Chul Paul Kim for writing the foreword to this book. Furthermore, I would like to express my sincere gratitude to the staff of Wipf and Stock Publishers for their efforts in designing, editing, typesetting, and printing this book in English. Finally, I give glory and thanks to God, who has guided me to write this book and has given me spiritual inspiration, grace, and blessings in abundance.

Byung Kook Hwang
July 7, 2025
Seoul, Republic of Korea

Foreword

THE SPECIAL PATH OF life often leads to highly creative achievements of the human spirit. In Christian ethics, this is often referred to as divine destiny or divine providence. My semantic understanding suggests the term "divine providence." In this book, Dr. Byung Kook Hwang, who studied life sciences with me in a divinely fated encounter at the University of Göttingen in Germany in the 1970s, explains the deep spiritual meaning of the Bible in a logical and scientific manner based on his profound understanding of life sciences. The cell, the basic unit of life created by God, is commonly referred to as a microcosm. Just as God controls the universe and all things in it, DNA controls life phenomena within cells. Interestingly, the author scientifically compares and analyzes the essence of the Trinity God (Father, Son, and Holy Spirit) in the Bible with the essence of life, DNA, messenger RNA, and proteins, explaining the Christian doctrine of the Trinity in an easy-to-understand manner. The essence of God is spirit. Genesis 1:2, written around 1450 BC, reveals the existence of water on earth and the fact that water is the reservoir of God's spirit. The connection between spirit, water, and life explains the true meaning of baptism. The author also analyzes the relationship between the Bible and science to help scientists in their creative research. Furthermore, this book analyzes the basic ideas and principles of the Bible and Christianity from a life science perspective in an easy-to-understand manner. It is recommended as a must-read book for Christians, non-Christians, and non-religious people to properly understand the Bible and Christianity. Finally, it is hoped that this book will be

Foreword

widely distributed in English-speaking countries, so that the gospel of Jesus Christ will be spread to the ends of the earth.

Dr. Wolf-Dieter Ibenthal,
Department of Biology,
University of Hamburg, Germany

Foreword

"THE BIBLE IS NOT a history book, but it is written historically. It is not a philosophy book, but it is written philosophically. The Bible is not a literature book, but it is written in a literary and entertaining style. The Bible is not a science book, but it is written scientifically and contains scientific facts. Therefore, the Bible contains a variety of readings that can provide spiritual nourishment for people in the world, whether they are Christians or not, to live wisely." (Excerpt from *The Bible and Christianity in the Scientific Perspective*)

To many people, the Bible and science seem to be opposites, far apart in their contents and relevance. Dr. Byung Kook Hwang, a life scientist, makes an audacious effort to bridge such a wide chasm. This book explores the reading of the Bible from multidimensional angles, especially from the perspective of a scientist, while providing an informative, accessible, and reader-friendly guide. Chapter 1, "Understanding the Bible," expounds foundational contents and themes of the Bible, such as the law, grace, faith, sin, works, salvation, and discipleship. Chapter 2, "Understanding Christianity," revisits the essence and significance of Christianity with regard to analogous scientific theories and their applications to today's world. Readers will learn how DNA represents cells as microcosms in God's creation, as humans were created in the image of God. Law entails righteousness, while grace is rooted in divine love. These two connect the two covenants and require Christians not to neglect observing the law. Thus, true faith must be accompanied by righteous actions led by repentance and honesty, which are far more important than self-centered prayer or empty praise. Reasserting how Christianity is ultimately rooted in divine love and human compassion

Foreword

to our neighbors, this concise book delivers a paramount wake-up call to the churches and Christians in Korea and around the world.

Dr. Hyun Chul Paul Kim,
Methodist Theological School in Ohio (MTSO),
USA

Prologue

Let's Get to Know the Bible and Christianity Properly and Anew

RELIGION HAS PLAYED A vital role in human history and life. Religion is necessary to resolve human anguish and spiritually heal the sickness of the heart, and it brings comfort and peace to human life. Religion gives universal consciousness and rational wisdom to the people of the world. The reason that all religions exist is that humans live in the world to control their physical lusts and desires religiously, so that they can live peacefully with joy and gratitude at all times. By believing in an almighty God or the words of Jesus, Buddha, Confucius, etc., religion enables us to abandon our greed and desires through self-discipline and to develop a good heart, a heart of compassion (惻隱之心), that has pity for others. In this way, religious people are helping to build a healthy society where people want less, give to others, and live together with consideration.

The Bible is mankind's greatest scripture, a logical and scientifically complete record of human life from the beginning of time to 100 AD, along with the revelations and words of God (Jesus). The Bible provides mankind with spiritual nourishment and wisdom to insight into the source and motives of human life and to live in peace in relationship with God. Christianity is a religion of practice that believes in God and Jesus Christ and is based on the Bible, which contains the words of God and Jesus. Christianity arose around the 1st century in the historical context of Israel, based on the teachings and gospel of Jesus the Messiah and the evangelistic mission of Jesus' apostles. Christianity is the world's largest religion and can be divided into the Roman Catholic Church, Protestantism, and the Eastern Orthodox Church. The substitutionary crucifixion and resurrection of Jesus in the New Testament is central to the Christian faith. Christianity is based on both the Old and New Testaments, but the New Testament is more fundamental to the faith.

The life, grace, and love of Jesus Christ in the New Testament are the central ideas of Christianity. Christianity exhorts people to believe in and worship God and Jesus Christ and to live a practical life in accordance with God's Word (will). In the Bible, God and Jesus Christ are the very idea of Christianity. In the beginning was the Word, and the Word was God (John 1:1). In him was life, and that life was the light of men (John 1:4). By the Word, he made all things (John 1:3). God's Word is eternal and unchanging. The Bible says, "And the Word became flesh and dwelt among us" (John 1:14). This means that we have Jesus Christ in us as the God of the Word. God is Word, life, and love (John 1:1–4; 1 John 4:16). Furthermore, God (Jesus) is the way, the truth, and the life (John 14:6). And God's grace has come through Jesus Christ (John 1:17). Grace is a gift from God.

In the 16th century, German Martin Luther (1483–1546) advocated the Reformation idea that "therefore being justified by faith" (Rom 5:1). It is the Christian doctrine that sinners are justified by faith in Jesus Christ alone, and it is based on God's grace. Furthermore, God is a God of justice and love. God is a God of justice (Ps 89:14), meaning he is righteous and just (Deut 32:4). God is also a God of love (1 John 4:16). The Bible says, "The one who does not love does not know God, for God is love" (1 John 4:8). God's love is poured out into our hearts by the Holy Spirit (Rom 5:5). Today is the age of the Holy Spirit. God's love is merciful and infinite. It reigns by grace through righteousness, leading to eternal life through Jesus Christ (Rom 5:21). And when we are with God, obeying and believing, we have peace of mind and God's grace. For God is the God of peace (1 Thess 5:23). Jesus said, "Peace I leave with you, my peace I give to you; not as the world gives, let not your hearts be troubled, neither let them be afraid" (John 14:27). After his resurrection, Jesus repeatedly told his disciples, "Peace be with you" (Luke 24:36; John 20:19). The ultimate goal of human life is peace. It's what we live for in the Christian faith. The Bible says, "So do not fear, for I am with you; do not be dismayed, for I am your God. I will strengthen you and help you" (Isa 41:10). Christians have God with them at all times in their lives.

Let's Get to Know the Bible and Christianity Properly and Anew

If we are to understand the Bible and Christianity correctly, we must first know exactly *what the nature of God is* and *who God is*. In the beginning, God created the heavens and the earth, all things, and man (Gen 1). The God of the Bible is creator, sovereign, and perfect. "In the beginning was the Word. And the Word is God" (John 1:1). The Bible explains God's Word in terms of the law of the universe and nature, that is, the way of heaven (天道). God created all things and established the laws of the universe, by which the universe operates accurately and perfectly. This description of God in the Bible is a common definition of God that you may encounter when reading the Bible. Interestingly, however, if we make a scientific comparison between the nature of God and the DNA of living things, we can easily understand the nature and power of God. In general, the cell, the basic unit of life created by God, is called a microcosmos. The essence of God is spirit; that is, God is spirit (John 4:24). The cells of living things divide and multiply under the sovereign control of DNA to create life. DNA is the source of life in a cell. It is responsible for the creation of everything in the cell and for all metabolism. DNA contains all the genetic information of the cell. The essence of DNA is genetic information. DNA has a God-like status in the cell. The DNA of life is perfect. God can be described as a perfect being like this DNA. Like this perfect DNA, the universe is governed by perfect universal laws created by God. The God of the Bible created everything in the universe with perfect principles and governs them with perfect laws. The DNA in a cell is sovereign and perfect, creating everything in the cell and governing all life phenomena in the cell with perfect laws.

Who is God? The Old Testament says that "God is who I am" (Exod 3:14). This means that God is uncreated and self-existent. God is a spirit (John 4:24), so he cannot be seen by human eyes. God's ways are perfect (Ps 18:30) and are the principles by which the universe operates. God is in control of the universe and the laws of nature. In the Old Testament, the Jews saw and recognized God's presence and omnipotent power in the wondrous works of God. In the New Testament, however, God's almighty power is made visible to human eyes through the words, signs, and wonders that Jesus showed as the Messiah. The Son of God (Jesus) is the image of the invisible God (Col 1:15). No one comes to God except through Jesus (John 14:6). Jesus Christ is the mediator between God and man (1 Tim 2:5). We believe in the coming of the kingdom of God through the words (the Gospels) of Jesus in the New Testament, and we believe in Jesus Christ as the Messiah, the Son of God. To know Jesus is to know God (John 8:19), to have seen Jesus is to have seen God (John 12:45), and to believe in Jesus is to believe in God (John 12:44; 14:1).

Christianity holds the doctrine of the Trinitarian God, which states that the Father, Son, and Holy Spirit are one God in three distinct persons. "I (Jesus) and the Father (God) are one" (John 10:30). God is spirit (John 4:24). Theologically, the essence of God the Father; his only Son, Jesus Christ; and the Holy Spirit is spirit, and they do the same thing. Messiah (any expected deliverer) means savior, deliverer, or messenger. From the DNA of an organism, messenger RNA is made that has the same genetic information. From the messenger RNA, proteins with the same genetic information are made. Similar to the cell's messenger RNA, which receives and transmits identical genetic information from DNA, in the New Testament, Jesus Christ delivers the Word of God (the gospel) as the "Son of God" and "Messiah". Messenger RNA and proteins derived from DNA have the same genetic information as DNA. In this way, the Christian doctrine of the Trinity can be easily understood by scientifically comparing and analyzing these DNA substances with the Father, Son, and Holy Spirit. The essence of the Holy Spirit is the spirit of God and the spirit of Christ (Rom 8:9). After Jesus, the present is the age of the Holy Spirit. The work of God's grace through the Holy Spirit (the Comforter), whom Jesus sent to mankind after his resurrection and ascension from the cross, is ongoing (John 1:16–17; 14:26).

Who is Jesus? Jesus is life. Jesus said, "I am the way, the truth, and the life" (John 14:6). The idea of "life" from the resurrection of Jesus is a central idea of Christianity that cannot be found in other religions. In the New Testament, the apostle Paul states emphatically, "If Jesus has not been raised, then the preaching of the gospel of God is in vain, and the faith of the believers is also in vain" (1 Cor 15:14). Jesus is the resurrection and the life, and whoever believes in him will never die (John 11:25–26). But even Jesus' disciples didn't believe in Jesus' resurrection until they saw him rise from the dead. "Do you believe because you have seen me? Blessed are they who have not seen and believe" (John 20:29). Not one of the disciples believed in the resurrected Jesus without seeing him. It was the experience of meeting the risen Jesus face-to-face that led Jesus' disciples to recognize his resurrection as a fact (John 20:19–23; 21:1–14). The resurrection of Jesus is the core of Christianity. The idea of resurrection sets Christianity apart from other religions as a religion of life. Many Christians question, "Did

Jesus really rise from the dead? Can Jesus be resurrected if he is the Son of Man? Can a person die and come back to life?" These questions are difficult to be answered from the life science perspective. If Jesus were a human being, it would be biologically impossible for him to die and come back to life. But Jesus is the "Son of God." He contains God's DNA. Therefore, Jesus, who has God's DNA, is not truly human. Jesus was resurrected as the "Son of God" after his substitutionary death on the cross (Matt 28:1–10; Mark 16:1–8; Luke 24:1–12; John 20:1–10). Without the resurrection, Jesus would be just an ordinary human being and could not be the Son of God. When asked "do you believe in the resurrection of Jesus?," if you answer, "I believe in the resurrection of Jesus," you are a true Christian. Most people who are trained in the natural sciences, especially life scientists, do not believe in the resurrection of Jesus scientifically. This is because they do not understand the theological implications of Jesus' resurrection in the Bible. Theologically, this is how the resurrection of Jesus is possible. Christianity begins with the resurrection of Jesus, and resurrection (life) is the core idea of Christianity. Christianity is a religion of life. Without the resurrection of Jesus, Christianity would not exist. A person who does not believe in God and Jesus cannot theologically be resurrected. However, Christians are saved by God's sovereign grace through true faith and obedience to God (Jesus) and have eternal life. And Christians who believe in God (Jesus) and live a life of grace through obedience to God (Jesus) have no cares, no worries, and are always at peace.

Christianity is a religion of love, life, and grace. Christianity is not a traditionally indigenous Korean religion. Christianity is a Western religion that is deeply rooted in Western culture, including Europe, the United States, Canada, South America, and Australia, etc. With a history of more than two thousand years (New Testament), Western Christianity entered the Korean Peninsula in the late 18th century during the Joseon Dynasty and has remained a major religion in Korea. As South Korea has industrialized and democratized following its liberation from Japanese rule in the 20th century, Christianity has continued to expand its presence in Korean society. However, along with the advanced Western culture, Christianity has also entered into the traditional Confucian, Buddhist, and Taoist cultures of the Korean peninsula and has been criticized by non-Christians for its many negative effects on Korean society. Today, for Koreans who have lived in various indigenous religions and Buddhist and Confucian cultures for five thousand years, Korean Christianity, which is originally derived from Western Christianity, is fading into a religion that seeks their own desires and well-being.

Today, Korean Christianity is in crisis in Korean society. Korean Christianity needs a revolution like the European Reformation that Martin Luther started in 1517. Korean Christianity and Christians must now be born again. Most Korean Christians practice their faith only in church, but they live a Confucian life at home and in society. There is a dichotomy between Christian faith and daily life in Korea, meaning that the Bible and Christianity are only in the church, and there is no biblical life outside the church that lives according to God's will. There is only a life that pursues self-love according to worldly selfish desires, and a life that gives and shares with neighbors with the agape love of God is lacking. Therefore, Christianity must now be reborn as a biblical, agape (selfless) religion of love and life, away from the religion of "salvation" and self-love that seeks personal blessing. God is love (1 John 4:8). Jesus is the source of life. There is life in Jesus Christ (John 1:4), and Jesus is the "Word of life" (1 John 1:1). The core of the Christian faith is "faith alone" in God and Jesus Christ. To be true Christians, we must understand the Bible correctly, obey and believe in God, and live righteously and well, according to the Bible and God's will. The life of Jesus Christ is the highest standard of life for people in our world to imitate. Christians should live a life of action in practice according to God's Word in the Bible at home and in society. And we are to love one another in deed and truth, not just in word or in tongue (1 John 3:18). Only when this agape-style life of God's love takes root in our society, a truly biblical Christian culture will be established in Korea. The Bible says, "The Lord is the Spirit, and where the Spirit of the Lord is, there is freedom" (2 Cor 3:17). "For those who are called in the Lord are free, belonging to the Lord, and servants of Christ; do not be slaves of men" (1 Cor 7:22–23). True Christians have freedom in the Lord Jesus Christ and live a life of faith in obedience to God and Jesus Christ, refusing to be servants of the world.

For the average Christian layperson, there is a difficulty in understanding fundamentally what the words and terms of the Bible mean and how the Bible contains the message of the gospel. Christians should not read the Bible literally but through a scientific analysis of the metaphorical and figurative words of God and Jesus Christ. God's truth is revealed in the words of God (Jesus) in the Bible. It is necessary for laypeople to read the Bible in English or Latin and compare and analyze it with the Korean version to have a correct view of the gospel and salvation. In addition, there

Let's Get to Know the Bible and Christianity Properly and Anew

are many mistranslations in the Korean Bible from the English (Latin) Bible. Sound Christian faith and doctrine are based on the Word of God and Jesus Christ. True doctrine creates a sound belief system that controls and guides Christian behavior. Christians in Korea need a new and correct understanding of the Bible and Christianity. The Bible and Christian doctrine are not the exclusive domain of theologians or church (cathedral) pastors. In churches and cathedrals, pastors should not distort the words of God (Jesus) in the Bible and preach worldly stories to laypeople. Christian laypeople living in the pluralistic era of the Fourth Industrial Revolution should wake up and read the Bible analytically and pay attention to bringing correct Christian ideas and doctrines to Korean Christianity.

In Part 1: Understanding the Bible, the origin and composition of the Bible is briefly described to make it easier for the general public to understand. Next, to make it easy to understand the doctrine of the Trinity of God in Christianity, the essence of the triune God (the Father, Son, and Holy Spirit) in the Bible is scientifically compared and analyzed with the DNA that is the essence of life. In addition, the meaning of God and the kingdom of God, the life and ministry of Jesus, the resurrection of Jesus, and the life history of Jesus are summarized and arranged, which the general public often wants to know. Furthermore, based on the words (the gospel) of God (Jesus) revealed in the Bible and the gospel preached by the apostles, "faith," "sin, death, and life," and "law and grace" are explained in an easy-to-understand manner. In particular, this book analyzes in depth how Jesus harmoniously completed "law and grace," the most important core themes of the Old and New Testaments, in his ministry. Furthermore, the book analyzes the "gospel" and "salvation" that Christians want to know based on the gospel of God preached by Jesus Christ and the apostles in the Bible.

In Part 2: Understanding Christianity, the origin and history of Christianity, the basic ideas of Christianity, and the main points of the Christian faith (the Lord's Prayer, the Apostles' Creed, baptism and the sacraments, and prayer) are scientifically analyzed and described in an easy-to-understand manner so that they can be properly applied to religious life. In particular, this book analyzes and presents the "right view of salvation" that Korean Christians should keep in mind. Furthermore, the book logically interprets the Bible and Christianity by relating them to science, so that Christians can easily understand the scientific facts deeply hidden in the Bible. Finally, by presenting "life guidelines for Christians" who live by the Bible and Christianity, the book attempts to help Christians root Christian culture

Let's Get to Know the Bible and Christianity Properly and Anew

in Korean society and live in spiritual abundance. The book is written by quoting, analyzing, and systematically organizing the Bible verses from the New International Version of the Bible (Korean Bible Society), the New International Version (NIV) Korean-English Commentary Bible (Agape), and Korean Bible (GOOD TV).

PART I

Understanding the Bible

구약 (Old Testament)
신약 (New Testament)

1

The Meaning and Origin of the Bible

CHRISTIANITY IS A RELIGION that believes in Jesus Christ and the word of God (Jesus) as written in the Bible. God's word is truth (John 17:17). "All scripture is given by inspiration of God, and is profitable for doctrine, for reproof, for correction, for instruction in righteousness" (2 Tim 3:16). The Bible is God's word of truth that sanctifies Christians to resemble Jesus Christ. Therefore, you are to believe everything that God (Jesus) says and describes in the Bible, which is written on the foundation of God's almighty power.

The Bible is a book of God's revelation, so we can recognize God through his Word. The Bible is the record of God's relationship with humans, and the truth is written by the word of God (Jesus) and the inspiration of the Holy Spirit. Along with the words of God, the Bible contains the inner thoughts and lives of humans from the beginning of time to AD 100. It gives us insight into the sources and motivations behind our behavior in this day and age and gives us wisdom to live righteously and peacefully in the world. The Bible is not a history book, but it is written historically; it is not a philosophy book, but it is written philosophically. The Bible is not a book of literature, but it is written in a literary and entertaining style. The Bible is not a science book, but it is written scientifically and contains scientific facts. Therefore, the Bible contains a variety of readings that can provide spiritual nourishment for people in the world, whether they are Christians or not, to live wisely.

Part I: Understanding the Bible

The Bible is humanity's greatest Scripture, with no revisions and a logical perfection that would have been impossible for humans to write. Since the Bible is a classic Scripture that contains the words of God and Jesus, we should not try to understand the contents of the Bible literally but rather analyze it scientifically to understand God's revelation accurately. The Bible is divided into the Old Testament and the New Testament. The Old Testament is the Scripture of Judaism, and both the Old and New Testaments are considered the Scripture of Christianity. However, Christians base their faith more on the New Testament. Christians see the gospel preached by Jesus in the New Testament as the fulfillment of the Old Testament. In the New Testament, Jesus said, "Do not think that I have come to abolish the Law or the Prophets; I have not come to abolish them but to fulfill them" (Matt 5:17). The Old and New Testaments complement each other in many ways, and the Old Testament is the basis for the New Testament. The Old Testament teaches God's law and foreshadows the coming of the Messiah. The New Testament tells the gospel of the birth, ministry, words, crucifixion, and resurrection of Jesus the Messiah and contains the ideas of the Christian faith: life, truth, grace, and love. To properly understand the Bible, you need to know the historical facts recorded in the Bible and the way people lived during its time.

The Bible was written from about 1450 BC to about AD 100. The original texts of the Bible were written primarily in Hebrew, with some Aramaic and Koine Greek. The words of God and Jesus were recorded in the Bible by the prophets and Jesus' apostles, with no errors. The Bible has traveled to many parts of the world, to many countries, and has been translated into many languages. The earliest translation is the Septuagint Old Testament, a translation of the Hebrew Bible into Koine Greek in the 1st century AD. The New Testament was written in Koine Greek. The Vulgate, a Latin translation of the Greek Bible by Roman Catholic theologian Hieronymus (Jerome, 347–420), was completed in 405. The Vulgate Latin Bible is currently used by the Roman Catholic Church. The English Christian theologian and Reformer John Wycliffe (1320–84) translated the Vulgate Bible from Latin into English and completed it in 1382. This was followed by an English translation, the King James Version (KJV), in 1611. In Germany, the Reformer Martin Luther (1483–1546) translated the Latin Bible into German and published the German Bible (Septemberbible) in September 1522. He made it possible for everyone, even the common people, to read the Bible and come to know the true words of God (Jesus). Later, in England, France,

The Meaning and Origin of the Bible

Switzerland, and other parts of Europe, the Bible was distributed and read by the common people, and the doctrine of Christianity was established.

On the Korean Peninsula, Christianity first began to spread when Seung-Hoon Lee (1756–1801) became the first Korean to be baptized as a Catholic in China and returned to Korea in 1784. In 1882, Sang-Ryun Seo, Hong-Jun Baek and others, who received the Korean Bible from Scottish missionaries John Ross and McIntyre in Manchuria, translated the Gospel of Luke into Korean for the first time. Later, in 1885, Soo-Jung Lee translated the complete Gospel of Mark into Korean. The first Bible books were the New Testament, translated and published by the Korean Bible Society in 1900, and the Old Testament, published in 1911. As a revised version of the Bible, the Old Testament was published in 1936 and the New Testament in 1938. Later, the Korean translation was revised again, the Korean spelling was unified, and the Korean Translation of the Bible, published in 1961, became the authorized standard Bible of the Protestant Church. Currently, the New Revised Version of the Bible (1998), the Bible (2005), and the Korean Language Bible (2007) are published and distributed by the Korean Bible Society, the Bible Translation Mission, the Korean Catholic Bishops' Conference, and Duranno Publishing.

2

The Structure of the Bible

CHRISTIANITY USES SIXTY-SIX BOOKS of the Bible, thirty-nine in the Old Testament and twenty-seven in the New Testament, all in the original Hebrew. The Bible contains the covenant (word) of God (Old Testament) and Jesus Christ (New Testament). The Bible says, "For the law was given through Moses, but grace and truth came through Jesus Christ" (John 1:17). In the Old Testament, God's covenant was preached as a law by Moses, "God's servant" (Deut 34:5). The Old Testament contains the history of Israel before Jesus and the covenants of God's word, revelation, etc. In the New Testament, God's new covenant is preached in grace and truth through Jesus Christ, the Son of God (Matt 16:16). The New Testament is the new covenant that God preached through Jesus Christ and his apostles to Jews, Gentiles, and people from all walks of life around the world.

The name of the Old Testament means Old Covenant. The Old Testament contains the old covenants and words of God during the time of God the Father. The Old Testament is what the Hebrew Bible is called in terms of Christian Scripture. The Old Testament is a collection of written stories that were passed down in Palestine, Egypt, Babylonia, and other places between the 1500s and 400s BC. The Old Testament also records the laws (Torah) given by God based on the history and lives of the ancient nation of Israel from 1500s BC onward. During the time of God the Father in the Old Testament, Moses, Joshua, and the prophets Isaiah, Jeremiah, Ezekiel, etc., preached the word of God. God's word, the Law, is written in the five books of

Moses, and Moses established Israel's religious doctrine by promulgating the Ten Commandments. Moses was the leader of the nation of Israel and one of the great prophets of Judaism. The Ten Commandments, which are the main commandments of Judaism and Christianity and the core of the Mosaic Law, are recorded in the Old Testament (Exod 20:1–17; Deut 5:6–21).

The New Testament, which Christianity treats as Scripture alongside the Old Testament, is the written word of God. It is based on the words and deeds and missionary activities of Jesus Christ and his apostles from the birth of Jesus, around 4 BC, to the writing of the book of Revelation, around AD 96. It was decided that the Scripture, newly enacted by the Council of Rome in 382, was called the New Testament by the Council of Carthage in 397. The New Testament contains the new covenant of God (Jesus), and Christians are saved by God's grace by keeping the new covenant. In the age of the Son of God, from the birth of Jesus to the resurrection of Jesus, Jesus preached the gospel of God, and in the age of the Holy Spirit, from Jesus' resurrection and ascension to today, Jesus' apostles and the Holy Spirit preach the word of God. The entire New Testament contains God's new covenant (Word) delivered through Jesus. Both the words of Jesus Christ and the gospel preached by his apostles are recorded in the New Testament in the same levels as the Word of God. The words of Jesus are written in the gospels of the New Testament, and the gospel of God that brings life, grace, love, and salvation, which is Christian thought and doctrine, was preached by Jesus and his apostles to all mankind. Jesus said, "I am the way, the truth, and the life. No one comes to the Father except through me" (John 14:6). Jesus Christ is the Messiah (John 4:26), Savior, and Lord (Luke 2:11). He served as a mediator between God and man (1 Tim 2:5).

1. THE OLD TESTAMENT

The Old Testament is the Scriptures that contain the history of ancient Israel before the birth of Jesus Christ, as well as God's covenants and revelations. The Old Testament, which consists of thirty-nine books, is divided into five parts: the Law Books (Torah, the Five Books of Moses), the Historical Books, Poetry/Wisdom Books, the Major Prophets, and the Minor Prophets. The Five Books of Moses (Genesis–Deuteronomy) were written by Moses as the covenant relationship between God and Israel was established. The Historical Books (Joshua–Esther) record the history of Israel's victories and defeats. The Poetry/Wisdom Books (Job–Song of Songs) provide a more intimate view of God's relationship with Israel and show God's earnest desire for Israel to worship and obey the Lord. The Major Prophets (Isaiah–Daniel) and Minor Prophets (Hosea–Malachi) record God's call to Israel to repent of their idolatry and disobedience to God and return to a relationship of spiritual obedience.

The Old Testament spans from around 1450 BC to roughly 400 BC. The Old Testament was written primarily in Hebrew, with some parts written in Aramaic (a variant of the original Hebrew). The descriptions in parentheses for each book of the Old Testament listed below indicate the book's author and the date of its composition (cf. Color New International Version [NIV] Korean-English Commentary Bible).

The Law Books (Torah, the Five Books of Moses)

The Torah (Law), also known as the Law of Moses, is the most important Scripture of Judaism. Today, Christianity also uses the Old Testament books as Scripture. The Torah was revealed by God through Moses. They are also known as the Five Books of Moses because they were written by Moses. In a broad sense, the Five Books of Moses contain the entirety of God's Word in the Old Testament. These books of law also record the history of the Israelites from the beginning of time until the Israelites entered Canaan, the Promised Land.

Genesis (Moses; ca. 1450–1400 BC)

Describes the creation of the heavens and the earth, the origins of man and the nation of Israel, and the lives and deeds of the ancestors of Israel, including Abraham, Isaac, Jacob, Joseph, etc.

Exodus (Moses; ca. 1450–1400 BC)

Recounts the Israelites' exodus from Egypt by God's appointed leader Moses, the Ten Commandments and other laws, covenants, regulations, rituals, etc.

The Structure of the Bible

Leviticus (Moses; ca. 1450–1400 BC)

Contains the rules for worshiping God and the rules and regulations for living a holy and pure life.

Numbers (Moses; ca. 1450–1400 BC)

Contains the census of the Israelites and their experiences in the wilderness and their hard wanderings.

Deuteronomy (Moses; ca. 1410–1395 BC)

Contains the sermon delivered by Moses just before entering the land of Canaan, recounting his time in the wilderness and reiterating the laws outlined in the previous four books. It summarizes the Five Books of Moses. Deuteronomy is often quoted in the New Testament and plays an important role in connecting the New Testament with the Old Testament. Deuteronomy is an explanatory book of God's law. It contains laws, rules, covenants, regulations, etc., about how people should live with God.

Historical Books

Joshua (Joshua; ca. 1370–1330 BC)

Judges (Samuel, uncertain; after the establishment of the monarchy but before David's capture of Jerusalem)

Book of Ruth (unknown; ca. 1011–931 BC, uncertain)

1 Samuel (presumably Samuel; ca. 1050–931 BC)

2 Samuel (presumed to be Gad and Nathan; ca. 1010–931 BC)

1 Kings (Jeremiah; estimated 561–538 BC)

2 Kings (Jeremiah; estimated 561–538 BC)

1 Chronicles (unknown, possibly written by Ezra; estimated 450–400 BC)

2 Chronicles (unknown; estimated 450–400 BC)

Ezra (Ezra; ca. 458–44 BC)

Nehemiah (Nehemiah; estimated ca. 420 BC)

Esther (a Jew who lived in Barsha; ca. 485–35 BC)

Part I: Understanding the Bible

Poetry/Wisdom Books

Book of Job (eyewitness; sometime between the time of Abraham and the return of the Jews from the Babylonian captivity)

Psalms (David, Moses, Solomon, Asaph, Ethan, Heman, the descendants of Korah, and others; ca. 1000 BC)

Proverbs (Solomon, Agag, King Lemuel, and others; ca. 1000–700 BC)

Ecclesiastes (Solomon; ca. 935 BC)

Song of Songs (Solomon; ca. 10th century BC)

Prophets

Isaiah (Isaiah; ca. 745–680 BC)

Jeremiah (Jeremiah; ca. 627–580 BC)

Jeremiah Lamentations (Jeremiah; ca. 586–585 BC)

Ezekiel (Ezekiel; ca. 593–71 BC)

Daniel (Daniel; ca. 605–530 BC)

Hosea (Hosea; ca. 790–710 BC)

Joel (Joel; ca. 830 BC or ca. 400 BC)

Amos (Amos; estimated 760 to 753 BC)

Obadiah (Obadiah; ca. 848–41 BC)

Jonah (Jonah; ca. 760 BC)

Micah (Micah; ca. 740–687 BC)

Nahum (Nahum; ca. 663–12 BC)

Habakkuk (Habakkuk; ca. 609–589 BC)

Zephaniah (Zephaniah; ca. 640–630 BC)

Haggai (Haggai; ca. 520 BC)

Zechariah [Zechariah; ca. 520–518 BC (Chapters 1–8), ca. 480–470 BC (Chapters 9–14)]

Malachi (Malachi; estimated to have been written after ca. 516 BC)

2. THE NEW TESTAMENT

The New Testament is the Christian Scripture that records God's covenant (Word) after the birth of Jesus. The New Testament consists of twenty-seven books, including the Gospels, which record the life, ministry, and teachings (gospels) of Jesus, the records of the Gospels and missionary activities of his apostles, the apostles' letters to the churches, and the Prophets. The New Testament is divided into the Gospels (Matthew–John), the historical book (Acts), Paul's epistles (Romans–Philemon), general epistles (Hebrews–Jude), and prophecy (Revelation). The New Testament was written from approximately AD 45–96 in Koine Greek, which as the ancient Greek language used in everyday life in the 1st century AD. The Gospel of Matthew, which has a strong continuity with the Old Testament, is the first book of the New Testament. The Revelation of John, which is a symbolic and apocalyptic revelation like the Old Testament book of Daniel, is the last book of the New Testament.

Jesus did not write himself about his deeds and life. His apostles (Matthew and John) and their companions (Mark and Luke) wrote about his birth, his words and deeds, his death on the cross, and his resurrection in the Gospels. The Gospels are the basis of the Christian faith. The Gospels Matthew, Mark, and Luke are called the Synoptic Gospels because they were written from a common point of view. The other, fourth Gospel, the Gospel of John, is philosophical, theological, and doctrinal in nature in terms of content. The Acts of the Apostles is a historical account of the apostles' evangelizing efforts after Jesus' resurrection and ascension. The Acts of the Apostles is also a historical chronicle of the experiences and activities of the first churches in the world. At that time, the early church did not have a Bible. The thirteen Pauline epistles (Romans–Philemon), written by the apostle Paul and centered around the book of Acts, are letters to the early church about the doctrines of the Christian faith, including salvation, the life of love, the spiritual church, the second coming of Christ, and pastoral guidance. The other eight epistles (Hebrews–Jude) were written by apostles other than Paul and teach additional Christian doctrines about the life of faith in God and Jesus Christ, the word of life, love, and the practice of righteousness. However, these epistles written by the apostles are based on the four Gospels. In the epistles, the apostles emphasize and preach the gospel of Jesus. The last book of the New Testament, the Revelation of John, is a symbolic and apocalyptic revelation of future events, including the return of Christ. However, the contents of Revelation are often symbolic and difficult to understand precisely, so interpretations vary.

The New Testament was written from about 4–6 BC (the birth of Jesus) to about AD 96 (the writing of the Book of Revelation). The New Testament was written in Koine Greek, followed by the Latin Bible (Vulgate) in 405. The New Vulgate is being used in the Roman Catholic Church today. The descriptions in parentheses for each book of the New Testament listed below indicate the book's author and the date of its composition (cf. Color New International Version [NIV] Korean-English Commentary Bible).

Gospels

Gospel of Matthew (Matthew; late 50s AD to before 70 AD)

Gospel of Mark (Mark; estimated AD 65–70)

Gospel of Luke (Luke, Greek physician; AD 61–63)

Gospel of John (John; ca. AD 80–90)

Historical Book

Acts of the Apostles (Luke, Greek physician; ca. AD 61–63)

Epistles

Romans (apostle Paul; ca. AD 57)

1 Corinthians (apostle Paul; ca. AD 55)

2 Corinthians (apostle Paul; ca. AD 55 or AD 56)

Galatians (apostle Paul; AD 48–49 or AD 55–56)

Ephesians (apostle Paul; AD 61–63)

Philippians (apostle Paul; AD 60–62)

Colossians (apostle Paul; ca. AD 62)

1 Thessalonians (apostle Paul; AD 51–53)

2 Thessalonians (apostle Paul; AD 51–53)

1 Timothy (apostle Paul; ca. AD 62, when the apostle Paul was released from prison and began his evangelistic journey again)

2 Timothy (apostle Paul; ca. AD 66–67)

Titus (apostle Paul; AD 63–65)

Philemon (apostle Paul; ca. AD 60–62)

Hebrews (unknown; ca. AD 64–67)

James (James, brother of Jesus; AD 45–49 or AD 60)

1 Peter (Peter; ca. AD 64–65)

2 Peter (Peter; ca. AD 64–65)

1 John (apostle John; ca. AD 85–96)

2 John (apostle John; AD 85–96)

3 John (apostle John; AD 85–96)

Jude (Jude, brother of James; ca. AD 60–80)

Apocalypse

Revelation (apostle John; AD 90–96)

Apocryphal Gospels

The apocryphal Gospels are not recognized as Scriptures in Christianity.

The Gospel of Judas: Not recognized as Scripture, because it was written by Judas Iscariot, who betrayed Jesus.

The Gospel of Mary: Partially lost. A Gospel written by Mary Magdalene, which is not recognized as Scripture because the author was a woman.

The Gospel of Thomas: While the Synoptic Gospels are based on the words and deeds of Jesus, the Gospel of Thomas is the "Gospel of Analects" that contains only the teachings of Jesus. It is similar to the content of the four Gospels, but some of it was newly discovered.

3

Scientific Understanding of the Essence of God

To properly understand the Bible and Christianity, you need to accurately know the essence of God. However, Christians often have a vague understanding of the nature of God, so they are often unable to say exactly "who God is like." This is because it is difficult to easily define the essence of God. In the Old Testament, God is defined as "I am who I am" (Exod 3:14). In the New Testament, Jesus says, "God is spirit" (John 4:24). This statement by Jesus means that God is not physical or visible but spiritual. Therefore, God's essence is best understood as "the Holy Spirit," a spirit of infinite perfection. God exists beyond time and space, and he always has unchanging perfection and eternity. God is eternal and immutable and governs the spiritual world. God is the Creator of the universe and the heaven and the earth, and he is the Lord of all (Gen 1). God is the creator and ruler of all things. God is in control of the universe and the providence of nature. God is sovereign and perfect. God is omnipotent, and God is personally and morally perfect.

The only one God exists as Father, Son, and Holy Spirit (Matt 28:19). Jesus is the Son of God (Matt 16:15–16), so Jesus Christ is God the Son clothed in flesh. The Father begets, the Son is born, and the Holy Spirit comes from the Father and the Son. Christianity holds the doctrine of the Trinity of God the Father, the Son, and the Holy Spirit. The three persons

Scientific Understanding of the Essence of God

of the Trinity, the Father, the Son (Jesus), and the Holy Spirit, are one God (John 10:30), though they are distinct in rank and form. The Father, Son, and Holy Spirit are the same in essence itself and equal in power and glory. Theologically, the essence (nature) of God is one God, the only God. God the Father, his only Son, the Lord Jesus Christ, and the Holy Spirit are always one God, with the same essence and performing the same roles. However, when analyzed scientifically, the essence of the Trinity (Father, Son, and Holy Spirit) is spirit. That is, God is a spirit (John 4:24). The spirit gives life (John 6:63). This means that there is no life without "spirit." God is the God of life. God gives life and creates living things. When the Bible refers to God, it is primarily referring to God the Father.

In the beginning, God created the heavens and the earth, all things, and man (Gen 1). God created the universe and everything in it. God is the creator, sovereign and perfect. In particular, God created man in his image (Gen 1:27). This biblical statement suggests that God and man are similar in image. Here, we try to make it easier to understand the essence (nature) of God by scientifically comparing God and the cell, the basic unit of life. To the general public, a living cell is known as a microcosmos. Cells continue to divide and multiply into countless numbers of identical cells that make up a living organism. Cells are created under the control of deoxyribonucleic acid (DNA) molecules in the cell. DNA creates cells. DNA contains the genetic information of the cell. The essence of DNA is genetic information. DNA has a God-like status in the cell. DNA is unchanging, creating everything in the cell and directing all cellular functions. In cells, DNA is the source of life. In cells, there are three substances that govern the genetic information of life: DNA (genes), messenger RNA (mRNA) derived from DNA, and proteins. The essence of DNA, messenger RNA, and proteins is the same: genetic information. Messenger RNA acts as a messenger (deliverer) that transmits the genetic information of DNA within cells. DNA makes messenger RNA, and messenger RNA is translated into amino acids to make proteins. The DNA in the cell is involved in the creation of everything in the cell and governs all life phenomena with a perfect law. Interestingly, these DNA and DNA-derived substances have different shapes, but the same essence, that is, the same genetic information. The basic structure of these DNA, messenger RNA, and proteins in the cell and their functions in all metabolic processes in the cell are analyzed below. The Christian doctrine of the triune God can be easily understood by scientifically comparing the triune Father, Son, and Holy Spirit with the DNA, messenger RNA, and protein in a cell. However, the logic that "God is DNA" never works, because God is an invisible spiritual image, while DNA is a nucleic acid substance that we can see. In particular, it is interesting to note that in the same way that God controls the universe, the laws of nature, and the spirit world, the DNA in the cell controls the phenomenon of life.

(1) THE FATHER (GOD, CREATOR): DNA (GENE)

Jehovah (Yahweh) is the proper name of God in the Bible. However, "God" is generally used rather than "Jehovah (Yahweh)." In English versions of the Bible, Jehovah is written as "the Lord." God is the only Sovereign, the King of kings and Lord of lords (1 Tim 6:15). God is sovereign and perfect. God is omnipotent and holy. God the Father is the transcendent Creator who rules the universe and is the source of all creation (Gen 1). The Bible says, "God is who He is (I am who I am)" (Exod 3:14). This means that God is uncreated. God was not created and exists by himself. God is uncreated and self-existent. God is a spirit (John 4:24), so he cannot be seen by human eyes. God is the Father of the Son Jesus, the Son comes from the Father, and the Holy Spirit is sent from God and Jesus (John 14:26). Thus, we can see that God, Jesus, and the Holy Spirit have the same phase but are in a vertical relationship. God said that in him is life (John 5:26). God is the one who exists as life. God is the source of life.

God and DNA are exquisite, perfect, and similar to each other. The perfection of God and the perfection of DNA are the same quality. The DNA in the cells of living things is on the same level as God in the universe. DNA is the source of life. The essence of DNA is genetic information. DNA contains the genetic information (base sequences) and perfectly controls all life phenomena in the cell. The genetic information in DNA is transferred to messenger RNA, which then translates the genetic information into amino acids to make proteins. These three DNA-derived cellular components are living substances that have different shapes but the same DNA genetic information and are in a vertical relationship to each other. DNA and its derivatives, messenger RNA and protein, are the essential components of living organisms, and they control the life processes of cells. DNA, messenger RNA, and proteins are living chemical molecules that are sensitive to heat and lose their structure when heated. The function of DNA in a cell is invisible; we can only see its structure. By observing the function

Scientific Understanding of the Essence of God

of messenger RNA and proteins in the cell, we can infer what DNA does. Intriguingly, God and DNA are similar in what they do.

(2) THE SON (MESSIAH, JESUS CHRIST): MESSENGER RNA

In the Bible, the Son is called the Son of God, the Son of Man, and the Lord Jesus Christ. The Son, Jesus Christ, is both divine and human. Jesus is God the Son, clothed in flesh. Jesus was conceived by the Holy Spirit and born to his mother, Mary, in Bethlehem around 4 BC (Matt 2:18–25; Luke 2:1–7). In the Gospels, Jesus performed wonders and signs several times to prove that he is the Son of God. "The Son of God is the image of the invisible God, the firstborn of all creation" (Col 1:15). Jesus said, "I and the Father are one" (John 10:30). Jesus Christ is the mediator between God and man (1 Tim 2:5). Jesus is life. Jesus said, "I am the way, the truth, and the life; no one comes to the Father (God) except through me" (John 14:6). To know Jesus is to know God (John 8:19), to have seen Jesus is to have seen God (John 12:45), and to believe in Jesus is to believe in God (John 12:44, 14:1). All things in heaven and on earth were created by and for the Son of God (Col 1:16).

Jesus Christ and messenger RNA are similar in what they do. Messiah (any expected deliverer) means savior, deliverer, messenger, etc. Christ (the Anointed) means the Savior and the one who preaches the gospel. The Messiah, Jesus Christ, was the Son of God who had God's genetic information (DNA) and delivered God's revelation, covenant, word, and gospel to people. The Messiah, Jesus Christ, played a similar role to messenger RNA in the cells of living things, which receives its genetic information from DNA. Messenger RNA receives its genetic information from DNA and makes proteins, which are responsible for all physiological and metabolic processes in the cell. We can visually see the expression of messenger RNAs in cells as transcripts. When messenger RNA was first identified and named in cells, it seems likely that life scientists were inspired by Jesus Christ's other name, Messiah.

Part I: Understanding the Bible

(3) THE HOLY SPIRIT (THE SPIRIT, SPIRIT OF GOD, SPIRIT OF CHRIST): THE GENETIC INFORMATION OR GENETIC CODE OF LIVING THINGS

The Holy Spirit, or the Spirit, is the spirit of God and the spirit of Christ (Rom 8:9). Christians have the Holy Spirit, the "spirit of Christ," within them. From a life science perspective, the Holy Spirit is compared with the genetic information or genetic code of living things. The role of the Holy Spirit is also compared to that of a protein that controls all metabolic processes in a cell, although they are different in shape. Almighty God created all things in the universe, and the resurrected Lord Jesus Christ appeared to his disciples. Afterward, Jesus ascended into heaven and promised to send the Holy Spirit (Comforter, Counselor) to live with us (John 16:17), teaching us the truth, protecting us with grace, and giving us peace (John 14:25–27). In the name of Jesus, God sent the Holy Spirit, the "Comforter (Counselor)," into the world (John 14:26). The Comforter is the Spirit of Truth who guides Christians to the path of truth on behalf of Jesus (John 14:17). Today, after Jesus' resurrection and ascension, the Holy Spirit is spreading the word (gospel) of God (Jesus). This is the age of the Holy Spirit. The Holy Spirit is witnessing to the world and the church about Jesus Christ. Pentecost is the day the Holy Spirit descended on the fiftieth day after Jesus' resurrection (Acts 2:1–21). It is considered the day when the early Christian church was founded. We are not Christians unless we have the Holy Spirit within us. "If the Spirit of God dwells in you, you are not in the flesh, but in the Spirit; and if anyone does not have the Spirit of Christ, he is not of Christ" (Rom 8:9). "God has sent his Son's spirit (the Holy Spirit) into our hearts" (Gal 4:6).

Cells are the basic unit of structure and function in living organisms. All of a cell's genetic information is contained in its DNA. The essence of DNA is genetic information. DNA is the source of life in a cell. The DNA molecule has a double-stranded structure made up of four bases: adenine (A), cytosine (C), guanine (G), and thymine (T). James D. Watson (1928–) and Francis H. C. Crick (1916–2004) discovered the helical structure of DNA in 1953 and were awarded the Nobel Prize in 1962. In every living organism, the sequence of the genetic code (A, C, G, T) that makes up the structure of DNA, called the base sequence, is constant and complete. Therefore, the perfection of God and the perfection of DNA are the same quality. The

Scientific Understanding of the Essence of God

function of DNA is only known when it is transcribed into messenger RNA and expressed as a transcript. In 1961, Francois Jacob (1920–2013) and others discovered the existence and function of messenger RNA and were awarded the Nobel Prize in 1965. Inside the cell, messenger RNAs are translated into amino acids to make proteins that carry the same genetic information. These DNA-derived messenger RNAs and proteins look different, but their essence, the genetic information, is the same. However, although we know the genetic code (base sequence) of DNA, we cannot directly observe the function of DNA itself in the cell. That is, we cannot see the function of DNA in the cell, only the structure of DNA. Thus, the functions of messenger RNAs and proteins are observed in the cell to infer what DNA is doing. As essential metabolites, proteins are the building blocks of living cells, from basic DNA duplication to the formation of biological structures, and are involved in all life phenomena such as physiology and metabolism. Therefore, DNA (gene), messenger RNA, and proteins have different shapes but the same genetic information (genetic code, base sequence) to perform the same functions in the cell.

We can only visually observe the expression of messenger RNA and proteins in cells. In the Gospels of the Bible, Jesus showed the invisible works of God by performing wonders and signs, and as a messenger of God, Jesus preached God's will and word (gospel) to his apostles and people. Similarly, messenger RNA, which transmits the genetic information of DNA in the cell as a messenger, is also expressed in the cell and shows various functions as a transcript. Just as the disciples of Jesus, such as the apostle Paul, preached the gospel (word) of God and Jesus Christ, messenger RNA and proteins receive genetic information from DNA and drive the metabolism and life phenomena of cells. In a microcosmic cell, DNA, messenger RNA, and proteins have different shapes, but they do the same thing (function). God, Jesus, and the apostles rule and govern the universe and all things by the Word of God (the Word), which is different in form but the same in function. In the beginning was God, and the Word was God (John 1:1). By the Word, God created all things (John 1:3).

4

God and the Kingdom of God

1. WHO IS GOD

GOD IS THE ABSOLUTE, the ruler of the universe and all things, and the controller of space and time. God is holy, righteous, and worthy of worship. In the beginning, God created the heavens and the earth (Gen 1:1). In the beginning, God created the invisible spiritual world (the heavens) and the visible material world (the earth). God created then the universe, nature, everything, and mankind (Gen 1). In the Bible, God says, "I am who I am" (Exod 3:14). This means that God is uncreated. God is spirit (John 4:24). Because God is a spiritual being, he cannot be seen by human eyes. God has an eternity that is unchanged by time. God is eternal. God is sovereign and perfect. God is the Creator and Lord of all things (Gen 1). Everything in the world was created for God's glory. God is one God and the Father of all things (everything in the universe) (Eph 4:6). God is the only true creator and ruler of the universe. The Bible says, "God is blessed, the only sovereign God, the King of kings and Lord of lords" (1 Tim 6:15).

To the frail human mind, God exists spiritually and is revered by mankind. "From everlasting to everlasting, you are God" (Ps 90:2). God exists beyond time and space and is always unchanging and eternal. Everything in the universe is dependent on God. "For from him and through him and to him are all things" (Rom 11:36). God is the source of all things, and he created everything and established the laws of the universe (the laws of heaven), so that the universe operates accurately and perfectly. He is the Almighty God who rules the universe. In the beginning was the Word, and the Word was with God, and the Word was God (John 1:1). By the Word he created all things (John 1:3). The Word of God is eternal and does not pass away or come into being. The Word does not change. God works in us through the Holy Spirit and outwardly through the Word. God is omnipotent, and what he does is perfect and accurate. Jesus said, "With man this is impossible, but with God all things are possible" (Matt 19:26). There is nothing wrong with what God is doing. Jesus says, "No one is good except God alone" (Luke 18:19). God is the standard of goodness.

The Old Testament Age

God was thought to be a spirit, omnipotent, and an object of worship, located in heaven or in a temple. God was perceived as high and distant and not easily accessible to humans. The Jews considered God (the one true God) to be the God of Israel (the Jews). The God of the Old Testament is the God who creates all things, loves, envies, punishes, and demonstrates creative power in human life. "God created the heavens and the earth and everything in them" (Gen 1:1; 2:1). The Lord God is a God who is perfect in his works, just and upright in all his ways, true and without deceit (Deut 32:4). God says, "You shall have no other gods before me, except me" (Exod 20:3; Deut 5:7). "The Lord your God is a jealous God" (Deut 5:9). God is jealous to keep his own glory. God loves those he loves and hates those he hates. "The Lord disciplines those whom he loves, just as a father disciplines his son in whom he is well pleased" (Prov 3:12). The God of the Old Testament is like a strict fleshly "Father" who refines (scourges) us in the human world.

The New Testament Age

In the New Testament era (Jesus) and afterward (the Holy Spirit), God is thought to be the God of humanity (Christians) everywhere and of all nations. God (Jesus) is a God of love who is in every Christian's heart, is accessible and friendly, giving grace and peace. The Word is God (John 1:1), and his eternal power and divinity can be seen in everything that he has made in the universe (Rom 1:20). God is spirit and is omnipotent, ruling and controlling humans and nature. God is the creator of the universe,

Part I: Understanding the Bible

a perfect, holy, righteous, good, forgiving, gracious, merciful, loving, and life-giving God. God (Jesus), whose Word became flesh and dwelt among us, is a God of grace and truth (John 1:14). The God (Jesus) of the New Testament is like a physical "mother" who gives endless love and grace to the human world.

(1) God Is the Way of the Universe and Nature

Nature refers to phenomena that are as they are without the addition of human power, or the order and phenomena of the universe that are beyond human power. In the Bible, God says, "I am who I am" (Exod 3:14). This definition of God is synonymous with nature, or "what is by itself." Lao Tzu's (老子) idea of "Idleness Naturalism" (無爲自然)" is not to try to force anything but to let things happen as they should. Nature is what it is. However, God is in control of the universe and the laws of nature.

"The way of God is perfect, and the word of the Lord is blameless" (Ps 18:30). God's ways are always the same and unchanging. The way of God is to live according to God's will (Word). Jesus said, "I am the way, the truth, and the life" (John 14:6). The way of God is the principle of all things in the universe and the way that governs the cycle of the universe. The way of God is the source of all things and the principle by which the universe operates. God is the creator of the universe and all things (Gen 1) and presides over it all as God's "way." The way of God is accurate, perfect, and without falsehood. The universe and all things operate and exist by God's way.

(2) God Is Spirit, Word, Life and Love

God is spirit (John 4:24) and therefore cannot be seen by human eyes. God is invisible. In the beginning was the Word, and the Word was God (John 1:1). God is Word, life, and love (John 1:1-4; 1 John 4:16). We can only know God through the Word because God is invisible. God is seen in the Word. God's Word is eternal, meaning it does not change and does not pass away. God's Word is truth (John 17:17). When we read and hear God's Word, our hearts are calmed and warmed. No one has ever seen God, but we have come to know God through his only Son (Jesus), who is in the bosom of God (John 1:18). Jesus says in the Bible, "He who has seen me has seen the Father; how do you say, 'Show us the Father'?"(John 14:9). We can see God through the person of Jesus Christ. The Son of God (Jesus) is the image of the invisible God (Col 1:15). "The Lord is your life" (Deut 30:20). In God was life, and this life is the light of men (John 1:3). God said that in him was life (John 5:26). God is the one who exists as life. God is the source of life. God himself gives life, breath, and all things (Acts 17:25). God creates life by giving life. And God is love (1 John 4:8). Love is born of God (1 John 4:7). God's love is the foundation of Christian thought. God's love is merciful, gracious, and infinite. God is a God of mercy and comfort (2 Cor 1:3). Jesus gave his disciples a new commandment of love. "Love one another. As I have loved you, so you must love one another"(John 13:34). "Whoever lives in love lives in God, and God in him" (1 John 4:16).

(3) God's Character: Justice and Love

The true image of God is seen in the harmony of "righteousness" through law and "love" through grace. God shows us justice through the law and love through grace. God is holy (Isa 6:3) and righteous (Ps 11:7). David says, "The Lord is my shepherd; he revives my soul and leads me in the paths of righteousness" (Ps 23:1–3). God has two attributes that go hand in hand: justice and love. God is both just and merciful. God's justice is revealed through the law, and God's love is revealed through grace. God is a God of justice (Ps 89:14). God is just and righteous (Deut 32:4). God walks in the paths of justice and walks in the midst of righteousness (Prov 8:20). When justice is done, the righteous rejoice, and the wicked are destroyed (Prov 21:15). God's justice is God's characterization of his public righteousness, which means that he punishes people for breaking the public law or committing a sin. God is a righteous judge (Ps 7:11). God judges with justice (1 Pet 2:23). God has set a day when he will judge the world with justice through a man (Jesus) whom he raised up (Acts 17:31). God rules the world righteously, justly, fairly, and equitably. God judges justly according to their deeds, rewarding the good and punishing the wicked. Those who do good find favor with God, but those who plot evil are condemned by God (Prov 12:2).

God is also a God of love (1 John 4:16). "He who does not love does not know God, for God is love" (1 John 4:8). Love is born of God (1 John 4:7). God's love is merciful, gracious, infinite, eternal, sovereign, and holy. God so loved us that he sent his Son, Jesus, to forgive us our sins (1 John 4:10). God loves us as he has loved his Son, Jesus Christ (John 17:23). God is love. God's love is poured into our hearts by the Holy Spirit (Rom 5:5). God's love covers transgressions and is compassionate. God is a god of mercy and comfort, who comforts us in all our tribulations (2 Cor 1:3–4). David says, "Goodness and steadfast love will truly be with me all the days of my life; I will dwell in the house of the Lord forever" (Ps 23:6). The apostle Paul says, "God, who is rich in mercy, through his great love for us, made us alive together with Christ, who were dead in our sins" (Eph 2:4–5). If we love one another, God is in us, and God's love is perfected in us (1 John 4:12). Since God so loved us, we ought to love one another (1 John 4:11). He who loves God also loves his brother (1 John 4:21). Let us not love one another in word and tongue only but in deed and in truth (1 John 3:18). We will be saved by love and grace. Through God's grace and love, spiritual blessings are given to humans. But love without justice is already not love. Without God's justice, God's love cannot exist. It is the true character of God that justice and love are seen together in harmony. Justice and love are inseparable from each other, like two sides of a coin. However, God's love is greater than his justice. God judges with justice, but God helps with mercy and love. The true believer lives by the agape love of God rather than the egotistic, selfish love of self.

2. WHERE IS GOD

God is not confined by time or space; he is everywhere in the universe. God is the Creator of the heavens and the earth and all things (Gen 1:1–31)—one God, who is above all things and in all things (Eph 4:6). God is in the heavens, everywhere in the universe, and in all time and space, answering those who seek him. God (Jesus, the Holy Spirit) is in every Christian. God (the Lord) is in us, and we are also in the Lord. In the Old Testament, Jehovah God showed the people the tree of life, rainbow, pillar of cloud, and pillar of fire as signs of his presence and covenant (Gen 2:9; 9:13–16; Exod 13:21–22). In the Old Testament era, the rite of baptism was not practiced to put the Spirit of God into the hearts of believers.

Where Jesus Christ is, there is God. Where Jesus' ministry is, there is God. God (Jesus, the Holy Spirit) is in the heart of the Christian. In the New Testament era, the ritual of baptism was performed to put God's Spirit into the heart of a repentant and believing person to make them one with God, i.e., to become a believer (Christian). Jesus was also baptized in water by John the Baptist (Matt 3:13–17), and all Christian believers are baptized (Matt 28:19). As such, Christians are the dwelling place of the Holy Spirit

(1 Cor 6:19–20). When you are baptized in the name of Jesus for the forgiveness of sins, you receive the gift of the Holy Spirit (Acts 2:38). Through faith, Jesus lives in the hearts of believers and builds them up with roots of love (Eph 3:17). In Christianity, would-be believers are baptized in water. From a bioscience perspective, this is because water contains the spirit of God. "The Spirit of God moved upon the face of the waters" (Gen 1:2). The apostle John says, "There are three that testify: the Holy Spirit, and the water and the blood. And these three are one in union" (1 John 5:7–8). Water is essential for the creation of life, as it has the source element of life. Water is life.

God does not dwell in houses made by men (Acts 7:48). God is life and therefore exists in living things as a spiritual being. God is a God of life and therefore does not reside in inanimate objects such as temples, churches, cathedrals, and other wooden and stone buildings. God is inherent in the body of the believer. When analyzed scientifically, idols are mostly dead things, so the God of life (the Holy Spirit) cannot reside in them. Therefore, we should not worship lifeless idols (Exod 20:4–5; Deut 5:8–9).

3. WHERE AND WHAT THE KINGDOM OF GOD IS

The kingdom of God is where God is. The kingdom of God, or the kingdom of heaven, is a theological concept found in the New Testament. The kingdom of God is the rule or reign of God and the display of his majesty and glory. The kingdom of God is an eternal kingdom where God reigns. The term "kingdom of God" is rarely used in the Old Testament; however, a similar concept, the "kingdom of the Lord (Jehovah)," is mentioned. "Your kingdom is an everlasting kingdom, and your dominion endures through all generations" (Ps 145:13). "The highest heavens belong to the Lord, but the earth he has given to man" (Ps 115:16). The heavens belong to Jehovah God.

In the Gospel of Matthew, Jesus says, "Repent, for the kingdom of heaven is at hand" (Matt 4:17). The kingdom of God (heaven) is near but not yet here, but "if I drive out demons by the finger of God, then the kingdom of God has come to you" (Luke 11:20). "Not everyone who says to me, 'Lord, Lord,' will enter the kingdom of heaven, but only he who does the will of my Father who is in heaven" (Matt 7:21). Instead of using the term "kingdom of heaven," in the other Gospels, Jesus speaks of the "kingdom of God." "The kingdom of God is near. Repent and believe the good news!" (Mark 1:15). Only those who repent and believe in the gospel of God can enter the kingdom of God. Jesus said to his disciples, "How hard it is for the rich to enter the kingdom of God!" (Mark 10:23). The kingdom of God is within us (Luke 17:20–21). The kingdom of God is not of this world (John 18:36). Jesus says, "No one can enter the kingdom of God unless he is born of water and the Spirit" (John 3:5).

(1) Where Is the Kingdom of God

The Bible commonly refers to the place where God dwells as "heaven." The apostle Paul says, "The kingdom of God is in heaven" (2 Cor 12:1-:2), through the visions and revelations the Lord gave us. Jesus taught us to pray "our Father in heaven" (Matt 6:9). The kingdom of God is in heaven. Peter says, "Jesus has ascended into heaven and is at the right hand of God" (1 Pet 3:22). The kingdom of God is also within us. Jesus says, "The kingdom of God does not come with your careful observation, nor will people say, 'Here it is,' or 'There it is,' because the kingdom of God is within you" (Luke 17:20–21). The kingdom of God is in heaven and in the hearts of believers. We also have an eternal home in heaven (2 Cor 5:1). When Jesus ministered, he proclaimed, "Repent, for the kingdom of heaven is at hand" (Matt 5:17). "And if I go and prepare a place for you, I will come back and take you to be with me that you also may be where I am" (John 14:3). The apostle Paul tells Christians. "And God raised us up with Christ and seated us with him in the heavenly realms in Christ Jesus" (Eph 2:6). The kingdom of God is not of this world (John 18:36). Thus, both Jesus Christ and the apostle Paul are saying that the kingdom of God is in heaven and in the person of the believer.

The Phenomenal Kingdom of God in the Old Testament

The Lord God created the garden of Eden and placed a man (Adam) there whom he had molded with his own hands (Gen 2:8). In the garden of Eden, Adam and Eve lived, and there were all kinds of trees that were beautiful and good for food and the tree of life (Gen 2:8–9). The garden of Eden is a place where man can eat of the fruit of the tree of life and live forever (Gen 3:22), a utopia where Adam and his wife Eve lived before they were driven out. For people in today's world, the garden of Eden is a phenomenal paradise on earth. However, after Adam and Eve were expelled, angels are guarding the way to the tree of life (Gen 4:24). Accordingly, no human being other than Adam and Eve has ever lived in Eden. In the Bible, the garden of Eden is the only place that people recognize as the kingdom of God where they can live forever.

(2) What Is the Kingdom of God Like

The kingdom of God is the realm where God sovereignly rules, and it is the realm of salvation. The kingdom of the Lord (God's kingdom) is an everlasting kingdom, where the Lord (God) reigns from generation to generation (Ps 145:13). The kingdom of the Lord has majesty and glory (Ps 145:11–12). The kingdom of God is where the power and glory of God resides, where there is no death but everlasting life, full of righteousness, peace, joy, and grace (favor). Jesus preached the gospel of God and spoke of the "kingdom of God" (heaven). "Repent, for the kingdom of heaven is near" (Matt 4:17). "Not everyone who says to me, 'Lord, Lord,' will enter the kingdom of heaven, but only he who does the will of my Father who is in heaven" (Matt 7:21). Not everyone who believes goes to the kingdom of God, but believers who live according to the will (Word) of God (Jesus). "The kingdom of God is near. Repent and believe the good news!" (Mark 1:15). Only those who are born again, repent, and believe in the gospel of God can enter the kingdom of God. The kingdom of God does not come to be seen but is within us (Luke 17:20–21).

In the Bible, the kingdom of God (the kingdom of heaven) is compared to a treasure that a man wants to obtain by selling everything he owns and buying a field. Jesus says, "The kingdom of heaven is like treasure hidden in a field" (Matt 13:44). In the same way, the kingdom of God is of great value to us. People of faith joyfully forsake all possessions to gain the kingdom of God. "But store up for yourselves treasures in heaven, where moth and rust do not destroy, and where thieves do not break in and steal" (Matt 6:20). The kingdom of God is a place where the "river of the water of life" flows in the middle of the road and there is the "tree of life," which bears twelve kinds of fruit and is free from curses (Rev 22:1–3). "For the kingdom of God is not a matter of eating and drinking, but of righteousness, peace and joy in the Holy Spirit" (Rom 14:17). As Romans says, the kingdom of God is not where humans eat and drink but where God and the Holy Spirit rule with agape (selfless) love and God's Word is kept, so that righteousness, peace, and joy always abound. The kingdom of God is a new heaven and a new earth where the righteous dwell, where there is no death, no sorrow, no weeping, no pain (2 Pet 3:13; Rev 21:1–4). The kingdom of God is free of worldly sin and evil. The kingdom of God is a kingdom of everlasting peace and righteousness, where there is no death, sorrow, or pain but everlasting life and peace. The kingdom of God is where we dwell in peace and live joyfully with the Lord.

5

Jesus Is the Messiah and the Life

JESUS CHRIST IS THE object of the Christian faith who came into the world as the Son of God (Matt 16:15–16) and ministered as the Messiah, a mediator with God (1 Tim 2:5). Jesus Christ is the Second Person of the Trinity, God the Son who is always with us, unchanging and eternal. The Bible says, "The Word became flesh and made his dwelling among us" (John 1:14). In this way, we have Jesus Christ in us as the God of the Word. God has established Jesus Christ as our mediator between us and God. Jesus Christ the Messiah is God's messenger who preached God's word (the gospel) to his apostles and people. Jesus was a descendant of Abraham and David, the fathers of the faith (Matt 1:1–17), and was born of his mother Mary by the Holy Spirit as the Son of God (Matt 1:18–25; Luke 1:35). He is our Lord Jesus Christ, who as to his human nature was a descendant of David, and who through the Spirit of holiness was declared with power to be the Son of God by his resurrection from the dead (Rom 1:3–4). "Jesus is the image of the invisible God, the firstborn of all creation" (Col 1:15). We see the image of God in Christ Jesus: "Christ is the image of God" (2 Cor 4:4). Christ Jesus is above all things and did God's work as mediator between God and man (1 Tim 2:5; John 5:19).

God gave Jesus life. Jesus is life. Jesus is the source of life. In Jesus Christ is life (John 1:4), and Jesus is the "word of life" (1 John 1:1). The "word of life" was from the beginning and we have heard it, seen it, and touched it (1 John 1:1). God himself had life in him, and he gave life to Jesus

Part I: Understanding the Bible

(the Son) so that life might come into him (John 5:26). In Jesus is life. Jesus said, "I am the way and the truth and the life. No one comes to the Father except through me" (John 14:6). The words of Jesus Christ are truth, eternal and unchanging. Jesus, the life, is the one who has life and does not change. And it is only through Christ Jesus that man can have life and approach God. Because of Adam's transgression, all have sinned and come to death, but because of Jesus Christ, all have eternal life (Rom 5:12–21). Adam's sin and fall brought death through disobedience to God's Word. However, Jesus obeyed God and lived a sinless life, taking the sins of men upon himself and dying as a sinner. Jesus suffered and died on the cross for our sins. The events of Jesus' substitutionary death on the cross and resurrection became the source of eternal life (salvation) through obedience to God. Jesus said, "I am the resurrection and the life; whoever believes in me will never die" (John 11:25–26). Jesus' resurrection from the dead after suffering severely and being crucified without sin is the divine proof that Jesus is the Son of God on the basis of eternal life.

Eternal life is knowing God and Jesus Christ (John 17:3). Whoever believes in Jesus Christ has eternal life (John 5:24). The Christian life is about believing, obeying, and getting to know God and Jesus Christ right. Those who have done good things will be resurrected to life, and those who have done evil things will be resurrected to the judgment of God (John 5:29). Jesus, the Good Shepherd, gives life abundantly to those who come to him (John 10:10). It is because of Jesus' death on the cross and resurrection that we have eternal life through faith in God and Jesus Christ. True believers who have received God's gift of grace and righteousness have life through Jesus Christ. If you believe in Jesus Christ, the source of life, you will be saved and live forever. Jesus said, "I am the light of the world. Whoever follows me will never walk in darkness, but will have the light of life" (John 8:12).

1. NAMES OF JESUS

In Christianity, Jesus Christ is referred to as God the Son in the Trinity—God the Father, God the Son, and God the Holy Spirit. The name of Jesus Christ encompasses all of the major Christian ideas. Jesus Christ was born in Bethlehem around 4 BC when the angel of the Lord appeared to the incarnate Son of God conceived by the virgin Mary by the Holy Spirit and gave him two names: "Jesus" and "Immanuel" (Matt 1:18–25; Luke 2:1–7). If we analyze the name Jesus Christ as a biological nomenclature, Jesus is a given name, and Christ is a family name. Therefore, there is only one Jesus in the world, but there can be multiple Christs. Jesus is the Messiah, the Savior, and the Lord (Luke 2:11). Jesus Christ is the mediator between God and man (1 Tim 2:5).

In the New Testament, Jesus is referred to as "Jesus of Nazareth" (Mark 10:47) or "the son of Joseph, Jesus of Nazareth" (John 1:45). The people of Nazareth, Jesus' hometown, called him "the carpenter," "Mary's son," "the brother of James, Joseph, Judas, and Simon" (Mark 6:3), "the carpenter's son" (Matt 13:55), "Joseph's son" (Luke 4:22), "the Son of God, the King of Israel" (John 1:49), etc.

Jesus

In the Gospel of Matthew, the angel of the Lord appeared in Joseph's dream and said, "She will give birth to a son, and you are to give him the name 'Jesus,' because he will save his people from their sins" (Matt 1:21). In other words, Jesus Christ was given the name "Jesus" by God. "Jesus" means saving his people from the yoke of sin. Etymologically, the name Jesus comes from the Hebrew word "Joshua" and means "to save."

Immanuel

God gave Jesus Christ another name: "Immanuel." It is written in the New Testament: "The virgin will be with child and will give birth to a son, and they will call him 'Immanuel,' which means, 'God with us' " (Matt 1:23). Immanuel, which means "God is with us," is also the name that the Old Testament prophet Isaiah gave to a baby to be born of a virgin. "The Lord himself will give you a sign: the virgin will be with child and will give birth to a son, and will call him Immanuel" (Isa 7:14).

Christ, Messiah, and Savior

Christ is a common noun, defined as the person who preaches the gospel and saves the world. However, Christ originally meant "the Anointed One," Messiah, and Savior. Christ, or "Anointed One," is the name given to the prophets and Messiah as the exalted one. In the Old Testament, prophets (1 Kings 19:16), priests (Exod 29:7), and kings (1 Samuel 10:1) were anointed with oil as a symbol of the Holy Spirit. When Jesus was conceived of the Holy Spirit and after his baptism, he was anointed by the Holy Spirit to preach the word of God (Luke 3:21–22; 4:18; Acts 10:38). Peter answered Jesus, "You are the Christ, the Son of the living God" (Matt 16:16). Jesus is the Christ.

Messiah (any expected deliverer, savior, messenger) means "one who delivers the gospel." Jesus acted as a messenger, delivering God's will and word (the gospel) to the apostles and people. In this way, Jesus the Messiah fulfills the same function as messenger RNA, which carries the genetic information of DNA in the cells of living things. Jesus Christ is referred to as "Jesus the Messiah." Jesus said, "I am the Messiah, the Christ" (John 4:26). There may be many Christs, but there is only one Jesus Christ. Savior means "to save the world (humanity)." In Christianity, Jesus Christ is called "the Messiah" or "Savior."

Son of God

Jesus is called "the Son of God" in the Bible (Matt 16:16; Acts 9:20). The name "Son of God" refers to Jesus' divinity. Jesus was called the Son of God because he was a holy man, born of his mother Mary by the supernatural power of the Holy Spirit (Matt 1:18–25; Luke 1:35; John 11:27). Biologically speaking, Jesus is the Son of God because he has God's DNA. Since Jesus is not created but "begotten," the idea of the Trinity is that God and his Son, Jesus, are essentially "one." Jesus is God the Son, the second person of the Trinity, who sent the Holy Spirit along with God the Father (John 14:26). He is the Lord Jesus Christ who was raised from the dead and proclaimed to be the mighty Son of God (Rom 1:4). "The Son of God is the image of the invisible God, the firstborn of every creature" (Col 1:15). All things in heaven and on earth were created by and for the Son of God (Col 1:16). "For there is one God and one mediator between God and men, the man Christ Jesus" (1 Tim 2:5). As the Son of God, Jesus mediates God's relationship with man. As the Son of God, Jesus was the messenger (mediator) between humanity and God, preaching God's will and word (the gospel) to the apostles and people.

Son of Man

The title "Son of Man" means that Jesus is the Messiah, the truly holy Son of Man. In the Old Testament, "Son of Man" is first used as a title for a transcendent being, the Messiah, who is foretold to come in the clouds (Dan 7:13–14). In the New Testament, "Son of Man" is applied to Jesus and is rarely used to refer to ordinary people. The name "Son of Man" represents the humanity of Jesus, who was born in a human body and fully possessed everything that humans have. "Son of Man" is not a title that people called Jesus. Jesus called himself the Son of Man when it was used in reference to his ministry, his passion, his resurrection, and his future coming. Rarely did anyone else call him "Son of Man." Jesus said, "Just as the Son of Man did not come to be served, but to serve, and to give his life a ransom for many" (Matt 20:28). "No one has ascended to heaven except the one who came down from heaven, the Son of Man" (John 3:13). When Jesus was being interrogated by the high priest, he said, "I am he, and you will see the Son of Man sitting at the right hand of the Mighty One and coming on the clouds of heaven" (Mark 14:62). In biological terms, Jesus' name, "Son of Man," means Son of Man with the DNA of his physical mother, Mary.

Lord

As an honorific title for Jesus, we call him "Lord" to express his high sovereignty and supreme spiritual authority. "God made Jesus both Lord and Christ" (Acts 2:36). Jesus is "Lord" (1 Cor 12:3). Christ is "Lord" of the dead and the living (Rom 14:9, Phil 2:11). The designation "Lord" refers to Christ giving grace and peace to believers in the church (Rom 1:7; Eph 1:2; Phil 4:23). Jesus is called "Lord" hundreds of times in the New Testament, including "acknowledging Jesus as Lord" (Rom 10:9) and "confessing Jesus Christ as Lord" (Phil 2:11). Lord is also used as a title for God (Matt 1:20–22; 22:37; 1 Cor 7:34; Phil 4:4–5). Christians refer to Jesus as "Lord" in their confessions of faith. If you confess Jesus as "Lord" and believe in his resurrection, you will be saved (Rom 10:9). Since Jesus' resurrection in the New Testament, the title "Lord" has been widely used to refer to Jesus from the apostles' preaching of the gospel to the Christian life of today. The apostle Paul said, "No one can say that Jesus is Lord except by the Holy Spirit" (1 Cor 12:3). This indicates that baptized Christians call Jesus "Lord." In Christianity in general, the title "LORD" or "Lord" is widely used to refer to

God, not just Jesus. "Believe in the Lord Jesus, and you will be saved—you and your household" (Acts 16:31). "For Moses said, 'The Lord your God will raise up for you a prophet like me from among your own people'" (Acts 3:22). "From everlasting to everlasting, Lord, you are God" (Ps 90:2).

2. JESUS' DIVINITY AND HUMANITY

Jesus is both the Son of God and the Son of Man. Jesus Christ has both the spiritual nature (divinity) of God (Rom 9:5) and the physical nature (humanity) of man (Luke 24:39). Jesus spoke of his divinity by identifying himself with God, calling God "my Father" and saying, "I and the Father are one" (John 10:30). Biologically speaking, Jesus has both God's DNA and the DNA of the Virgin Mary. As such, the divinity and humanity of Jesus Christ are united as one. Jesus became the eternal Son of God by the Holy Spirit, uniting man and God (the Holy Spirit) in Jesus Christ. We are Christ's people because we have the Spirit of God (Jesus) in us (John 8:9). Jesus' conception by the Holy Spirit (Matt 1:18) and resurrection from the dead (Matt 28:6–7) are supernatural, indicating his divinity. The supernatural resurrection of Jesus implies the divinity of Jesus. In reality, earthly people who do not have God's DNA cannot resurrect themselves. Jesus Christ is called "the son of Abraham and David," born in the flesh (Matt 1:1). Jesus, the Son of God, was born of a descendant of David in the flesh (Rom 1:3). But Jesus Christ is also the Son of God, begotten of the Holy Spirit, and a holy human being, born of the virgin Mary (Matt 1:18–25; Luke 2:1–7). Through the work of the Holy Spirit in the body of his mother Mary, Jesus was born with both humanity and divinity. Jesus said, "I am from above and am not of this world" (John 8:23) and "before Abraham was, I am" (John 8:58). Jesus was glorified with God before the foundation of the world (John 17:5), and as the Son he did exactly what he saw God doing (John 5:19). The Lord Jesus Christ was raised from the dead by the Spirit of sanctification and declared to be the Son of God with power (Rom 1:4). In this way, Jesus spoke of his divinity and did the works of God as the Son.

Jesus performed many signs and wonders to prove to people that he was the Son of God—that is, his divinity. He made wine out of water at a wedding feast in Cana of Galilee (John 2:1–11) and fed five thousand people with five loaves and two fish (Mark 6:38–44). He raised Lazarus from the grave (John 11:1–44). He healed a demon-possessed man (Mark

1:23–28), a leper (Matt 8:2–4), a man with a severe leprosy (Luke 5:18–26), a man who was blind and mute (Matt 12:22–37), a woman with a hemorrhage (Mark 5:25–34), and a man who was blind from birth (John 9:1–11). In these ways, Jesus demonstrated what God was doing with signs and wonders. These signs and wonders testified to what Jesus did in God's name (John 10:24–25). The signs and wonders that Jesus performed were supernatural and superhuman. They are acts of God, not of man. Through these signs and wonders, Jesus testified to his divinity as the Son of God and confirmed God's revelation and word.

Jesus was born in the flesh, justified by the Spirit, preached the gospel of God to mankind, became the object of faith in the world, and demonstrated his true divinity in glory (1 Tim 3:16). Jesus has humanity along with divinity, and his humanity cannot be expressed independently. Being the Son of God is the personal manifestation of humanity in divinity. In the Bible, Jesus' divine nature sometimes appears as a personality derived from his humanity (John 3:13; Rom 9:5). Jesus said, "No one has ever gone into heaven except the one who came from heaven, the Son of Man" (John 3:13). Christ Jesus did God's work as a mediator between God and man (1 Tim 2:5; John 5:19). Jesus Christ fulfilled the office of mediator by taking on the garments of flesh and delivering the word of God (the gospel) as the Messiah, the Son of God. Jesus denied himself to do the will of God (John 5:30), did not seek his own glory (John 8:50), and glorified God in all things (1 Pet 4:11). Jesus lived a life of complete conformity to the will of God, and Jesus lived a life of loving service to God and man (Matt 7:12; 20:27).

3. THE LIFE AND MINISTRY OF JESUS

The New Testament records the life and ministry of Jesus Christ in detail. Jesus is the forty-second generation descendant of Abraham, the patriarch of the faith (Matt 1:1–17). Jesus was born in Bethlehem as the Son of God by his mother Mary, who was conceived by the Holy Spirit (Matt 1:18–25; Luke 2:1–7). Jesus was circumcised (Luke 2:21), and he was a Jew (Gal 3:16). He grew up in Nazareth, the hometown of his parents, Joseph and Mary (Matt 2:22–23). As the baby Jesus grew, he became stronger, full of wisdom, favored by God, and loved by God and people (Luke 2:40, 52). He was baptized in water by John the Baptist (Matt 3:13–16; John 1:33) and preached the gospel of God to the nation of Israel (Jews) (Mark 1:14–15). He was arrested the night he took the Lord's Supper (1 Cor 11:23–26) and was crucified and died around AD 30 (Mark 15:21–37). He then rose from the dead (Matt 28:1–10; Mark 16:9; John 20:11–18), spoke about the things of the kingdom of God for forty days (Acts 1:3), and ascended into heaven (Mark 16:19; Luke 24:51).

Jesus was born of the virgin Mary, became the incarnate Son of God, and lived a life of suffering in soul and body, being attacked and tempted by Satan and oppressed by an unrighteous world. He was born under the law (Gal 4:4). To redeem us from the curse of the law (Gal 3:13), Jesus was crucified (Mark 15:21–37), descended into Hades (hell) (Apostles' Creed), and entered the lowest place (Eph 4:9). As such, Jesus was in a state of humiliation, forsaking his divine majesty and dying in submission to the law. After Jesus died and received the sour wine, he said, "It is finished" (John 19:30). Jesus' redemptive work was accomplished when the sinless Jesus died on the cross as a complete atonement for sin. Jesus paid the full penalty for our sins, and he rose from the dead in a spiritual and physical body, finally free from the curse of the law and exalted in status (1 Cor 15:44–46). Jesus' resurrection gave us the hope that if we are born again, we too can be raised from death by sin (John 3:3; Eph 2:1; 1 Pet 1:3). Jesus also rose from the dead to become Lord of the dead and of the living (Rom 14:9). After his resurrection, the human Jesus appeared to his disciples on earth (Acts 1:3) and then ascended into heaven (Mark 16:19; Luke 24:51). Now, Jesus is at the right hand of God and participates in God's rulership over all things in the universe (Eph 1:20–21; 1 Pet 3:22). In the final stage, Jesus' supreme glorious exaltation will be his bodily return from heaven to the world (Acts 1:11; Rev 1:7–8). The work of Jesus will be completed when Jesus Christ descends into this world to judge and save the living, the dead, the lawless, and those who love unrighteousness (1 Cor 4:4–5; 1 Thess 4:13–17; 2 Thess 2:1–12).

Jesus Christ came into the world and fulfilled the offices of prophet, priest, and king (Heb 5:1–7). Even after his ascension, he sent his Comforter (Counselor), the Holy Spirit, to continue his ministry (John 14:26). The Old Testament predicted the coming of a prophet (Deut 18:15), and Jesus identified himself as a prophet (Matt 23:37; Luke 13:34). As a prophet, Jesus fulfilled Old Testament prophecy, preaching the word of God and leading people to the way of truth and life (John 14:6). As a priest who became a sin offering to atone for human sin, Jesus served as a mediator to establish the relationship between God and humans and bring reconciliation (Mark 10:45; Rom 3:24–25; Heb 4:14–16; 5:1–10). As a priest, Jesus Christ bore the sins of the people, performed sacrificial ministry, and acted as a mediator for his people, giving them grace and peace. In his kingly office, Jesus is a ruler with eternal spiritual and cosmic kingship, now and in the future, entrusted by God with the authority to destroy the power of Satan, rule the church, and reign over creation (Ps 72:17; Matt 28:18; Luke 1:32–33; 10:18–19; 19:38; John 18:37; Eph 1:22; 1 Cor 15:25; 2 Pet 1:11).

As man's substitute, Jesus Christ performed the work of atonement, which is a vicarious atonement, to take the punishment of sin and save sinners, humans. In the Old Testament, an anointed priest (Christ) offered a sin offering to receive forgiveness of sins (Lev 4:20, 31, 35). Jesus took on the sins of the world (John 1:29) and gave his life as a ransom for many guilty people (Mark 10:45; Gal 1:4). As a righteous man, Jesus Christ died in the place of the unrighteous and was buried in the flesh but was raised in the spirit to save a sinful people (1 Pet 3:18). Jesus said, "I have not come to call the righteous, but sinners" (Matt 9:13). Jesus came into this world to forgive and save by grace those who are sinful, hopeless, and desperate. Jesus gives us everything that belongs to life and godliness by his glory and virtue (grace) (2 Pet 1:3). The righteous and holy God punishes sin (Gen 3:3, Exod 20:5, Rom 6:23), but Jesus Christ of love did the work of atonement, giving us "justification by faith" and saving people by grace (Rom 1:17; 3:23–26). To mankind under the Old Testament law, God continues his work of grace through the Comforter, the Holy Spirit, whom Jesus ascended and sent after his resurrection from the cross (John 1:16–17; 14:26).

4. THE RESURRECTION AND LIFE OF JESUS

(1) The Resurrection of Jesus

The resurrection of Jesus is the central idea and doctrine of Christianity. The resurrection is not a human event but a divine event, an event of God. The resurrection of Jesus is also a creative event in which God gave spiritual life to a lifeless human being. Jesus suffered harshly at the hands of the Romans, was crucified, died, was buried, and on the third day rose from the dead and ascended into heaven (Matt 28:1–10; Mark 16:1–8; Luke 24:1–12; John 20:1–18). Peter, Jesus' apostle, spoke of Christ's resurrection in his Pentecostal sermon, saying, "He was not abandoned to the grave, nor did his body see decay" (Acts 2:31). Jesus' resurrection is proof that Jesus Christ is the Son of God (Rom 1:4). Jesus' resurrection is the revelation of his divinity to mankind. Without his resurrection, Jesus would have been just an ordinary human being, not the Son of God. The resurrection of Jesus is both a historical fact and a theological event. Through Jesus' death on the cross and resurrection, righteousness is restored and new life is given to us.

Jesus was raised by the Spirit of sanctification and declared to be the Son of God (Rom 1:4). Afterward, Jesus' disciples, who were in despair over his death, preached the gospel with all their lives for the name of Jesus Christ (Acts 15:25–35). Jesus' disciples' belief in his resurrection was a testimony to the historical Jesus and the starting point for the proclamation of the early church. Christians celebrate the resurrection of Jesus on Easter Sunday, three days after Good Friday, when Jesus was crucified. In Christianity, Easter is celebrated on the Sunday following the first full moon (lunar month) after the vernal equinox. If this full moon falls on a Sunday, then the following Sunday is Easter. The timing of Easter closely coincides with Passover, which is associated with the Old Testament Exodus. The apostle Paul emphasized, "And if Christ has not been raised, our preaching is useless and so is your faith" (1 Cor 15:14). In the preaching of the gospel of God, the resurrection of Jesus has become a central idea of Christianity. The resurrection of Jesus means that Jesus has overcome human sin and death, and this speaks of God's revelation of death and life.

(2) The Idea of Life in the New Testament

Most of the humans who lived in the Old Testament era, including Adam, Eve, and Moses, are dead (1 Cor 15:22). With the exception of Enoch, everyone else in the Old Testament is dead (Gen 5:24; Heb 11:5). Therefore, the Old Testament is very sparse on the idea of life. The New Testament states that "in Jesus Christ was life" (John 1:4) and calls Jesus "the Word of life" (1 John 1:1). Jesus is the source of life. The New Testament contains the idea of salvation (eternal life), that only God the Creator can give life through the resurrection of Jesus. The resurrection of Jesus is the saving event of God who raised life from lifeless death. Adam of sin and death is the founder of the Old Testament era, and Jesus Christ of life, grace, and love is the founder of the New Testament era. Resurrection refers to the reviving of the dead by gaining life again, and like Jesus's resurrection, the belief that the dead are resurrected also spread to people (John 6:39–40; 1 Cor 15:12–13). Resurrection and eternal life are the covenant of Jesus Christ himself and the revelation of God in advance to his disciples. In

Jesus Is the Messiah and the Life

the Bible, Jesus says, "I am the bread of life. If anyone eats of this bread, he will live forever" (John 6:48, 51). This means that Jesus' body is given to us as the divine bread of life. In the church's communion service, Christian believers share the bread of life, which symbolizes the flesh of Jesus. Jesus himself said, "I am the resurrection and the life. He who believes in me will live, even though he dies; and whoever lives and believes in me will never die" (John 11:25–26). Jesus' resurrection is proof that those who believe in Jesus Christ will be raised from the dead and live forever. The apostle Paul says, "By his power God raised the Lord from the dead, and he will raise us also" (1 Cor 6:14). Thus, if we obey God by faith, we too can be resurrected, saved, and live forever.

Believers' faith in the death and resurrection of Jesus Christ on the cross is the foundation of the Christian faith. Jesus clearly prophesied that he would suffer many things, be killed, and be resurrected (Matt 16:21). The resurrection is accomplished by the power of God (Matt 22:28–29). Resurrection is the coming back to life of the body through the resurrected Jesus (John 11:25–26). The resurrection of Jesus means that the spirit is reunited with a perfect body of flesh and bones (Luke 24:39). The apostle Paul speaks of salvation (eternal life): that because Jesus rose from the dead, everyone who believes in Jesus will have life (1 Cor 15:20–22). By the spirit of sanctification, Jesus was raised from the dead so that he might be recognized as the Son of God with power (Rom 1:4). The resurrection of Jesus was the event that revealed Jesus to be the Son of God. His resurrection is a symbolic event of salvation, as Jesus rose again from the dead as a substitutionary atonement for all people who believe in him. The resurrection of Jesus means the salvation of all mankind. Jesus' resurrection restored righteousness to humans and gave them life. Jesus' resurrection from the dead brings us out of the bondage of the rigid rules and regulations of the Old Testament law and into the new age of grace, love, and life of the New Testament. Jesus gave his disciples a new commandment: "Love one another" (John 13:34). Those who keep the commandment will love God and Jesus and be loved by God (Jesus) (John 14:21). Through the two events of Jesus' death on the cross and resurrection, God showed that Jesus has authority over life. God and Jesus have the power to save Christians by grace and give them eternal life. After his resurrection, Jesus appeared to his disciples and gave them peace, the Holy Spirit, and forgiveness of sins (John 20:19–23). True life-giving faith cannot be attained by one's own efforts, however; it can only come in God and in Christ through Jesus Christ.

6

What Is Faith

FAITH IS BELIEVING IN God and Jesus Christ and accepting Jesus as "Lord." Christians are united by faith with Jesus Christ, the Son of God. A person of faith worships and praises God and Jesus Christ and does God's will. Those who truly believe are with God and Jesus Christ until death. Jesus said to his disciples, "Trust in God; trust also in me" (John 14:1). He was asking them to believe in both God and Jesus Christ. The beginning of faith is to believe that God exists (Heb 11:6). Without faith it is impossible to please God. The object of Christian faith is God, the Trinity of Father, Son, and Holy Spirit. The Holy Spirit gives us faith (1 Cor 12:9). Faith is passive and obedient. Faith is a gift of God, given by grace. Faith is not earned by human will but is sovereignly given to us by God. Faith is given by God, so we humans cannot become Christians on our own. Only those who come to Jesus because God causes them to come believe in Jesus (John 6:65). A person of faith is righteous, poor in spirit, and merciful. The poor in spirit, the meek, those hungry for righteousness, the merciful, the pure in heart, and the peacemakers are blessed by faith, for theirs is the kingdom of heaven (Matt 5:3–9).

Faith is built on the Word (John 1:1). Faith is obeying God and keeping the Word and the gospel of God and Jesus Christ. God's Word is truth (John 17:17). Faith is hearing and believing the words of Jesus Christ. "Consequently, faith comes from hearing the message, and the message is heard through the word of Christ" (Rom 10:17). Obedience comes from a heart of faith. True faith in Jesus begins with unconditional obedience. True faith produces a humble, submissive heart. Obedience to Jesus requires self-denial. The life of true faith is a life of daily self-denial and following the Lord. Jesus says, "If anyone would come after me, he must deny himself and take up his cross daily and follow me" (Luke 9:23). Christian self-denial is the renunciation of physical desires and the spiritual belief in and obedience to Jesus Christ. Jesus rebuked those who disobeyed him by claiming to believe with their mouths only. "Why do you call me, 'Lord, Lord,' and do not do what I say?" (Luke 6:46). You must not just say you believe, but you must believe by doing righteous and good deeds. "For just as the body without the soul is dead, so faith without works is dead" (Jas 2:26). Saying you believe in God without doing righteous deeds is not true faith in God. It is pretense and hypocrisy. True faith is accompanied by righteous deeds. The believer does righteous deeds. True faith should be our life. The life of faith is living according to the Word of God. A life without righteousness is a life of false faith. Many people in the world say they believe in Jesus Christ, but they live a worldly life of self-love. The life of faith is to do God's will and live for the glory of God with the Lord in us.

Faith is a marvelous thing, and when we believe, we are born again, regenerated, changed in character, and become a new person spiritually. A fallen man becomes a new man, establishing a right relationship with God and living a life of spiritual faith in Jesus Christ. "There is no one righteous, not even one" (Rom 3:10). In God's eyes, there is no righteous person in this world. "There is not a righteous man on earth who does what is right and never sins" (Eccl 7:20). We are sinners, but when we believe in God and Jesus Christ, we are made righteous, and we hate sin and long for righteousness. "Since we have been justified through faith, we have peace with God through our Lord Jesus Christ" (Rom 5:1). This justification frees us from sin to do God's will and live a life of faith in a reconciled relationship with God. The faith that the Bible speaks of is a faith that works through love and grace. Faith regenerates sinners and makes them righteous in the sight of God. True faith is demonstrated by trusting in God (Jesus) and believing by acting on the Word. Our faith is seen by the Lord in our works and obedience. True faith works in love and produces a humble heart that serves, cares, and humbles and abandons itself. "The Lord knows those who are his" (2 Tim 2:19). God knows our faith. True faith is not something we can earn through our own efforts but is obtained in union with Jesus Christ and through him. Our good works of faith bring grace. The Christian of faith lives in gratitude for God's grace. It is by grace that we are saved through faith, and that is a gift from God (Eph 2:8).

1. THE MEANING OF FAITH

True faith is trusting and relying on God and Jesus Christ for everything in our lives. Jesus said, "Come to me, all you who are weary and burdened, and I will give you rest" (Matt 11:28). Faith is going to Jesus Christ. Jesus declared, "I am the bread of life. He who comes to me will never go hungry, and he who believes in me will never be thirsty" (John 6:35). "Yet to all who received him, to those who believed in his name, he gave the right to become children of God" (John 1:12). All Christians become sons of God by faith in Jesus Christ (Gal 3:26). They receive the Holy Spirit by hearing the gospel and believing (Gal 3:2). When you believe in Jesus, you become a child of God. As children of God, we can call God our Father (Rom 8:15). A person of faith calls God "Father."

By faith the worlds were formed by the word of God (Heb 11:3). "Hebrews 11" in the New Testament defines faith and explains it in detail. Here it tells us exactly what faith is and what it does. Here is how Hebrews defines faith: "Now faith is the substance of things hoped for, the evidence of things not seen" (Heb 11:1). Faith is the assurance of what we hope for and the confirmation of what we do not see. Even though we have not seen God, with glorious joy we believe in him. In the Old Testament, God called Abraham righteous because he believed in him (God) (Gen 15:6). Furthermore, the Lord God said, "The righteous will live by his faith" (Hab 2:4). From these words of God in the Old Testament, Martin Luther's Reformed idea of "justification by faith" in the New Testament was established. "The righteous will live by faith" (Rom 1:17), or "we have been justified through faith" (Rom 5:1). "It is God who justifies" (Rom 8:33). All have sinned and fall short of the glory of God but are justified freely by God's grace through the redemption that is in Christ Jesus (Rom 3:23–24). The righteous live by faith (Gal 3:11). As such, a person of faith lives righteously. In the gospel, the righteousness of God is revealed so that faith may be by faith (Rom 1:17). There is righteousness in the Word of God and in the gospel. Righteousness is not from the law but from God through faith in Christ (Phil 3:9). God's righteousness is revealed by his grace (mercy). Only the righteous live according to God's will by faith in God. The righteous always do God's will. In

What Is Faith

the way of righteousness is life, and there is no death (Prov 12:28). Faith is the way to life, and without faith it is impossible to please God (Heb 11:6).

True faith is an absolute acceptance of God's Word, repentance, and absolute trust and obedience to God (Jesus). A person of faith obeys God and does what is righteous. "You are slaves to obedience, which leads to righteousness" (Rom 6:16). Faith is manifested in obedience to God (Jesus). Trust and obedience come from the heart. A Christian of true faith obeys God. "Trust" is the highest volitional component of faith. "Ask God, and it will be given to you; but ask only in faith, and do not doubt" (Jas 1:5–6). Faith is based on trust. Trust results in devotion and obedience to the object of faith. Only faith based on trust is accepting Jesus Christ as Lord and obeying him. If we do not trust in Jesus Christ, we do not have true faith. Abraham was confident that God would fulfill what he had promised (Rom 4:21). God cannot lie and has promised eternal life (Titus 1:2). God does not change (Mal 3:6), so he is infinitely trustworthy. We must also rely on and believe in Jesus Christ and trust that he will do what he has promised. It is following what Jesus said. This means "do whatever he tells you" (John 2:5).

Faith has an objective reality, and we must have faith based on objective truth. To be saved, one must acknowledge Jesus Christ as Lord and believe in his heart the events of his crucifixion for human sins and his resurrection from the dead (Rom 10:9; 1 Cor 15:1–4). In other words, humans cannot be saved and have eternal life without believing in Jesus' death and resurrection for our sins. Through baptism, the Spirit of God (the Holy Spirit) enters the human heart, leading to the beginning of actual faith. Those who believe in Jesus have eternal life (John 3:36), but there are differences in the intensity of faith among Christian believers. Faith is not great at first, and it gradually grows bigger. Jesus compared the size of faith to a mustard seed. "If you have faith as small as a mustard seed, you can say to this mountain, 'Move from here to there' and it will move. Nothing will be impossible for you" (Matt 17:20). Only faith that works by love is true faith (Gal 5:6). True faith is a work of love. Our faith overcomes the world (1 John 5:4), and whatever we do not do by faith is sin (Rom 14:23). A Christian of true faith overcomes worldly tests and lives according to God's will. A person of faith should not be a servant of the world but a servant of God and Jesus Christ (1 Cor 7:22–23).

Part I: Understanding the Bible

2. FAITH, REGENERATION, AND REPENTANCE

Regeneration, which means "to be born again," or "to be born anew," is the process by which fallen human beings are made spiritually new in order to live in a right relationship with God. Regeneration causes us to repent and begin a life of faith. Faith without regeneration and repentance is not true faith. We never approach God in response until we are born again, which means that an unregenerate person cannot hear God's Word and believe in God and Jesus Christ. It is God who regenerates us. Regeneration (rebirth) is not accomplished by human will and effort. When we are spiritually born again, God recreates us daily and gives us new life. To be born again spiritually is to receive new life. When we are born again, a spiritual change occurs in our attributes, temperament, personality, and mind, giving us a new nature. Our sanctifying transformation through faith in Jesus Christ is a repeated rebirth, dying daily and being born anew daily. "If anyone is in Christ, he is a new creation; the old has gone, the new has come" (2 Cor 5:17). The believer in Jesus Christ is born again and undergoes a spiritual transformation.

In a broad sense, regeneration is the entire process of being born again spiritually, from repentance (conversion) and faith to justification and sanctification. Regeneration, repentance, and faith bring justification. Sanctification is the process by which we become holy and gloriously conformed to the life of Jesus Christ by a godly life of faith. A holy life is a life of righteousness and goodness lived according to God's will. Jesus emphasized the need to be born again when he told the Jewish leader Nicodemus, "I tell you the truth, no one can see the kingdom of God unless he is born again" (John 3:3). "No one can enter the kingdom of God unless he is born of water and the Spirit" (John 3:5). As such, "water and the Holy Spirit" are necessary for regeneration in order to be saved and enter the kingdom of God. This is because one must be born again of water and the Spirit to have life. "Everyone who believes that Jesus is the Christ is born of God" (1 John 5:1). He who is born of God overcomes the world (1 John 5:4). When we are born again, we will be freed from worldly things. "Put off your old self, which is being corrupted by its deceitful desires; and be made new in the attitude of your minds; and put on the new self, created to be like God in true righteousness and holiness" (Eph 4:22–24). God is a God of truth. We must be born again from a life of fleshly desires to a new man after God's righteousness and truth. The spiritual truth of God does not enter the hearts of the unbelievers. The person of faith overcomes the desires of the flesh by walking according to the Spirit (Gal 5:16). "Because of his mercy, He saved us through the washing of rebirth and renewal by the Holy Spirit" (Titus 3:5). The born-again person is freed from selfish self-love and empowered by the Holy Spirit to work the agape (selfless) love of God. "You know that everyone who does what is right has been born of him" (1 John 2:29).

To repent is to be sorry for a sin or wrongdoing, to turn away from it, and to come to God. Repentance results in a spiritual change of heart and a change of behavior. To follow God, we must forsake our sins. Repentance leads to the forgiveness of sins (Luke 24:47). Repentance frees you from the evil thoughts, evil deeds, and bad habits in your heart and brings you closer to God and Jesus Christ. Jesus Christ said, "Repent, for the kingdom of heaven is at hand" (Matt 4:17), and he wanted the believer's entire life to be a life of repentance. God has given us repentance that leads to life (Acts 11:18). In the worldly life, repentance should happen to the believer every day, every moment. When we repent, we receive life. The true Christian life is a life of repentance. Repentance keeps us Christians on the path of faith. Faith without repentance is not true faith. A truly repentant person lives righteously and well. Repentance produces faith, so that God saves the believer and welcomes him into the kingdom of God.

"Conversion" is the act by which a human being in disobedience to God turns away from sin and returns to God by his grace. Conversion is the work of the Holy Spirit that allows a person to repent of sin, be born again, and turn to Jesus Christ to believe in Jesus. Conversion is an important component of repentance. A classic example of human conversion is the conversion of the apostle Paul. He was converted from a law-abiding Jew to a Christian who preached the gospel of Jesus. On the road to Damascus, Paul heard the voice of Jesus Christ, who appeared to him as a light, and he was converted, born again, baptized, and became a true apostle of Jesus (Acts 9:1–19; 22:6–16; 26:12–18). In this way, Paul received the revelation of God through Jesus Christ. Jesus said, "No one knows the Father except the Son and those to whom the Son chooses to reveal him" (Matt 11:27). God's revelation is an important element of conversion. However, many Christians today do not understand the terms repentance and conversion correctly. Repentance happens every moment in the Christian's life. When a person who has no religion or is a practitioner of another religion, such as Buddhism or Islam, converts to Christianity and believes in God and Jesus Christ, this can be called "conversion." It is also a type of "conversion" for an atheist who lives a worldly life to be baptized and born again—and to become a Christian who believes in God and Jesus Christ. However, repentance in a broad sense includes these types of "conversions."

Repentance is turning away from your past sins and showing that you no longer sin. When you repent and believe in Jesus Christ, you are given new spiritual life. Jesus said, "The kingdom of God is near. Repent and believe the good news" (Mark 1:15). Only those who repent and believe the gospel of God can enter the kingdom of God. John the Baptist cried out in the wilderness of Judea: "Repent, for the kingdom of heaven is near" (Matt 3:2). Peter encouraged people to believe in Jesus by preaching, "Repent and be baptized, every one of you, in the name of Jesus Christ" (Acts 2:38). The apostle Paul also said, "Repent and turn to God and prove their repentance by their deeds" (Acts 26:20). Repentance is the result of faith, and we repent when we fear God. God causes us to repent. Repentance is a gift from God (Acts 11:17–18; 2 Tim 2:25). We can only repent if God gives it to us by grace (2 Cor 7:10). With genuine repentance, the sinner receives remission (forgiveness) of sins (Luke 5:31–32, 24:47; 1 John 1:9). Genuine repentance results in a change of heart, which in turn leads to a change in behavior. Repentance is not regret. Judas Iscariot, who betrayed Jesus and sold him for thirty pieces of silver, regretted seeing Jesus convicted but did not truly repent (Matt 27:3). "The love of money is the root of all evil" (1 Tim 6:10). Judas loved the money of the world, but he lacked true obedience and faith in Jesus. Judas drew near to Jesus to learn the truth and confess his faith, but he was not saved because he did not submit to Jesus. Judas's faith was a false faith that loved the world of sin and darkness. True faith, believed with the heart, is accompanied by true repentance and obedience. Repentance demands obedience to God. "Repent" was the central message of Paul and the other apostles as they preached the gospel of Jesus Christ.

Repentance is being set free from sin and returning to God and Jesus for forgiveness and a change in behavior (Acts 3:26; 8:22; 20:21; 26:20). "The Lord is a forgiving God" (Neh 9:17). If we confess our sins, God is faithful and just to forgive us our sins and purify us from all unrighteousness (1 John 1:9). Abraham, Jacob, Moses, David, Peter, and Paul, some of the most revered servants of God in the Bible, all committed worldly sins during their lives. However, they all repented and were forgiven, freed from their sins, obeyed God, and lived righteous lives by faith, and are worshiped by mankind forever. Only those who obey God by faith are made righteous. Those who repent and are born again, clothed in new life, do God's will through faith in God and the guidance of the Holy Spirit. The fruit of

What Is Faith

repentance is manifested in the life of faith. A person of faith forsakes selfish desires and serves people with compassion. Furthermore, out of selfless love of God, he does his best to fulfill his duties with honesty and integrity in his own position.

3. FAITH, WORKS, AND GRACE

True faith is believing that God exists, seeking him, and receiving Jesus Christ. "You will seek me and find me when you seek me with all your heart" (Jer 29:13). "Anyone who comes to him must believe that he exists and that he rewards those who earnestly seek him" (Heb 11:6). Those who seek God will find and to them who knock, it shall be opened (Matt 7:7–8; Luke 11:9–10). True faith is seeking God and receiving Christ Jesus to have peaceful fellowship with him. We open the door of our hearts to receive and believe in the Lord Jesus Christ and enjoy a life of joy together in him. "I stand at the door and knock. If anyone hears My voice and opens the door, I will come in and eat with him, and he with me" (Rev 3:20). The life of faith is a life of receiving Jesus Christ and living with him.

True faith is manifested in trusting God and Jesus Christ and acting on their words. A believing heart toward God is an obedient heart. A person of faith obeys God. Obedience is an essential component of true faith. Faith and obedience do not come from the mouth but from following God's will in action. The slavery of sin results in death, or the slavery of obedience results in righteousness (Rom 6:16). True faith produces righteous behavior through obedience. Faith in action is true faith. True faith is manifested in good and righteous deeds. It is impossible for a person without faith to perform righteous works. True faith and righteous works always go together. "The righteous will live by his faith" (Hab 2:4). A righteous person lives by true faith. Righteousness is the inevitable result of true faith. A person of true faith relies on Jesus Christ and receives the gift of grace from him. True faith looks to Jesus as the Lord and perfecter of faith (Heb 12:2). Furthermore, the believer is conformed to the image of Jesus (Rom 8:29). Once this justification by faith occurs, sanctification begins. In the life of faith, sanctification is the process of being set free from sin and conformed to the likeness of Jesus Christ as a child of God. Sanctification is the transformation of the sinner's nature in the human heart. To be sanctified is to have the Word of God abundantly in our hearts and to live in obedience to God according to the Word under the guidance of the Holy

Spirit. A Christian of faith lives for the glory of God by being conformed to the likeness of Jesus Christ. "Make every effort to live in peace with all men and to be holy; without holiness no one will see the Lord" (Heb 12:14). A person of true faith is sanctified. Without holiness, we will not see the Lord. "Those he justified, he also glorified" (Rom 8:30). God has glorified and sanctified those whom he has justified by faith. The life of faith is a life of righteousness and holiness.

We must be doers of the word of God but not hearers only, deceiving ourselves (Jas 1:22). A true believer hears and does the word of God. "Everyone who hears these words of mine and puts them into practice is like a wise man who built his house on the rock" (Matt 7:24). In this way, Jesus described the doer of faith as a wise man who built his house on a rock. "If anyone considers himself religious and yet does not keep a tight rein on his tongue, he deceives himself and his religion is worthless" (Jas 1:26). The Bible gives a very clear and logical definition of faith and works (Jas 2:14–26). "For those who repent and are born again, faith in Jesus requires works," James says. "As the body without the spirit is dead, so faith without deeds is dead" (Jas 2:26). Faith without deeds is useless (Jas 2:20). Faith and actions are inextricably linked and work together. True faith must be accompanied by righteous works, meaning that faith without righteous works is not true faith. "His faith was made complete by what he did" (Jas 2:22). If you say you have faith but do not act righteously, you do not really believe in God and Jesus Christ. Faith without works is vain and pretentious (Jas 2:20). "You have faith; I have deeds. Show me your faith without deeds, and I will show you my faith by what I do" (Jas 2:18). Saying pity to the poor is not a true deed. "Suppose a brother or sister is without clothes and daily food, and if you say to him, 'Go, I wish you well; keep warm and well fed,' but does nothing about his physical needs, what good is it?" (Jas 2:15–17); it is not faith of works. We cannot show faith without works (Jas 2:18). Faith without works is hypocritical.

What is true faith? True faith is to practice the will and word of God (Jesus) by doing. Anyone who does not do the will of God is not a true believer. Those who believe in Jesus will do what Jesus does (John 14:12). However, living according to God's will does not mean living according to the rigid rules and regulations of legalistic Christianity. We are justified by faith in Christ, but not by the works of the law (Gal 2:16). We are not justified by keeping all the laws. A life of faith means a life of righteous works in the sight of God. The righteous do God's will. "Was not our ancestor

Abraham considered righteous for what he did when he offered his son Isaac on the altar" (Jas 2:21). "A person is justified by what he does and not by faith alone" (Jas 2:24). We are not justified by faith alone, but righteousness and good works must go together. We have a good conscience to do everything good (Heb 13:18). It is one thing to know intellectually who Jesus is, but it is another to have a faith that involves obeying, trusting, and acting according to his Word. Righteous and good works are seen in the lives of Christians who truly believe in Jesus Christ. When we believe in God, God works in us to do righteous and good works. A person of true faith does what is right. "For we walk by faith, not by sight" (2 Cor 5:7).

The ancestors of faith obeyed, worshiped, endured, and sacrificed to God by faith (Heb 11). "Without faith it is impossible to please God" (Heb 11:6). The people (the ancestors) of faith devotedly obeyed God to please God and died by faith. The people of faith recorded in the Bible were those who obeyed God with a good thought, heart, and soul. By faith, Abel offered a better sacrifice to God than Cain and became a righteous man (Heb 11:4). By faith, Enoch pleased God and was transferred to God without dying (Heb 11:5). By faith, Noah built the ark and saved his house (Heb 11:7). By faith, Abraham obeyed and sojourned in the promised land as if he were in a foreign land (Heb 11:8–9). By faith, Abraham offered his only son Isaac when he was tempted (Heb 11:17). By faith, Isaac, Jacob, and Joseph endured difficult lives and were blessed (Heb 11:20–22). By faith, Moses was humiliated in Egypt, saved the Israelites, and crossed the Red Sea like dry land (Heb 11:26–29). By faith, the prostitute Rahab received the spies in peace (Heb 11:31). In this way, Rahab was justified by her works (Jas 2:25). Furthermore, Samson, David, Samuel, and the prophets overcame the neighboring nations by faith, practiced righteousness, received promises, and destroyed the forces of unrighteousness (Heb 11:32–34). Some did not want to be released from severe torture in order to obtain a better resurrection (Heb 11:35). Some people of faith were mocked and scourged, killed with swords, afflicted and abused, and wandered in the wilderness, mountains, caves, and dens (Heb 11:36–38). However, all of these people received evidence of their faith, but they did not yet receive what was promised (Heb 11:39). This was so that God could perfect the works of these fathers of the faith. Today, Christians around the world continue the righteous deeds of the fathers of the faith. The Bible says, "A person is justified by what he does and not by faith alone" (Jas 2:24).

Part I: Understanding the Bible

For every believer who is loved by God and called to be a saint, there is grace and peace from God and the Lord Jesus Christ (Rom 1:7). The apostle Paul says, "We have gained access by faith into this grace in which we now stand"(Rom 5:2). God is a "God of grace" (1 Pet 5:10). In this way, this visible faith brings forth God's grace. God gives grace freely to us (Eph 1:6). God wants all grace to abound in us so that every good work may abound in us (2 Cor 9:8). Because God's grace abounds in us, we enjoy doing good works. We have forgiveness of sins in Christ Jesus through the riches of his grace (Eph 1:7). The "Spirit of grace" (Heb 10:29) works grace in us. Grace reigns through righteousness (Rom 5:21). "For it is by grace you have been saved, through faith and this not from yourselves, it is the gift of God" (Eph 2:8). We are not saved by works because human works are not perfect in the sight of God, but we are saved by grace through faith in Jesus Christ. The gift of grace of Jesus Christ abounded to many people (Rom 5:15). We are saved by grace to do righteous and good works in life. Righteous and good works are the result of salvation. There is grace for all who sincerely love our Lord Jesus Christ (Eph 6:24). By grace, Jesus Christ cares for and protects people of faith, so we can live a life of righteousness, good works, and peace.

7

What Is Sin

1. THE NATURE OF MAN AND SIN

SIN IS DEFINED AS anything that is contrary to God's laws (commandments), laws, or truth. It is sin to live worldly, according to human will, rather than following God's will. Breaking the law, whether it is God's law or the law of the world, is sin. Sin is lawlessness (1 John 3:4). All wrongdoing is sin (1 John 5:17). To know to do good and not to do it is sin (Jas 4:17). Therefore, anything that we do not do according to the will of God by faith is sin (Rom 14:23). Sin is disobedience and rebellion against God. Sin occurs when we fail to obey God and have a right relationship with him. Sin is the breaking of a relationship with God. As a result of Adam and Eve's sin of disobedience to God in the garden of Eden (Gen 3:1–24), their relationship with God was severed, leading to spiritual death as well as physical death through sickness and pain. If a man is a slave to sin, he will die, but if he is a slave to obedience, he will be made righteous (Rom 6:16). Obedience to God by faith results in righteousness. "For the wage of sin is death, but the gift of God is eternal life in Christ Jesus our Lord" (Rom 6:23). However, through the blood of Jesus, shed on the cross, we have made peace, reconciling all things to God through Jesus (Col 1:20).

God created man in the image of God (Gen 1:27). Humans were created in the holiness of righteousness and truth, just like God (Eph 4:24). Humans are born with good and evil natures. We humans have both a good and an evil nature. The evil nature emerged when the first humans, Adam and Eve, sinned in disobedience to God (Gen 3:1–24). By disobeying God's command not to eat the fruit of good and evil, Adam and Eve ate the fruit out of a desire to become like God, who knows good and evil (Gen 3:1–6). As a result, Adam and Eve became aware of good and evil. Accordingly, biblically speaking, humans are more likely to display their evil nature to the world than their good nature. The nature of sin is greed and lust. The evil nature, the lusts and desires in the human heart, are the source of evil and sin. Man has a desire to do what God says not to do. Sin is in us. Sin dwells in the heart (Rom 7:17). Sin comes from the human heart. Sin occurs when we do things according to our own will instead of God's will. We are all under sin (Rom 3:9). We humans die to sin and live to righteousness (1 Pet 2:24). No one is good but God alone (Mark 10:18). There is no one who does good, not even one (Ps 14:3). There is no righteous person in the world who does nothing but good and never sins (Eccl 7:20). There is none righteous, no one who does good (Rom 3:10–12), so no one can say that he is without sin before God the Creator. "There is no one who does not sin" (1 Kgs 8:46). Humans have greed in their hearts, which is fundamentally the root of evil and sin. When people are tempted, it is because they are drawn away by their own desires and fall into temptation (Jas 1:14). "After desire has conceived, it gives birth to sin; and sin, when it is full-grown, gives birth to death" (Jas 1:15). The nature of sin is an evil that stems from greed, desire and lust. There is a wickedness in the human heart that falls short of goodness. It is sin that dwells in man to do evil (Rom 7:20). This puts man under condemnation.

Conscience is the nature of human beings toward good. Conscience is the source of goodness. We have a good conscience to do good in all things (Heb 13:18). Conscience is given by God but not earned through human effort. Conscience is our natural inclination toward truth and a good heart to do righteously. "Holding on to faith and a good conscience" (1 Tim 1:19). However, humans are greedy by nature and therefore inherently sinners. The sin that is in our flesh does not do good but does evil (Rom 7:19). But evil does not overcome good. It is only the Lord God who does good. Jesus said, "No one is good except God alone" (Luke 18:19). God is the standard of goodness. God's love drives us to do good. A good heart is a heart that has compassion for its neighbors, a compassionate heart. The Lord God is good to all and has compassion (mercy) on all that he has made (Ps 145:9). "When Jesus landed and saw a large crowd, he had compassion on them and healed their sick" (Matt 14:14). In our worldly lives, in order to manifest our good nature, we must strive to do good to our neighbors in love, according to God's will.

2. ORIGINAL SIN AND SIN

(1) Original Sin

Original sin is traced in the Old Testament to the sin of disobedience by the first humans, Adam and Eve, who broke God's command (Gen 3:1–24). For this reason, original sin means that humans are condemned from birth, regardless of their will. The first humans, Adam and Eve, inherently had greed and desire, the root of sin, and thus all humans who descend from Adam are born in a state of sin. The psalmist confesses, "Surely I was sinful at birth, sinful from the time my mother conceived me" (Ps 51:5). Thus, humans are sinners from birth. Even the most spiritual people admit that they are sinners. The apostle Paul said, "Of sinners I am chief" (1 Tim 1:15). Peter also confessed, "Go away from me, Lord; I am a sinful man!" (Luke 5:8).

Our ancestors, Adam and Eve, broke God's command to "not eat of the fruit of the tree of the knowledge of good and evil in the garden of Eden, for when you eat of it you will surely die" (Gen 2:17), were tempted by the deceitful serpent (Satan), and ate of the fruit of good and evil out of a desire to be like God (Gen 3:1–6). This human nature of Adam and Eve's, that is, desire and pride, led to disobedience to God. Adam and Eve were judged for their disobedience to God and lost their intimate relationship with God (Gen 3:16–19), were expelled from the garden of Eden, where the tree of life was located, and died, losing eternal life (Gen 3:22–24; 5:5). Adam and Eve's disobedience to God is the beginning of the man's fall and pride. Through the disobedience of one man, Adam, sin entered the world, and all men became sinners (Rom 5:12, 19). Adam and Eve were guilty of disobeying God by doing their own will. As a result, their sin was inherited by their offspring, the human race. Sin arose when humans lost their good nature and sought an independent self, trying to be "I am who I am" (Exod 3:14) like God. Man's desire and pride led him (Adam) to try to become God on his own.

Curses and punishments were given to those who were guilty of disobeying God (Lev 26:14–33). God punished Adam and Eve for their sin of disobedience. God said to Eve, "I will greatly increase your pains in childbearing; with pain you will give birth to children" (Gen 3:16). God also punished Adam in this way. God said to Adam, "Cursed is the ground because of you; through painful toil you will eat of it all the days of your life" (Gen 3:17). "By the sweat of your brow you will eat your food, until you return to the ground" (Gen 3:19). God told Adam that he would have to sweat and toil all his life to eat anything from the ground. Humans must sweat and work all their lives to survive and get food from the ground. It is also a sin for humans not to sweat and work.

(2) Sin

God created man in the image of God (Gen 1:27). In this way, God made people right and upright, but they do everything they can with their schemes (Eccl 7:29). As descendants of Adam and Eve, we were children of wrath by birth, who lived out the desires of our flesh, doing what the body and mind desire according to our lusts (Eph 2:3). Humans are born with greed and lust by nature; we have a self-centered, selfish need to possess. The original sin of Adam and Eve's disobedience to God is the source of sin, which means that humans do evil acts of their own free will. The Bible says, "We all, like sheep, have gone astray, each of us has turned to his own way" (Isa 53:6). Sin dwells in the human heart (Rom 7:17). There is one original sin but many real sins. Sin comes from man's malice and fallen self in disobedience to God. The Bible says, "All that is in the world, the lust of the flesh, and the lust of the eyes, and the pride of life, is not of the Father, but is of the world" (1 John 2:16), and from these desires comes sinful behavior. Even if humans do good things on the outside, they are under God's judgment because they are corrupt and have evil on the inside. However, "No one who is born of God will continue to sin, because God's seed [DNA] remains in him" (1 John 3:9). Therefore, Jesus Christ, the Son of God, is sinless. However, all humans sin. "There is no one who does not sin" (1 Kgs 8:46).

To do good is to do according to the will of God, and to do evil is to do according to the will of the flesh. The desires of the flesh oppose the Holy Spirit and make it impossible for us to do what we want, which is to do good (Gal 5:17). "There is no one who does good, not even one" (Ps 14:3). "Seek good, not evil, that you may live" (Amos 5:14). The apostle Paul says, "Hold on to faith and a good conscience" (1 Tim 1:19). Conscience is the good nature of human beings. We have a good conscience to do good in all things (Heb 13:18). All people, whether they believe in God or not, have a

What Is Sin

"law of their own (heart)" called a conscience. God wants us to live our lives doing good works (Eph 2:10). But humans do not do the good they want to do; they do the evil they do not want to do (Rom 7:19). The human heart is deceitful above all things and desperately corrupt (Jer 17:9). Humans have a corrupt and deceitful heart that does not do what is good, but what is evil (sin) and disobeys God (Jer 16:12). Because man's nature is corrupt, there is nothing good in his flesh, so he is incapable of doing good (Rom 7:18). Within man is a wicked heart that is inclined toward evil, which stems from greed and lust. To know to do good and not to do it is sin (Jas 4:17). "Everyone who sins is a slave to sin" (John 8:34). Humans are sinners by nature and are under the yoke of sin. From within, sin is working in their hearts to do evil, not good (Rom 7:19–20). People love the darkness more than the light because their deeds are evil (John 3:19). All unrighteousness is sin (1 John 5:17). For to those who want to do good, evil is present, so that the mind serves the law of God, but the body serves the law of sin (Rom 7:21, 25). Inwardly we delight in the law of God, but in our members we wage war against the law of our minds, so that we are held captive by the law of sin in our members and cannot escape from sin (Rom 7:22–23). Our wicked hearts and the bad behavior (bad habits) of the law of sin overcome our good conscience and take our hearts captive to do evil.

Anything that goes against God's law (will) and a person's good conscience is sin. In the Bible, sin is disobedience to God's commandments and breaking the law (1 John 3:4). The lusts and desires of the human heart give rise to the "works of the flesh" (Gal 5:19). We sin because we are driven by our own greed and desires. There are evil thoughts, lewdness, theft, murder, adultery, greed, lying, debauchery, slander, pride, and foolishness in the human heart, and these "evil works of the flesh" defile the man (Mark 7:21–23). Sin includes consciously sinful thoughts, acts that are contrary to conscience or morality, evil desires, carnality, lust, condemnation of others, pride, jealousy, envy, hatred, causing mental and material harm, living idle and not working in the sweat of our brow, fraud, theft, murder, rape, and other evil thoughts and evil acts. "All these evils come from inside and make a man 'unclean'" (Mark 7:23). A crime is an outward manifestation of an evil thought in the heart. Among sins is the sin of resisting or blaspheming the Holy Spirit, which is eternally unforgivable (Matt 12:31–32; Mark 3:29; Luke 12:10; Heb 6:6). Blasphemy against the Holy Spirit is an unforgivable and eternal sin. "Walk in the Spirit, and you shall not fulfill the lust of the flesh" (Gal 5:16). All humans commit sins in their lives because there is evil in their hearts through greed and lust. Even Abraham, Jacob, Moses, David, Peter, and Paul, who are most revered by Christians as servants of God in the Bible, all committed human sins during their lives. However, they are all worshiped by mankind because of their sincere repentance to God, forgiveness, being born again, turning away from sin, obeying God, and believing. We should live righteously and good, doing God's righteousness and goodness according to the Holy Spirit who has come into us.

3. THE WAGES OF SIN: DEATH

Because of the sin of disobedience to God by our ancestors, Adam and Eve, humans are born with a spiritual sin nature. Since Adam's blood (DNA) flows through the human body, humans are inherently sinners. Therefore, no human being in the world is perfect. Even if you don't recognize yourself as a sinner, you are still a sinner and subject to the penalty of death. This is because sin must be paid for. "The sinful passions aroused by the law were at work in our bodies, so that we bore fruit for death" (Rom 7:5). Failure to obey God results in death and destruction (Deut 30:15–18). God is just and righteous (Deut 32:4). God is a God of justice (Ps 89:14). A God of justice demands that humans be punished for their sins, and that punishment must be paid. In the Bible, the apostle Paul said, "The wages of sin is death" (Rom 6:23). You must die to pay for your sins. When a person becomes a slave to sin, he leads to death (Rom 6:16). If you sin, you are given death. "Just as sin entered the world through one man (Adam), and death through sin, and in this way death came to all men, because all sinned" (Rom 5:12). We are dead in our "trespasses and sins" (Eph 2:1). Where there is no sin, there can be no death. "After desire has conceived, it gives birth to sin; and sin, when it is full-grown, gives birth to death" (Jas 1:15). Human death began with the original sin of Adam and Eve, and death spread to the human race in the world. The penalty for sin is physical and spiritual death. Death is the separation of body and spirit in a human being. For Christians, spiritual death is the separation of the Spirit of God from the body and their departure from God. "Your iniquities have separated you from your God" (Isa 59:2). Sin brings spiritual death, severing our relationship with the God of life.

4. REPENTANCE, FORGIVENESS OF SIN, AND LIFE

According to the Scriptures, Christ died for our sins and rose on the third day (1 Cor 15:3–4). Jesus died for our sins and was raised from the dead. Through his death on the cross and resurrection, Jesus paid the full penalty for humanity's sins. As a result of Jesus' payment for the sins of mankind, we receive the forgiveness of sins. "For the wages of sin is death, but the gift of God is eternal life through Christ Jesus our Lord" (Rom 6:23). The forgiveness of sins is not earned by human will or works. There is no condemnation because the law of the Spirit of life in Christ Jesus has set us free from the law of sin and death (Rom 8:1–2). Those who are in Christ Jesus are not condemned. Those whom God has justified are forgiven of their sins. Those who follow the path of righteousness lead to life, but those who pursue evil lead to sin (Prov 10:16).

We repent to God for the forgiveness of our sins and are born again, free from sin and given life by God's grace. God says, "Repent, and turn yourselves from all your transgressions" (Ezek 18:30). "He who conceals his sins does not prosper, but whoever confesses and renounces them finds mercy" (Prov 28:13). To follow God, we must forsake our sins. Repentance leads to the forgiveness of sins (Luke 24:47). If we confess our sins, God is faithful and just and will forgive us our sins and purify us from all unrighteousness (1 John 1:9). In other words, if we repent of our sins, the righteous God will forgive us our sins and make us righteous.

God, who is rich in mercy, made us alive together with Christ, because of his great love for us, even though we died of sins (Eph 2:4–5). Jesus said in the preaching of the gospel, "Repent, for the kingdom of heaven is near" (Matt 3:2; 4:17). "For as in Adam all die, so in Christ all will be made alive" (1 Cor 15:22). Those who believe in Jesus Christ receive forgiveness of sins and life when they repent. Jesus made us alive when we were dead in our trespasses and sins (Eph 2:1). Jesus Christ says, "Whoever finds his life will lose it, and whoever loses his life for my sake will find it" (Matt 10:39). Whoever lays down his life for Jesus Christ receives forgiveness of sins and gains eternal life. "For to be carnally minded is death, but to be spiritually minded is life and peace" (Rom 8:6). If we repent, by the grace of God we can change the mind of the flesh into the mind of the spirit and be born again.

8

Harmony of Law and Grace

THE LAW OF THE Bible, as taught by God, is the standard of life of faith that we should strive to keep. "The Law" refers to the Law of Moses and is recorded in the five books of Moses in the Old Testament. The Law sometimes refers to the entire Old Testament. The laws of the Old Testament were given to the Jews (the nation of Israel). "Blessed is the man who delights in the law of the Lord, meditating on it day and night" (Ps 1:1–2). The Bible says, "The law was given by Moses, but grace and truth came by Jesus Christ" (John 1:17). Only those who do the law are justified before God (Rom 2:13). God's covenant cannot be broken or annulled because it is based on the law (Gal 3:15–18). There is no binding requirement for Christians to keep all of the law today. However, Christians should not neglect to keep the law. Properly kept, the law is beneficial for living righteously and well in this worldly life. The purpose of the law is to produce a pure heart, a good conscience, and the love that comes from a faith without deceit (1 Tim 1:5). Blessings come to those who obey the law out of fear of God (Deut 10:12–13; Lev 26:1–13), but punishment, curses, and chastisement are given to those who disobey (Lev 26:14–33). Blessed are those who keep the law (Prov 29:18). Many commandments in the law, such as "love the Lord your God with all your heart and with all your soul" (Deut 6:5) and "love your neighbor as yourself" (Lev 19:18), foreshadow Jesus' commandment to "love God and love your neighbor" (Matt 22:37–39). Likewise, the Old Testament emphasizes God's love and grace. God said, "But showing

Harmony of Law and Grace

love (mercy) to a thousand generations of those who love me and keep my commandments" (Exod 20:6).

God's grace and love are based on God's covenant (law). God's law is made perfect in love and grace through Jesus Christ (Matt 5:17). Love and grace perfect the law. Grace is a gift from God. It is a gift that God gives to us without payment, not earned by our own merit, and it serves to connect us to God (Jesus). God gives sunshine and sends rain equally to the bad and the good, the righteous and the unrighteous (Matt 5:45). God's grace is extended to all people in the world in this way. There is grace for all who love Jesus Christ (Eph 6:24). The grace of Jesus Christ is in our hearts (Gal 6:18). While the law is important in Christianity, Jesus' words make grace and love central to the faith.

God's law is always and everywhere the same and does not change with time and place. God shows justice through the law and love to humans through the grace. God is a God of justice and righteousness (Ps 89:14), but God is also a God of love (1 John 4:8). "Righteousness and justice are the foundation of your throne; love and faithfulness go before you (the Lord)" (Ps 89:14). If people break public law (the law) by doing bad things, they are punished as judged by worldly standards. God is publicly righteous, just, and impartial. God judges people's behavior fairly, rewarding good behavior and punishing bad behavior. "To those who by persistence in doing good seek glory, honor and immortality, he (God) will give eternal life. But for those who are self-seeking and who reject the truth and follow evil, there will be wrath and anger" (Rom 2:7–8). God is sovereign, his grace and love are infinite and eternal, and he gives spiritual blessings. Without God's justice, however, God's grace and love could not exist. God has both the stick of the law and the carrot of grace. God's justice through the law and God's love through grace are seen together in harmony with each other. Jesus, the Son of God, obeyed the law and the will of God. In the New Testament, Jesus said, "Do not think that I have come to abolish the Law or the Prophets; I have not come to abolish them but to fulfill them" (Matt 5:17). This means that the law is fulfilled by Jesus' grace and love. Furthermore, Jesus teaches: "If you love me, keep my commandments" (John 14:15). Love is the fulfillment of the law. Jesus who loves another has fulfilled the law (Rom 13:8). "Love does no harm to its neighbor. Therefore love is the fulfillment of the law" (Rom 13:10). Thus, grace and love are at the heart of God's law. Along with the law, grace and love are central to the Christian faith. Those who have received grace are at peace and are with God (Luke 1:26).

Part I: Understanding the Bible

1. THE LAW, SIN, AND PUNISHMENT

Each of the Five Books of Moses is known as a part of the Law. The Bible says, "The law is holy, and the commandment is holy, and righteous and good" (Rom 7:12). The most important law is the Ten Commandments, which Moses received from Jehovah God on Mount Sinai. Commandments 1–4 deal with man's obligations to God, while commandments 5–10 are universal moral rules for man's neighbor (Exod 20:1–17; Deut 5:1–21). You are to worship God as the only God, do not make and serve idols, do not call the Lord your God in vain, and remember the Sabbath day to keep it holy (commandments 1–4). These four commandments describe what reverence for God is. We are to serve and love God with all our heart, soul, and mind (Matt 22:37). We practice sincere worship of God and obey God by aligning our words and actions. "These people come near to me with their mouth and honor me with their lips, but their hearts are far from me. Their worship of me is made up only of rules taught by men" (Isa 29:13). Thus, honoring God only with words is not true honor to God. We must obey and worship God in true acts of faith. We rest our bodies and minds on the Sabbath to worship and serve God. Commandments 5–10 of the Ten Commandments tell us to love our neighbors, honor our parents, and eliminate covetousness in our lives. That is, honor your parents, do not murder, do not commit adultery, do not steal, do not bear false witness against your neighbor, and do not covet your neighbor's house, wife, servant, or any of his possessions. Jesus continued to speak of the new commandment (law) in the New Testament. "Love your neighbor as yourself" (Matt 22:39). "Anyone who looks at a woman lustfully has already committed adultery with her in his heart" (Matt 5:28). We must love our neighbors, forsake lust and greed, and have a self-sufficient heart.

The Bible associates sin with the law (Rom 2:12–14; 4:15; Jas 2:9–10). In a broad sense, sin is a violation of God's law, or the will of God. Greed and lust in the human heart are the source of sin. Man has a desire to do what God forbids him to do. Sin occurs when we act according to our own will and not God's will. In our hearts there is both good and evil. Therefore, sin dwells in our flesh (Rom 7:17), and nothing good dwells in our flesh (Rom 7:18). "The good that I would I do not: but the evil which I would not, that I do" (Rom 7:19). "With the mind I myself serve the law of God; but with the flesh the law of sin" (Rom 7:25). We humans live worldly lives in a conflict between our good heart, which wants to keep the "law of God," and our evil heart, which wants to practice the "law of the flesh" of greed.

Although we delight in the law of God in our hearts, we are captivated by the law of sin in our flesh (Rom 7:22–23). Without the Old Testament law, "You shall not covet" (Exod 20:17), we would not have known the sin of covetousness (Rom 7:7). Without the law, sin is dead (Rom 7:8). The law makes sin visible. Paradoxically, the law causes us to sin. James said, "For whosoever shall keep the whole law, and yet offend in one point, he is guilty of all" (Jas 2:10). As such, God's law is strict. "Everyone who sins breaks the law; in fact, sin is lawlessness" (1 John 3:4). Human sin existed in the world before there was a law, but when there was no law, sin was not considered sin (Rom 5:13). Without the law, it is difficult to know sin, and therefore sin is not recognized as sin. Because there is a law, it is through the law that people are made aware of sin (Rom 3:20). The law shows the dreadful nature of sin (Rom 7:8–13). In the law, human beings are made aware of their sinfulness, and greed and lust are restrained in their lives. In general, because there is a "law," humans recognize "sin."

Through the law, we know what God's will and teachings are, and we become aware of human sin. God judges and punishes people for their sins to prevent them from sinning and to make them do good works that are pleasing to God. God punishes human sin with justice. In the Old Testament, punishment, curses, and chastisement were given to guilty people who disobeyed God's laws (commandments) (Lev 26:14–33). God's Law (Torah) entails appropriate punishment for sin. Cursed is everyone who does not walk in accordance with the law (Gal 3:10), the law brings wrath, and where there is no law, there is no transgression (Rom 4:15). Where there is law, sin is revealed. The law was made for lawbreakers and the ungodly (1 Tim 1:9–10). The apostle Paul defines the law as a law of sin and death (Rom 8:2). A law that does not punish is only good advice. It is very wrong to remove divine punishment from God's Law (Torah). Without punishment, people's minds would be confused and they would ignore or disregard either the laws of men or the laws of God. Thus, without chastisement, the law loses its absolute sanctity, and sin ceases to be considered a wrongdoing. "He is God's servant, an agent of wrath to bring punishment on the wrongdoer" (Rom 13:4). "The Lord knows how to rescue godly men from trials and to hold the unrighteous for the day of judgment, while continuing their punishment" (2 Pet 2:9). God disciplines people who do evil and unrighteous things. Punishing worldly sins that lead people to turn away from God has the effect of causing them to repent and return to God. "The Lord disciplines those he loves, and he punishes everyone he accepts as a son" (Heb 12:6; Prov 3:12). God's loving discipline (chastening) refines us to bring about righteousness and peace. As we become his true sons, we are refined by the rod of his discipline to produce a harvest of righteousness and peace (Heb 12:11).

2. JESUS AND THE LAW

The law book (Old Testament) says, "Cursed is the man who does not uphold the words of this law by carrying them out" (Deut 27:26). The New Testament also says, "Cursed is everyone who does not continue to do everything written in the Book of the Law" (Gal 3:10). In this way, both the Old and New Testaments tell us to walk according to the law. Anyone who does not live by the law before God is unrighteous (Gal 3:11). Also, Jesus did not come to abolish the Law but to fulfill it (Matt 5:17). Jesus came to fulfill the Law of Moses (Luke 24:44), and the apostle Paul preached the Law of Moses to the people (Acts 28:23). The apostle Paul says, "Women, be in submission, as the Law says" (1 Cor 14:34). As written in the Old Testament Law (Lev 19:18), Jesus said, "Love God and love your neighbor" (Luke 10:26–27). However, Jesus said, "On the Sabbath the priests in the temple desecrate the day and yet are innocent" (Matt 12:5) and "it is lawful to do good on the Sabbath" (Matt 12:12). God's law says, "Remember the Sabbath day by keeping it holy" (Exod 20:8). But Jesus is saying that not keeping the Sabbath is not a sin. Jesus did not mind people not keeping the formalities of the law, such as "keeping the Sabbath." However, this does not mean that Jesus is saying that you do not have to keep the entire law.

God's law is an inseparable and unified law. If anyone keeps the whole law and breaks one of its points, he is guilty of the whole law (Jas 2:10). In the same light, the apostle Paul testifies that the "circumcised" are those who are obligated to do the whole law (Gal 5:3). Jesus also speaks of the eternity of the law and the need to do and teach it. "Until heaven and earth disappear, not the smallest letter will by any means disappear from the Law, and whoever practices and teaches these commands will be called great in the kingdom of heaven" (Matt 5:18–19). In the Old Testament, it is recorded that the Lord put his covenant (law) made with the house of Israel on their hearts and wrote it down (Jer 31:33). In the New Testament, similar words of the Lord are also quoted and recorded as follows: "This is the covenant I will make with the house of Israel after that time, declares the Lord. I will put my laws in their minds and write them on their hearts. I will be their God, and they will be my people" (Heb 8:10, 10:16).

Harmony of Law and Grace

In the Sermon on the Mount, Jesus is clearly teaching the Law of Moses. He declares: "I have not come to abolish the Law, but to fulfill it. Until heaven and earth disappear, not the smallest letter will disappear from the Law. Anyone who breaks one of the least of these commandments and teaches others to do the same will be called least in the kingdom of heaven" (Matt 5:17–19). Jesus did not try to abolish the Law of Moses but to put his own new law (the New Testament) in its place. In this strong tone, Jesus is reaffirming the integrity and sanctity of the Mosaic Law. Jesus adamantly refused to break even the smallest commandment of the law. In principle, Jesus submitted to and kept the law. Jesus' Sermon on the Mount contains all the moral, ceremonial, and civil elements of the Mosaic Law, along with its penalties. There was no separation of religion and politics at this time, and the penalties of the law had temporary or permanent sanctions.

God's law is perfect, without flaw (Ps 19:7). Jesus kept the law perfectly. The Law of Moses is the law under which the Lord Jesus was born, and it is the law that Jesus obeyed. The New Testament records that Jesus was born under the law. "God sent his Son, born of a woman, born under law" (Gal 4:4). Baby Jesus was circumcised according to the Law of Moses and offered sacrifices in the temple in Jerusalem (Luke 2:21–24). Joseph and Mary performed a purification ritual according to the law of the Lord and returned to Nazareth, having done everything for baby Jesus (Luke 2:22–39). The Lord Jesus became a follower of circumcision for the sake of God's faithfulness, which was to confirm the promises given to the fathers (Rom 15:8). The Lord Jesus was obedient to the Law of Moses and came to fulfill the Law but not to abolish it (Matt 5:17). He was baptized to fulfill righteousness (Matt 3:15–16), and even when death approached, he had his disciples prepare the Passover meal for the Last Supper so that they could eat together according to the Mosaic Law (Luke 22:8). Jesus commanded people to observe the Mosaic Law, telling them to keep the commandments to inherit eternal life (Matt 19:17). The new commandments in the New Testament, which Jesus also spoke of, are "do not murder, do not commit adultery, do not steal, do not give false testimony, honor your father and mother, and love your neighbor as yourself" (Matt 19:18–19). However, after Jesus' time, the apostle Paul preached Jesus' gospel of grace, saying, "If you are led by the Spirit, you are not under law" (Gal 5:18). In the New Testament, the apostle John said, "Everyone who sins breaks the law; in fact, sin is lawlessness. But He appeared so that he might take away our sins. And in him is no sin." (1 John 3:4–5). John emphasized that Jesus was sinless and appeared for the forgiveness of sins by grace.

Part I: Understanding the Bible

3. THE LAW: DOES NOT GIVE LIFE AND SALVATION

God's law is the Law of Moses, which is well known from the Old Testament. God's law is perfect, without flaw (Ps 19:7). Indeed, if humans kept the law perfectly, the law would give them life and salvation (eternal life). However, because of Adam and Eve's disobedience to God (Gen 3), humans are sinners by nature from birth. Therefore, humans under sin (Rom 3:9) are unable to keep the law perfectly in their lives. Accordingly, humans cannot save themselves through the law and have eternal life. God says, "Keep my decrees and laws, for the man who obeys them will live by them. I am the Lord" (Lev 18:5). Similarly, the Old Testament also says, "I gave them my decrees and made known to them my laws, for the man who obeys them will live by them" (Ezek 20:11, 13, 21). Jesus Christ used the same principle when he told the rich young ruler who wanted to inherit eternal life, "If you want to enter life, obey the commandments" (Matt 19:17). The apostle Paul said, "Moses describes in this way the righteousness that is by the law: 'The man who does these things will live by them'" (Rom 10:5). However, at this time, the keeping of the law must be perfect. Cursed is everyone who does not keep the whole law (Gal 3:10). But it is impossible for humans to keep the whole law perfectly. "For whoever keeps the whole law and yet stumbles at just one point is guilty of breaking all of it" (Jas 2:10). Thus, it is not possible for humans to perfectly keep the whole law on their own.

No one can perfectly keep the law except Jesus Christ. "Everyone who sins breaks the law; in fact, sin is lawlessness. But he appeared so that he might take away our sins. And in him is no sin" (1 John 3:4–5). All have sinned and fall short of the glory of God (Rom 3:23). This testimony is recorded in many passages of Scripture, from Genesis to Revelation. In reality, the law cannot save a sinner to eternal life; therefore, the law does not give life or salvation. The Bible fully testifies to this point. "No one will be declared righteous in his sight by observing the law; rather, through the law we become conscious of sin" (Rom 3:20). However, "Through him everyone who believes is justified from everything you could not be justified from by the law of Moses" (Acts 13:39). "No one is justified before God by the law, because the righteous will live by faith. The law is not based on faith" (Gal 3:11–12). It is through faith in Jesus Christ that a person is justified (Gal 2:16). If being justified is by the law, then Jesus died in vain on the cross (Gal 2:21). If the law could give life, then righteousness would be from the law (Gal 3:21). Thus, since the law cannot give life, righteousness does not come from the law. By the works of the flesh, humans cannot perfectly keep God's law, and they are saved by grace through faith.

It is written in the New Testament that the law is good and holy, and the commandments are holy, righteous, and good (1 Tim 1:8; Rom 7:12). However, the apostle Paul writes in the New Testament that the law cannot give life and salvation to sinful man. After declaring the law to be holy and good, the apostle Paul goes on to show in Romans why God's law cannot save humans. "I am unspiritual, sold as a slave to sin" (Rom 7:14). The weakness is in man, not in the law. "What the law was powerless to do in that it was weakened by the sinful nature, God did by sending his own Son in the likeness of sinful man to be a sin offering. And so he condemned sin in sinful man" (Rom 8:3). "God made you alive with Christ and forgave us all our sins" (Col 2:13).

4. GOD'S LAW AND JESUS' GRACE

If God's law cannot save us, why do we care about it? Why did God give us the law? God gave the law because of human sin. God gave the law to humans, so that they would be made aware of sin by the law (Rom 3:20). Without the law, humans would be corrupted by greed and lust and would sin more by doing evil deeds. The law was added because of our transgressions until the coming of the promised seed (Jesus) (Gal 3:19). But the law is not the most important thing in God's dealings with man under sin. The law is added and provisional. God gave us the law to save us and to deal with the problem of sin, but the law is not necessary. The law was given because of lawbreakers and ungodly people (1 Tim 1:9-10). The apostle Paul tells us that we can recognize sin because we have the law. "With the mind I myself serve the law of God; but with the flesh the law of sin" (Rom 7:25). "I was alive without the law once: but when the commandment came, sin revived, and I died" (Rom 7:9). Where there is no law, there is no transgression (Rom 4:15). This law (commandment) does not actually kill sin but makes it alive.

Those who do the law live in the law (Gal 3:12). Before we were led by Jesus Christ to be justified by faith, we were under the law and subject to the law (Gal 3:23-24). The apostle Paul was concerned about keeping the first law (covenant) when he said, "Do not be enslaved to things that are not God by nature, that is, to elementary things that are weak and worthless" (Gal 4:8-9). The law did not lead people to Christ Jesus but rather brought

Part I: Understanding the Bible

them into bondage. The law was not born of faith. In the New Testament, the Lord declares, "God found fault with the first covenant. The time is coming, when I will make a new covenant" (Heb 8:7-8). God made the first covenant obsolete and he said, "What is obsolete and aging will soon disappear" (Heb 8:13). In this way, he foreshadowed the disappearance of the first covenant, the Mosaic Law, and the establishment of a new covenant. The letter of Jesus Christ (the New Covenant) was written by the Spirit of the living God (2 Cor 3:3). Jesus Christ became the end of the law for righteousness to all who believe (Rom 10:4). In the age of the Holy Spirit after Jesus, we were freed from the law to serve the new one of the Spirit (Rom 7:6). Before God, no one is justified by the law, but the righteous live by faith (Hab 2:4, Gal 3:11). We are justified by faith in Jesus. Those who walk in the paths of righteousness find life (Prov 11:19).

Through Jesus Christ, God's law was made perfect in love and grace (Matt 5:17). By grace, God enables us to keep the law. The law came in and increased offenses, and where sin increased, grace abounded even more (Rom 5:20). The presence of the law increased sin, making us need the grace of Jesus Christ even more in our lives. The purpose of God's law is to produce love, which comes from a pure heart, a good conscience, and a faith without deceit (1 Tim 1:5). "Love does no harm to its neighbor. Therefore love is the fulfillment of the law" (Rom 13:10). It is written in God's law: "'Love the Lord your God with all your heart and with all your soul and with all your mind' [Deut 6:5]. This is the first and greatest commandment. And the second is like it: 'Love your neighbor as yourself'" (Matt 22:37-39; Mark 12:30-31; Luke 10:27). "Love your neighbor as yourself" (Rom 13:9) contains all of God's commandments (Exod 20:13-15). The God of the Old Testament also said, "Showing love to a thousand generations of those who love me and keep my commandments" (Exod 20:6). The entire New Testament is about the grace of Jesus Christ. The Lord Jesus Christ shines the light of grace upon us. The grace of God (Jesus) is to "not take the yoke of a servant." Jesus says, "Come to me, all you who are weary and burdened, and I will give you rest. Take my yoke upon you and learn from me, for I am gentle and humble in heart, and you will find rest for your souls" (Matt 11:28-29). Jesus Christ invites people to learn from his meek and humble nature and live a life of rest full of his grace. He told the story of the "Parable of the Prodigal Son" (Luke 15:11-32) to his disciples to make them feel God's love, God's infinite mercy, and God's infinite grace. All have sinned and fall short of the glory of God (Rom 3:23). But because of the

Harmony of Law and Grace

redemption that is in Jesus Christ, people are justified by God's grace, free of charge (Rom 3:24).

Just as sin reigns in death, so also grace reigns in righteousness, leading to eternal life through Jesus Christ (Rom 5:21). If you are led by the Holy Spirit, you are not under the law (Gal 5:18). Sin does not have dominion over people because they are under God's grace (Rom 6:14). Jesus Christ saves us by grace through faith. In fact, Almighty God can only save sinners by grace. "Let the wicked forsake his way, and the unrighteous man his thoughts: and let him return unto the Lord, and he will have mercy upon him; and to our God, for he will abundantly pardon" (Isa 55:7). In the same way, if you come to God and believe, he will have compassion on the wicked and the unrighteous and forgive your sins. "It is by grace you have been saved, through faith and this not from yourselves, it is the gift of God" (Eph 2:8). In the age of the Holy Spirit after Jesus, there is no other gospel than the gospel of the grace of Jesus Christ (Gal 1:6–9). The salvation of the Christian is by grace, and not by works, otherwise grace would no longer be grace (Rom 11:6). Grace is not earned by human ability or merit. Grace is a gift of God's unconditional love. Only by grace, we can know the truth, avoid sin, act righteously, and keep our faith. Grace provides the nourishment for God's will to be realized in the Christian life. God gives grace to the humble (1 Pet 5:5). In God's grace, we are strong (2 Tim 1:8), built up, and secured for life (Acts 20:32). Christians live by God's grace (Acts 13:43). It is only through Jesus Christ that we can be forgiven of our sins and receive grace. We receive grace from God (Jesus) without merit, so we are humble in our lives and do good works for the glory and joy of God.

9

What Is the Gospel

1. THE MEANING OF THE GOSPEL

THE GOSPEL, OR GOOD news, is Jesus' death on the cross, his resurrection, and the coming of the kingdom of God. Jesus' substitutionary crucifixion and resurrection are the proof that he brings salvation for humans to be freed from sin and death. The gospel is Jesus' proclamation of the coming of the kingdom of God to mankind. Jesus proclaimed the "good news of God" and said, "The time has come and the kingdom of God is near. Repent and believe the good news" (Mark 1:14–15). The gospel is the promise that Jesus the Messiah died on the cross to atone for human sin and rose from the dead to save humans from sin and death and bring them into the kingdom of God for eternal life. The gospel is the power of God for salvation to all who believe (Rom 1:16). "In the gospel a righteousness from God is revealed, a righteousness that is by faith from first to last" (Rom 1:17). There is righteousness in the words and gospel of God. Only the righteous live by faith in God (Rom 1:17). But salvation is a result of the gospel rather than the gospel itself. Jesus said, "Whoever loses his life for me and for the gospel will save it" (Mark 8:35). We are saved by living according to the word of God and Jesus Christ. The crucifixion of Jesus, the resurrection of Jesus, and the words of God and Jesus are the core of the gospel. In a broader sense, however, the gospel is the words of God and Jesus Christ. It includes the covenant and word of God and Jesus Christ, and the gospel

What Is the Gospel

of Jesus' apostles who preached in both of their names. The gospel is the word of truth (Col 1:5). The gospel is constantly bearing fruit and growing in us and in the whole world, since the day we heard it and did it and truly realized the grace of God in truth (Col 1:6).

The Gospels of the New Testament contain the gospel or the good news of Jesus Christ. The "kingdom of God" is central to Jesus' gospel. The very first verse of what is known to be the earliest of the Gospels (Mark 1:1) declares, "The beginning of the gospel about Jesus Christ, the Son of God." Jesus proclaimed the gospel of God to the nation of Israel (Jews) (Mark 1:14–15). Jesus preached the good news of the kingdom of God to the poor and the sick (Matt 4:23; 11:5; Luke 4:18–19; 16:16). For forty days after his resurrection, Jesus appeared to the apostles and spoke to them about the things of the kingdom of God (Acts 1:3). The gospel of Jesus Christ is at the center of Christianity. The gospel is the foundation of Christian life, and the preaching of the gospel brings unbelievers to faith. Christian churches and Christians are obligated to preach the gospel of Christ exactly, as it is written in the Bible. Only the gospel proclaimed by Jesus Christ is to be preached. This is because there is no other gospel but the gospel of Jesus Christ. The apostle Paul warns that those who preach a corrupted "other gospel" are cursed (Gal 1:6–9). The gospel of Jesus Christ must be fully understood in order to preach the word of new life (Acts 5:20). The gospel works in believers to sustain their faith in Jesus Christ through the trials of their lives, giving them comfort and peace by God's grace. Those who are not ready to receive the gospel cannot approach God. We become like Jesus Christ, when we faithfully believe the gospel and the words of Jesus and follow him.

Jesus' apostles preached the gospel (good news) of Jesus' death on the cross, resurrection, and the coming of the kingdom of God to both Jews and gentiles. The centerpiece of the gospel they preached was Jesus' substitutionary death on the cross and resurrection. As historical figures in the New Testament, the apostles are the disciples who met Jesus, followed him, and learned his teachings. Among these groups of disciples, the twelve apostles Jesus raised up were Peter (Simon), James (the son of Zebedee), his brother John, Andrew, Philip, Bartholomew, Matthew, Thomas, James (the son of Alphaeus), Thaddaeus, Simon, and Judas Iscariot, who betrayed Jesus (Matt 10: 2–4; Mark 3:16–19). In Luke's Gospel, Judas, the son of James, is recorded as an apostle instead of Thaddeus (Luke 6:16). After the death of Judas Iscariot, who betrayed Jesus, Matthias was chosen to replace him

Part I: Understanding the Bible

as an apostle (Acts 1:16–26). Matthias was a disciple of Jesus, who was with the other disciples throughout Jesus' ministry until the day that Jesus died on the cross and was taken up to heaven (Acts 1:21–23). After Jesus' resurrection and ascension, these apostles were sent out as witnesses of Jesus to preach the gospel in Jerusalem, Judea, Samaria, and to the ends of the earth (Matt 28:18–20; Acts 1:8).

The apostles of Jesus were chosen by Jesus and were witnesses of his resurrection. In a position of absolute authority and glory, the apostles testified with signs and wonders, preaching the gospel of God and Jesus Christ to the whole world. The evangelizing ministry of Jesus' apostles was empowered by the Holy Spirit (Acts 1:8). The work of the Holy Spirit was done through the apostles (Acts 2:4, 14–41; 8:29; 9:31; 10:45). After Jesus' resurrection and ascension into heaven, the evangelizing efforts of Jesus' apostles, led by Peter, John, Philip, and Paul (AD 5–ca. AD 64–67), are recorded in the book of Acts. It contains information about the origins of Christianity, including how it was created and how it spread. Saul (Paul), the persecutor of the church of God (Acts 2:1–47), which was born on Pentecost (the Day of the Holy Spirit), never actually met Jesus Christ. Saul was circumcised on the eighth day, and he was of the house of Israel, of the tribe of Benjamin, a Hebrew, and a Pharisee (Phil 3:5). Saul persecuted the church in Jerusalem and was blameless in the righteousness of the law (Acts 8:1–3; Phil 3:6). However, when Saul heard the voice of Jesus, he was converted and became an apostle (Acts 9:1–19; 22:6–16; 26:12–18; 1 Cor 15:9–10). After his conversion from Judaism to Christianity, Saul changed his name to "Paul" as he traveled on his missionary journeys. Paul confesses, "Paul, an apostle—sent not from men nor by man, but by Jesus Christ and God the Father, who raised him from the dead" (Gal 1:1). The gospel that Paul preached was received through the revelation of Jesus. God and Jesus Christ made Peter the apostle to the circumcision (Jews) and Paul the apostle to the gentiles (Gal 2:8). The apostle Paul traveled to the major cities in the Mediterranean region of the Roman Empire, preaching the gospel of Jesus and writing thirteen epistles. The gospel was to be proclaimed to every creature in the world, and Paul became a laborer of the gospel (Col 1:23). The apostle Paul preached the gospel of Jesus primarily to gentiles rather than Jews, leading early Christianity to separate from Judaism. The apostles of Jesus, such as Peter, Paul, Barnabas, John, Philip, James, and Judas, preached the gospel of Jesus with signs and wonders in Jerusalem, Judea, Samaria, and to the ends of the earth.

2. THE GOSPEL OF JESUS

The life, ministry, and teachings of Jesus, that is, the "gospel" of Jesus, are recorded in detail in the "four Gospels" of the New Testament (Matthew, Mark, Luke, and John). Jesus' gospel and teachings were given orally and recorded in writing by his disciples and followers. The Gospel of Mark is the first gospel to record the life of Jesus and is the prototype for the Gospels of Matthew and Luke. These three Gospels (Matthew, Mark, and Luke) are called the Synoptic Gospels because they share a common view of Jesus. The Gospel of Mark is the oldest of the three, written by Mark, and was used by Matthew and Luke to write the Gospel of Matthew and the Gospel of Luke, respectively. The fourth gospel not included in the synoptic gospels is the Gospel of John. Unlike the three synoptic gospels, the Gospel of John describes the life, characters, and words of Jesus. The Gospel of John, written by John, contains profound Christian philosophy and doctrine. The Gospel of John begins with this statement: "In the beginning was the Word, and the Word was with God, and the Word was God" (John 1:1). "Grace and truth came through Jesus Christ" (John 1:17). The Logos (Word, Reason) is God. The purpose of writing the Gospel of John is to help people believe that Jesus is the Christ, the Son of God, and to believe in Jesus and have life in the name of Jesus Christ (John 20:31).

Jesus Christ exhorted, "Repent, for the kingdom of heaven is near" (Matt 4:17), and he wanted believers to live a life of repentance. A gospel that does not include repentance is not the true gospel. This is how Jesus described the gospel: "The time has come. The kingdom of God is near. Repent and believe the good news!" (Mark 1:15). "No one can enter the kingdom of God unless he is born of water and the Spirit" (John 3:5). "Not everyone who says to me, 'Lord, Lord,' will enter the kingdom of heaven, but only he who does the will of my Father who is in heaven" (Matt 7:21). "Unless you change and become like little children, you will never enter the kingdom of heaven. Whoever humbles himself like this child is the greatest in the kingdom of heaven" (Matt 18:3–4). "It is hard for the rich to enter the kingdom of God" (Mark 10:23). "It is easier for a camel to go through the eye of a needle than for a rich man to enter the kingdom of God" (Mark 10:25; Luke 18:25). Jesus also said, "I am the way and the truth and the life. No one comes to the Father except through me" (John 14:6). The kingdom of God is not for everyone who believes in God. One must live according to the will of God (Jesus) to enter the kingdom of God. Jesus said, "The kingdom of God is within you" (Luke 17:21). God is a God of peace (1

Thess 5:23). Jesus preached a gospel of peace. "My peace I give you. I do not give to you as the world gives. Do not let your hearts be troubled and do not be afraid" (John 14:27). After his resurrection, Jesus continued to say to his disciples, "Peace be with you" (Luke 24:36; John 20:19, 21, 26). The gospel of Jesus is "peace." After his resurrection, Jesus Christ emphasized the word "peace" and offered it to the world in his gospel. Jesus Christ is a resting place for those of us who are struggling and suffering in the world. "Come to me, all you who are weary and burdened, and I will give you rest" (Matt 11:28). The One who is the very foundation of God's creation (Rev 3:14) said, "Behold, I stand at the door and knock; if anyone hears My voice and opens the door, I will come in to him and eat with him, and he with Me" (Rev 3:20). In this way, Jesus is with all those of faith who receive him.

Jesus performed many signs and wonders to prove that he is the Son of God and to make people believe in God. These signs and the fact of his resurrection were recorded in the Bible, so that his disciples could believe that Jesus is the Christ, the Son of God, and have life in his name (John 20:30–31). The signs and wonders that Jesus performed demonstrated his almighty power as the Son of God. In his first sign, Jesus made wine out of water at a wedding feast in Cana of Galilee (John 2:1–11). In this sign, Jesus foreshadowed the manifestation of the gospel of grace to fulfill the existing law, just as he turned water into wine. Jesus fully knew the past of the Samaritan woman he first met, revealing that he is the Messiah, the Christ (John 4:7–26). Jesus had compassion on people and fed five thousand people with five loaves and two fish (Mark 6:38–44). Jesus said, "I am the light of the world" and demonstrated what God was doing by healing a man who had been blind from birth (John 9:1–7). Jesus said, "I am the resurrection and the life" (John 11:25), and he raised Lazarus from the dead after he had been in the tomb for four days (John 11:1–44). In this way, Jesus demonstrated the signs of the resurrection by raising the dead. He also healed an unclean demon-possessed man (Mark 1:23–28), a leper (Matt 8:2–4), a paralytic (Luke 5:18–26), a blind and mute man (Matt 12:22–37), a woman with a hemorrhage (Mark 5:25–34), a man who was born blind (John 9:1–11), and ten lepers (Luke 17:11–19). Jesus healed them to demonstrate his compassion and what God was doing in wonders. These signs and wonders testified to what Jesus was doing in God's name (John 10:24–25). The signs and wonders that Jesus performed were supernatural, superhuman, perfect, and permanent. These signs and wonders are acts of God but not of man. Jesus used these signs and wonders to testify to his divinity as the Son of God and to confirm God's revelation and word. In today's world, however, the power of God is not manifested in these superhuman signs and wonders. The power of God is manifested in godliness and holiness through a life of faith based on the Word of God, guided by the Holy Spirit.

When Jesus saw the crowds, he went up on a mountainside and gave a discourse (sermon) (Matt 5:1–2). The Sermon on the Mount, recorded in the Gospel of Matt (chapters 5–7), contains Jesus' teachings and Christian precepts, including the Lord's Prayer. In the Sermon on the Mount, Jesus spoke of eight blessings for those who believe (Matt 5:3–12). Blessed are the poor in spirit, those who mourn, the meek, those who hunger and thirst for righteousness, the merciful, the pure in heart, the peacemakers, and those who are persecuted for the sake of righteousness. He urged believers to be salt and light, showing good deeds and bringing glory to God (Matt 5:13–16). Jesus encouraged believers to practice righteousness by fulfilling the law (Matt 5:17–20). He continued, "Do not murder, do not get angry, do not commit adultery, do not swear, do not oppose the weak, and love your enemy and your neighbor" (Matt 5:21–48). "Be careful not to do your 'acts of righteousness' before men, to be seen by them" (Matt 6:1). "When you give to the needy, do not let your left hand know what your right hand is doing" (Matt 6:3). "When you pray, do not be like a hypocrite, for they love to pray standing in the synagogues and on the street corners to be seen by men. But when you pray, go into your room, close the door and pray to your Father, who is unseen. Then your Father, who sees what is done in secret, will reward you" (Matt 6:5–6). In the Sermon on the Mount, Jesus gave us the Lord's Prayer that we should pray: "Our Father in heaven, hallowed be your name, your kingdom come. Your will be done on earth, as it is in heaven. Give us today our daily bread. And forgive us our debts, as we also have forgiven our debtors. And lead us not into temptation, but deliver us from the evil one. For yours is the kingdom and the power and the glory forever. Amen" (Matt 6:9–13). "Do not worry about tomorrow" (Matt 6:34); "Do not judge, or you too will be judged" (Matt 7:1); "Ask and it will be given to you; seek and you will find" (Matt 7:7), etc., are some of the teachings that Jesus shared with the crowds on the mountain.

Jesus continued to teach his disciples in the gospel. "Do to others as you would have them do to you" (Luke 6:31). "Many who are first will be last, and the last first" (Mark 10:31; Luke 13:30). "Whoever wants to become great among you must be your servant, and whoever wants to be first must be slave of all" (Mark 10:43–44). Jesus said, "Blessed rather are those who hear the word of God and obey it" (Luke 11:28). "Whoever does God's will is my brother and sister and mother" (Mark 3:35). Jesus also said, "The Son of Man did not come to be served, but to serve, and to give his life as a ransom for many" (Mark 10:45). "Love the Lord your God with all your heart and with all your soul and with all your mind and with all your strength. The second is this: 'Love your neighbor as yourself.' There is no commandment greater than these" (Mark 12:30–31). After his resurrection, Jesus told his disciples, "Go into all the world and preach the gospel to all creation" (Mark 16:15).

3. THE GOSPEL PREACHED BY THE APOSTLES

Jesus went to God his Father and sent us the Comforter (Counselor), the Holy Spirit (John 16:7). In the age of the Holy Spirit after Jesus, the apostles, including Paul, preached the gospel (good news) of God that Jesus preached. The four Gospels (Matthew, Mark, Luke, and John), which record the gospel and sayings (words) of Jesus, became the basis for the epistles, which contain the gospel preached by the apostles. The Epistles of the Apostles in the New Testament are pastoral letters for the church. Of the twenty-seven books of the New Testament, twenty-one were written by the apostles. The twenty-one epistles consist of thirteen of Paul's epistles to the church, disciples (sons) and coworkers of faith, and eight of the other apostles' epistles. In these epistles, God and Jesus spoke the gospel through Paul, Hebrews's writer, James, Peter, John, and Jude. Of the epistles, Hebrews has no known author. Apostles were members of the body of Jesus who were inseparable from Jesus Christ and worked together with him (1 Cor 12:27). The apostles saw the life, ministry, crucifixion, and resurrection of Jesus Christ. Because the apostles speak as members of the body of Jesus, the entire epistles are the words of God and Jesus Christ spoken by the apostles in Jesus Christ. The apostle Paul recorded his theology in the book of Romans from the gospel that he preached. Peter, Paul, John, and others preached the gospel of God's (Jesus') grace, peace, and hope to the church. "Grace to you and peace from God our Father and the Lord Jesus Christ" (Rom 1:7; 1 Cor 1:3; Gal 1:3; Eph 1:2; 1 Pet 1:2; 2 John 1:3). God is a God of peace (Rom 15:33; Phil 4:9; 1 Thess 5:23). The God of hope fills us with all joy and peace in faith, so that we may overflow with hope by the power of the Holy Spirit (Rom 15:13).

In the age of the Holy Spirit, there is no other gospel than the gospel of Jesus about grace (Gal 1:6-9). Paul warned that those who preached any other gospel than the one Jesus preached would be accursed. The apostle Paul was established for the gospel of God (Rom 1:1). Paul proclaimed to the people of Judea and Hellas that they needed to repent, turn to God, and believe in the Lord Jesus (Acts 20:21). Paul became a minister in the church to fulfill the word of God (Col 1:25). Paul preached Christ crucified (1 Cor 1:23). The gospel that Paul preached was neither received nor learned from men but received through the revelation of Jesus Christ (Gal 1:12). Paul sought to fulfill with all his life the commission given to him by the Lord Jesus Christ, which was to bear witness to the gospel of God's grace (Acts 20:24). Paul said himself, "If I were still trying to please men, I would not be a servant of Christ" (Gal 1:10).

(1) Justification and True Faith

God is the Savior of all people, especially of those who believe in him (1 Tim 4:10). The book of Romans, written by the apostle Paul, contains the main Christian theological ideas about the gospel. In Romans, Paul discusses the truth of justification. "In the gospel a righteousness from God is revealed, a righteousness that is by faith from first to last. The righteous will live by faith" (Rom 1:17; Gal 3:11). In the New Testament, Paul is the advocate of "justification by faith." Then in 1517, Martin Luther of Germany (1483-1546) advocated "justification by faith" (Rom 5:1) as a Reformation idea. Paul's theology greatly influenced the establishment of this "justification by faith" as a Christian doctrine. Paul saw righteousness as the inevitable result of true faith. The righteous live by faith (Gal 3:11). The person of faith lives righteously. "We through the Spirit wait for the hope of righteousness by faith" (Gal 5:5). It is by faith that a person is justified but not by the works of the law (Rom 3:20; Gal 2:16). The law was not established for the righteous but for the lawbreakers, the disobedient, and sinners (1 Tim 1:9-10). Paul saw death in sin, and he saw life in Jesus Christ (Rom 6:11). If you are a slave to sin, you will die, but if you are a slave to obedience, you will be made righteous (Rom 6:16). The prayer of a righteous man is powerful (Jas 5:16).

People of true faith obey God and do what is righteous. "Whether you are slaves to sin, which leads to death, or to obedience, which leads to righteousness?" (Rom 6:16). We are justified by faith as slaves of obedience to God. Obedience comes from the heart. Faith that works righteousness is true faith. "As the body without the spirit is dead, so faith without deeds is dead" (Jas 2:26). A person is justified by works, but not by faith alone (Jas 2:24). Thus, James emphasizes that both faith and works are necessary for a person to be good and righteous. The apostle Paul also emphasizes good works in the life of faith. God wants us to live by doing good works (Eph 2:10). Christians are set free from sin to become servants of righteousness (Rom 6:18) and have eternal life in the Lord Jesus Christ (Rom 6:23). The Bible gives us wisdom for salvation through faith in Christ Jesus (2 Tim 3:15). Not by works of righteousness but by his mercy he saved us by the washing of regeneration and renewing by the Holy Spirit (Titus 3:5). This tells us that while our works are important, we cannot be saved without God's mercy (grace). However, no one is saved without righteous and good works. We are justified by faith and have peace with God through our Lord Jesus Christ (Rom 5:1). The apostle Paul exhorted us to live in this world prudently, righteously, and godly, instructing us by the grace of God that saves (Titus 2:11–12).

(2) The Gospel Preached by the Apostle Paul

The apostle Paul became a minister for Jesus Christ and carried out his ministry by preaching the gospel of God to the gentiles (Rom 15:16). The gospel that Paul preached was not according to the will of man, nor did he receive it from man, nor was he taught it, but he received it through the revelation of Jesus Christ (Gal 1:11–12). The gospel is the coming of the kingdom of God. Paul defined the kingdom of God: "The kingdom of God is not a matter of eating and drinking, but of righteousness, peace and joy in the Holy Spirit" (Rom 14:17). In the Son of God, we have redemption, the forgiveness of sins (Col 1:14). The apostle Paul preached the gospel in the manifestation and power of the Holy Spirit. "My message and my preaching were not with wise and persuasive words, but with a demonstration of the Spirit's power, so that your faith might not rest on men's wisdom, but on God's power" (1 Cor 2:4–5). However, through the sanctification by the Holy Spirit and faith in the truth, you are saved (2 Thess 2:13). "Our citizenship is in heaven. And we eagerly await a Savior from there, the Lord Jesus Christ" (Phil 3:20). God loves us and graciously gives us eternal comfort and good hope (2 Thess 2:16). All the treasures of wisdom and knowledge are hidden in Christ (Col 2:3). Christians live in the Lord, as if they had received Christ Jesus as Lord (Col 2:6). Our faith and love come from the hope stored up in heaven (Col 1:5). "Now these three remain: faith, hope and love. But the greatest of these is love" (1 Cor 13:13). Paul says, "Love your neighbor as yourself" (Rom 13:9). All the commandments of God and Jesus Christ are contained in this word of love. Love comes from a pure heart, a good conscience, and faith without deceit (1 Tim 1:5). "Hold faith and a good conscience" (1 Tim 1:19). "Be an example for the believers in speech, in life, in love, in faith, and in purity" (1 Tim 4:12). "God did not give us a spirit of timidity, but a spirit of power, of love and of self-discipline" (2 Tim 1:7).

Paul urges people to remember the words of the Lord Jesus: "It is more blessed to help the weak and to give than to receive" (Acts 20:35). Paul also tells people, "The unrighteous, the fornicators, the idolaters, the greedy, the envious, and the drunkards will not inherit the kingdom of God" (1 Cor 6:9–10; Gal 5:19–21). He who is in union with the Lord is spiritually one with the Lord, and he who commits fornication sins against his own body (1 Cor 6:17–18). Paul also detailed the ethics that wives and husbands, children and parents, and servants and masters should observe with one another (Eph 5:22–33; 6:1–9). "Each one of you must love his wife as he loves himself, and the wife must respect her husband" (Eph 5:33). "Children, obey your parents in the Lord, for this is right" (Eph 6:1). "Fathers, do not exasperate your children; instead, bring them up in the training and instruction of the Lord" (Eph 6:4). Servants are to obey their masters as they would Christ, and masters are to stop threatening them and do good to them, not judging them by appearances (Eph 6:5–9). "Whatever you do, work at it with all your heart, as working for the Lord, not for men" (Col 3:23). "Anyone who does wrong will be repaid for his wrong, and there is no favoritism" (Col 3:25).

The house of God is the church of the living God and the pillar and ground of the truth (1 Tim 3:15). The apostle Paul speaks of the church in the book of Ephesians. God made Jesus the head of the church over all things, and the church is the body of Jesus (Eph 1:22–23). Through the church, he wanted to make known the manifold wisdom of God to the rulers and authorities in the heavenly realms (Eph 3:10), so that in the church he might be glorified throughout all generations, forever and ever (Eph 3:21). Paul became a worker in the church, according to the office God gave him, to fulfill the word of God for us (Col 1:25). Paul fulfilled his calling to build up the body of Jesus Christ, the church of God, through the gospel. When Paul heard that there were quarrels in the church at Corinth, he said, "I appeal to you, brothers, in the name of our Lord Jesus Christ, to be perfectly united in mind and thought" (1 Cor 1:10–11). Paul also speaks of the qualifications of bishops and deacons in the church. A bishop must be blameless, temperate, self-controlled, respectable, hospitable, able to teach (1 Tim 3:2). Deacons, likewise, must be men worthy of respect, sincere, not pursuing dishonest gain, and holding the deep truths of the faith with a clear conscience (1 Tim 3:8–9). "The elders who direct the affairs of the church well must be worthy of double honor, especially those whose work is preaching and teaching" (1 Tim 5:17). The Lord's servant must not quarrel; instead, he must be kind to everyone, able to teach, and patient (2 Tim 2:24).

"Food does not bring us near to God; we are no worse if we do not eat, and no better if we do" (1 Cor 8:8). This means that what we eat does not determine our wealth or poverty. "When the plowman plows and the thresher threshes, they ought to do so in the hope of sharing in the harvest" (1 Cor 9:10). "Whoever sows sparingly will also reap sparingly, and whoever sows generously will also reap generously" (2 Cor 9:6). "A man reaps what he sows" (Gal 6:7). Paul warned against laziness, saying, "If a man will not work, he shall not eat" (2 Thess 3:10). "For we brought nothing into the world, so we can take nothing out of it" (1 Tim 6:7). The love of money is the root of all evil (1 Tim 6:10). "Command them to do good, to be rich in good deeds, and to be generous and willing to share" (1 Tim 6:18). "Flee the evil desires of youth, and pursue righteousness, faith, love, and peace, along with those who call on the Lord out of a pure heart" (2 Tim 2:22). Paul continued to exhort us, "Lead a quiet life, mind your own business, and work with your hands" (1 Thess 4:11). "Even as I please all men in all things, not seeking mine own profit, but the profit of many, that they may be saved" (1 Cor 10:33). "Be kind to each other; be joyful always; pray continually; give thanks in all circumstances, for this is God's will for you in Christ Jesus" (1 Thess 5:15–18). Paul wrote to Timothy, his true son in the faith, "Grace, mercy and peace from God the Father and Christ Jesus our Lord" (1 Tim 1:2).

(3) The Gospel Preached by Other Apostles

In addition to the apostle Paul, James, Peter, John, Jude, and the writer of Hebrews wrote their own epistles and preached the gospel to both Jews and gentiles. When Jesus came to do God's will, he abolished the first law in order to establish a second, new covenant (Heb 10:9). By faith the whole world was created by the word of God (Heb 11:3). Hebrews 11 defines exactly what faith is and tells us what it does. "Now faith is the substance of things hoped for, the evidence of things not seen" (Heb 11:1). We have not seen Jesus Christ, but we believe in him with all our glory and joy. Without faith it is impossible to please God (Heb 11:6). The ancestors of faith endured, sacrificed, obeyed, and worshiped God in faith to please him. The ancestors of faith, such as Abraham, Sarah, Isaac, Jacob, Joseph, Moses, Rahab, Gideon, Barak, Samson, Jephthah, David, and Samuel, died according to their faith in devoted obedience to God (Heb 11:4–40). "He should ask God, who gives generously to all without finding fault, and it will be given to him" (Jas 1:5). When a person of faith asks God, he will one day grant it right according to his will. God tempts no one, so when a person is tempted, it is because he is drawn away and deceived by his own desires (Jas 1:14). It is the devil (Satan) who tempts us, not God. The apostle John said, "This is how we recognize the Spirit of Truth and the spirit of falsehood" (1 John 4:6). We must distinguish between the things of the world and the things of God. The victory that overcomes the world is our faith in God (1 John 5:4). We can overcome worldly temptations by faith.

James exhorts us to draw close to God by faith in him and to live a life of genuine faith. "Everyone should be quick to listen, slow to speak and slow to become angry, for man's anger does not bring about the righteous life that God desires" (Jas 1:19–20). "We all stumble in many ways. If anyone is never at fault in what he says, he is a perfect man" (Jas 3:2). "Judgment without mercy will be shown to anyone who has not been merciful" (Jas 2:13). If we do not have compassion on the poor or those in need, we will not receive eternal life, which is freely and graciously given by God. "For the wisdom that is on earth is unspiritual, of the devil; but the wisdom that comes from heaven is first of all pure; then peace-loving, considerate, submissive, full of mercy and good fruit" (Jas 3:15–17). "Anyone who chooses to be a friend of the world becomes an enemy of God" (Jas 4:4). "Come near to God and He will come near to you" (Jas 4:8). "God opposes the proud, but gives grace to the humble" (Jas 4:6; 1 Pet 5:5). "Brothers, do not slander and grumble against one another" (Jas 4:11; 5:9). The prayer of faith saves the sick (Jas 5:15). "The Lord's coming is near" (Jas 5:8). James says, "Be patient, then, brothers, until the Lord's coming," analogizing to the heart of a farmer who waits patiently for the harvest of fruit (Jas 5:7).

The apostles Peter, John, and others spoke of a good conscience and good works. God does not look at outward appearances but judges each person by their deeds (1 Pet 1:17). "We trust we have a good conscience, in all things willing to live honestly" (Heb 13:18). "Have a good conscience. It is better, if it is God's will, to suffer for doing good than for doing evil" (1 Pet 3:16–17). We have a good conscience by nature to do good. "Do not imitate what is evil but what is good. Anyone who does what is good is from God" (3 John 1:11). "He must turn from evil and do good; he must seek peace and pursue it" (1 Pet 3:11). "Anyone, then, who knows the good he ought to do and does not do it, sins" (Jas 4:17). "Do not forget to do good and to share with others" (Heb 13:16). Doing good is the most important virtue of a believer.

Peter exhorts Christians to live by faith, holy deeds, godliness, and love, while looking forward to the kingdom of God and the return of Jesus Christ. "Cast all your anxiety on Him (the Lord) because he cares for you" (1 Pet 5:7). The Lord rescues the godly from temptation and keeps the unrighteous under punishment until the day of judgment (2 Pet 2:9). "Make every effort to add to your faith, goodness; and to goodness, knowledge; and to knowledge, self-control; and to self-control, perseverance; and to perseverance, godliness; and to godliness, brotherly kindness; and to brotherly kindness, love" (2 Pet 1:5–7). All prophecy in the Bible did not come by the will of man, but men spoke from God as they were moved by the Holy Spirit (2 Pet 1:21). "The day of the Lord will come like a thief" (2 Pet 3:10). Therefore, "you ought to live holy and godly lives, as you look forward to the day of God and speed its coming" (2 Pet 3:11–12). "In keeping with his promise we are looking forward to a new heaven and a new earth, the home of righteousness" (2 Pet 3:13).

"The word of God is living and active, and sharper than any two-edged sword" (Heb 4:12). Jesus is the "Word of life" (1 John 1:1). The "Word of life" was from the beginning, and we have heard it, seen it, and touched it with our hands (1 John 1:1). What Jesus Christ has promised us is eternal life (1 John 2:25). God is light, and in him there is no darkness at all (1 John 1:5). "Just as man is destined to die once, and after that to face judgment" (Heb 9:27). Those who know that God is righteous know that everyone who does what is right has been born of God (1 John 2:29). If anyone lives in God, he must walk as Christ did (1 John 2:6). The world will pass away, and with it the lusts of the world, but whoever does the will of God will live forever (1 John 2:17). Christ appeared to take away our sins, but in him is no sin (1 John 3:5). Jesus Christ is sinless. Whoever is born of God does not sin (1 John 5:18). It takes our patience to receive what God has promised after we have done his will (Heb 10:36). "Keep your lives free from the love of money and be content with what you have" (Heb 13:5).

Paul, John, Peter, and Jude also exhort us to live in God's love. God is love (1 John 4:8). "Do not love the world or the things in the world. If anyone loves the world, the love of the Father is not in him" (1 John 2:15). "Let us not love with words or tongue, but with actions and in truth" (1 John 3:18). "If we love one another, God lives in us, and his love is made complete in us" (1 John 4:12). "Whoever lives in love lives in God, and God in him" (1 John 4:16). "Whoever loves God must also love his brother" (1 John 4:21). "Show proper respect to everyone: Love the brotherhood of believers, fear God" (1 Pet 2:17). "Above all, love each other deeply, because love covers over a multitude of sins" (1 Pet 4:8). "Beloved, build yourselves up in your most holy faith and pray in the Holy Spirit. Keep yourselves in God's love as you wait for the mercy of our Lord Jesus Christ to bring you to eternal life" (Jude 1:20-21).

10

What Is Salvation

1. THE MEANING OF SALVATION

WHEN YOU BELIEVE IN God and Jesus Christ, you are saved. Salvation is the sovereign work of God. Salvation is when a person is born again through Jesus' substitutionary death on the cross and resurrection, repents and receives forgiveness of sins, is freed from the yoke of sin, and is reconciled to God through the Holy Spirit. Salvation is when a person is freed from all evil and sin. Salvation requires being spiritually born again (John 3:7). There is no salvation without being spiritually born again. Jesus said, "No one can see the kingdom of God unless he is born again" (John 3:3). If we are not fully regenerated by true faith, that is, born anew, we are not saved and cannot enter the kingdom of God. The purpose of salvation is to be spiritually born again and completely transformed into a person of true faith. A person of faith who is saved can change his heart and mind anew, so that he can do good and righteous deeds to please God.

In the Bible, God, through the angel of the Lord, gave the name of the Messiah (Savior) "Jesus" to the Son of God, born of his Virgin Mary. The true meaning of "salvation" is found in the meaning of Jesus' name: "He (Jesus) will save his people from their sins" (Matt 1:21). Jesus said, "I am the door: by me if any man enter in, he shall be saved" (John 10:9). Accordingly, man's salvation comes only through the Lord Jesus Christ, the Son of God. Jesus himself said, "For the Son of Man (Jesus) came to seek and to save what was

What Is Salvation

lost" (Luke 19:10). The apostle Paul says, "Christ Jesus came into the world to save sinners" (1 Tim 1:15). In the same way, Jesus Christ came to this earth to seek and save the lost and sinners. We are not saved by human will and effort. We cannot enter the kingdom of God in our own strength. Salvation does not come from man but is a gift of God (Eph 2:8). The life of salvation is about becoming children of God (John 1:12), turning away from sin and being born again through faith in Jesus. "God was reconciling the world to himself in Christ, not counting men's sins against them" (2 Cor 5:19). Salvation is when God (Jesus) frees Christians from the yoke of physical sin and keeps them living by the Holy Spirit. "If we live in the Spirit, let us also walk in the Spirit" (Gal 5:25). We must live according to God's will, guided by the Holy Spirit.

Jesus' substitutionary death on the cross and resurrection are the events of salvation for us. To be saved, you must believe in your heart that Jesus died on the cross to atone for your sins and that he rose from the dead (Rom 10:9; 1 Cor 15:1–4). The resurrection of Jesus is God's saving event shown to all mankind who believe in him. God foreshadows the salvation of all mankind by showing the resurrection of Jesus. The resurrection of Jesus with humanity is evidence of salvation. Jesus said, "I am the resurrection and the life. He who believes in me will live, even though he dies; and whoever lives and believes in me will never die" (John 11:25–26). Those who believe in Jesus have eternal life, and God intends to save the world through Jesus (John 3:16–17). "Believe in the Lord Jesus, and you will be saved, you and your household" (Acts 16:31). "Now that you have been set free from sin and have become slaves to God, the benefit you reap leads to holiness, and the result is eternal life" (Rom 6:22). Those who believe in Jesus Christ, who rose from the dead in a substitutionary crucifixion, will have their sins forgiven, be reconciled to God, enjoy peace, and receive eternal life (salvation).

"From him (the Lord) and through him and to him are all things" (Rom 11:36). Christians are born of God and return to God after death. From a Christian doctrinal perspective, salvation means that Christians will be judged by God after death (Heb 9:27) and enter the kingdom of God (heaven) to live forever. To enter the kingdom of God is to have eternal life. Eternal life is living where God dwells. The kingdom of God is the realm of salvation. Both the kingdom of God and eternal life refer to salvation. "Now this is eternal life: that they may know you, the only true God, and Jesus Christ, whom you have sent" (John 17:3). Jesus Christ is the only door through which we may gain life and enter into salvation (John 10:9). "You are in Christ Jesus, who has become for us wisdom from God—that is, our righteousness, holiness and redemption" (1 Cor 1:30). Jesus Christ is the door to our salvation. Jesus says, "My sheep listen to my voice; I know them, and they follow me. I give them eternal life, and they shall never perish" (John 10:27–28). If we follow Jesus Christ, we have eternal life. There is no salvation apart from through Jesus Christ. Christians who live a life of faith believe that after they die, they will be resurrected like Jesus, saved, and have eternal life. However, God leads to salvation through faith, repentance, obedience, and sanctification work. Sanctification requires being born again (regeneration). Christians are sanctified when they obey God's word by faith. "Follow peace with all men, and holiness, without which no man shall see the Lord" (Heb 12:14). Salvation is accomplished by God's sovereignty, but we must live a life of faith by doing God's will. "Not everyone who says to me, 'Lord, Lord,' will enter the kingdom of heaven, but only he who does the will of my Father who is in heaven" (Matt 7:21). Those who say they serve the Lord only with their mouths but do not do the will of God cannot be saved. After repenting and turning away from sin, then being born again by faith, Christians live a life of obedience to God. Those who believe in and obey Jesus have eternal life (John 3:36). "The servant of obedience leads to righteousness" (Rom 6:16). A person of faith obeys God and does good and righteous deeds. Moreover, blessed are the poor in spirit, for theirs is the kingdom of heaven (Matt 5:3). However, those who practice the "works of the flesh," such as fornication, self-indulgence, idolatry, witchcraft, strife, envy, heresy, speculation, drunkenness, debauchery, etc., will not inherit the kingdom of God (Gal 5:19–21).

God's will is cherished in God's mercy. Mary's obedience to God brought about the birth of Jesus and the beginning of God's salvation work. Man's salvation comes through the mercy of Jesus (Titus 3:5). God sees our faith. True faith accompanies good works and brings forth God's grace. Grace comes through Jesus Christ (John 1:17), and in Jesus Christ we can see God's will and grace. We are saved by grace through faith, and salvation is the gift of God (Eph 2:8). A good God offers salvation by grace without cost to the people of true faith. After his resurrection, Jesus said, "Whoever believes and is baptized will be saved" (Mark 16:16). Believing in Jesus Christ is the way for the people of the world to be saved and live forever in the kingdom of God. Therefore, believers should live a life that resembles Jesus. Jesus said, "Whoever loses his life for me and for the gospel will save it" (Mark 8:35). Giving up oneself for the sake of Jesus Christ is an essential requirement of faith that leads to salvation by grace.

Salvation does not depend on human works to keep the law but comes entirely from God's grace. We enter the kingdom of God by grace through faith in and obedience to Jesus Christ. Salvation does not come from the law (Gal 3:22-23). No one, Jew or gentile, is saved through the law by keeping it. This is because, by the works of the law, a person is not recognized as righteous before God (Rom 3:20). One is justified by faith in Jesus Christ but not by the works of the law (Rom 3:28; Gal 2:16). Grace reigns through righteousness, resulting in eternal life through Jesus Christ (Rom 5:21). Salvation is a work of God by grace but not of man. If it is by grace, it is not of works (Rom 11:6). The gift of God is eternal life in Jesus Christ (Rom 6:23). Only when we have faith to live righteously by grace, God gives us the gift of salvation (eternal life) through grace for our true faith. A person of faith lives righteously. Salvation is not achieved through human free will and works. We are not saved by works. This is not to say that righteous works are not necessary for salvation but that humans should not "boast in their works" (Eph 2:9). Human works are not perfect in God's sight. Human works of righteousness fall short of God's standard of righteousness. As it is written, there is none righteous, not even one (Rom 3:10). This is because human righteousness is not perfect. The Bible clearly records that we are saved by grace through faith in Jesus Christ but not by human works. We cannot keep God's law perfectly by works of the flesh, so we are saved by grace through faith. However, while salvation is accomplished by God's grace, no one is saved without righteous and good works. In the path of righteousness there is life and no death (Prov 12:28). Those who believe are justified by true faith and saved by grace, enjoying eternal life in the kingdom of God.

2. REGENERATION, REPENTANCE, AND SALVATION

Regeneration, which means "to be born again," is an essential requirement of spiritual salvation that believers must possess. To be born again spiritually is to be given new life. Regeneration is the source of the Christian life, as we imitate God and become more like Jesus Christ through true faith. Faith without regeneration is not true faith. Jesus said to Nicodemus, "I tell you the truth, no one can see the kingdom of God unless he is born again" (John 3:3). This means that humans cannot be saved without spiritual regeneration. Those who believe in Jesus are born of God (1 John 5:1). "Everyone born of God overcomes the world" (1 John 5:4). When we are spiritually born again, we can overcome the things of this world. The apostle Paul says, "You were taught, with regard to your former way of life, to put off your old self, which is being corrupted by its deceitful desires; to be made new in the attitude of your minds; and to put on the new self, created to be like God in true righteousness and holiness" (Eph 4:22–24). "If anyone is in Christ, he is a new creation; the old has gone, the new has come" (2 Cor 5:17). If you are in Jesus Christ, you are born again, and there is a spiritual change. To be saved, we must break free from a life of fleshly desires and be reborn as new spiritual people who follow God's righteousness and truth. As we see in the conversion of Zacchaeus, a tax collector and rich man (Luke 19:1–10), God's work of salvation necessarily involves a spiritual renewal in us. Not by works of righteousness which we have done, but according to his mercy, God our Savior saved us, by the washing of regeneration, and renewing of the Holy Spirit (Titus 3:5).

The human ancestors, Adam and Eve, sinned by disobeying God. As a result of Adam and Eve's original sin, humans sin by doing evil of their own free will with the greed and desire of their hearts. Man is a sinner because he is naturally under the yoke of sin. Man without faith disobeys God by practicing evil (sin). The sin in our hearts causes us to do evil things that God does not want us to do (Rom 7:19–20). "After desire has conceived, it gives birth to sin; and sin, when it is full-grown, gives birth to death" (Jas 1:15). Humans die because of sin. "Your iniquities have separated you from your God; your sins have hidden his face from you, so that he will not hear" (Isa 59:2). Sin results in spiritual death, a departure from God, which cuts off right relationship and communication with the God of life. A person who is cut off from God is already spiritually dead. Sin alienates us from God and our neighbors, locking us in.

Repentance is the prerequisite for salvation. The Baptist John and Jesus began preaching the gospel by saying, "Repent, for the kingdom of heaven is near" (Matt 3:2; 4:17). This indicates that repentance is a prerequisite for salvation. Jesus came into the world to call sinners to repentance (Luke 5:32). Repentance leads to the forgiveness of sins (Luke 24:47). Peter also told the people, "Repent, then, and turn to God, so that your sins may be wiped out" (Acts 3:19). When a person is completely born again, repents, and believes in Jesus, he receives the forgiveness of sins. Human repentance, the turning away from sin and being born again, is a key element of faith that obtains salvation. "God has granted even the Gentiles repentance unto life" (Acts 11:18). Repentance brings life. In a life of faith, we must be born again and repent daily to receive forgiveness of sins, life, and salvation. Repentance is confessing the sins of the world, taking off the old clothes and putting on the new clothes of life, being born again, turning to God, and living according to God's will. True repentance is when sinful human beings are born again and turn to Jesus, the source of life, who died bearing human sins and was resurrected. True repentance is confessing your sins and turning to the Lord and following him. "Godly sorrow brings repentance that leads to salvation and leaves no regret" (2 Cor 7:10). Repentance leads to the forgiveness of sins, which leads to salvation. Repentance is a result of faith and is a gift from God. There is no salvation without repentance that leads to a new birth, confession of sins, and asking for forgiveness.

True repentance is truly hating sin and turning away from it. Those who do not repent of their sins cannot be saved. Jesus commanded his disciples to preach about repentance: "Repentance and forgiveness of sins will be preached in his name to all nations, beginning at Jerusalem" (Luke 24:47). "Repent" was also a theme that the apostle Paul taught everyone (Acts 17:30). James emphasized to his brothers, "For those who repent and are born again, faith in Jesus requires works." "What good is it, if a man claims to have faith but has no deeds? Can such faith save him? " (Jas 2:14). "As the body without the spirit is dead, so faith without deeds is dead" (Jas 2:26). James also says, "Show me your faith without deeds, and I will show you my faith by what I do" (Jas 2:18). Faith without works is false faith (Jas 2:20). A believer who repents but has no works cannot be saved. A true believer does good and righteous deeds. True faith, "believing with a good heart," leads to salvation. "To those who by persistence in doing good seek glory, honor and immortality, he will give eternal life" (Rom 2:7). Jesus said, "Every good tree bears good fruit, but a bad tree bears bad fruit" (Matt 7:17). If we are faithful in our faith and act righteously, our lives will bear good fruits of salvation.

3. GRACE, WORKS, AND SALVATION

The key terms that characterize Christianity are grace, life, and salvation. In his New Testament epistles, the apostle Paul says that "grace" means all things to the Christian faith. The Lord Jesus Christ is the God of grace. According to the Reformer Martin Luther (1483–1546), Christians are saved and enter the kingdom of God only by "sola fide" and "sola gratia" in Jesus Christ. Luther's Reformation idea of "justification by faith" (Rom 5:1) is a key Christian doctrine. And in the New Testament, "justification by faith" is the core of soteriology. Justification by faith is the forgiveness of all sins by God's mercy (grace) to the sinner through faith and the rebirth of the sinner to a sinless, righteous person. The believer lives righteously. In the gospel, "The righteousness of God is revealed from faith to faith. The righteous will live by faith" (Rom 1:17), and God's righteousness is revealed in his mercy. In the Bible, the Pharisee, who believed he was righteous and was proud and despised others, was not justified by faith (Luke 18:9–14). Those who firmly believe in their own righteousness like the Pharisees are not saved. This is because human righteousness is not perfect. But the publican who repented, saying, "God be merciful to me, for I am a sinner," was "justified by faith" through Jesus on the spot (Luke 18:13–14). Jesus rebuked the Pharisee, saying, "For everyone who exalts himself will be humbled, and he who humbles himself will be exalted" (Luke 18:14). In this way, God forgives sinners like the poor tax collector and saves them by justifying them by faith through grace. The salvation of a believer like the tax collector who is born again and repents of his sins is based on God's grace. Grace is the abundant favor and gift of God in Jesus Christ. Those who receive grace are at peace and with God (Luke 1:26); however, those who confess their sins but do not repent do not come to the grace of salvation. God's grace is extended to those who truly believe in Jesus Christ and want to be saved, like the lowly outcast Samaritan woman (John 4:1–42).

Salvation is the gift of God through faith, by grace but not from man (Eph 2:8). Salvation is a work of God. While salvation does not deny works itself, it is not earned by human will and effort. This is because human works are not perfect in God's sight. Jesus said, "It is easier for a camel to go through the eye of a needle than for a rich man to enter the kingdom of God" (Matt 19:24; Luke 18:25). "There is none righteous, not even one" (Rom 3:10). There is no righteous person in this world. We humans are all under sin (Rom 3:9). The apostle Paul goes on to say, "Salvation is not by works, so that no one can boast" (Eph 2:9). De-emphasizing human works for salvation is because man boasts of his imperfect works as righteous deeds. What man considers righteous and good is not perfect in God's sight. No human work can be righteous and good enough to please God. Human righteousness falls short of God's standard of righteousness. Human righteousness is not perfect. No one is perfect enough to reach God's

What Is Salvation

standard of righteousness by works and be saved. Therefore, salvation is obtained by God's grace. The human will, which is inherently sinful, cannot accomplish salvation. As Jesus said, "With man this (salvation) is impossible, but with God all things are possible" (Matt 19:26; Luke 18:27). God saves us not according to our works but by his will and the grace he has given us in Christ Jesus (2 Tim 1:9). Not because of our righteous deeds, but because of the mercy and love of God our Savior, who has appeared and saved us by the renewing of the Holy Spirit (Titus 3:4–5). Salvation is a gift of God and is accomplished by sovereign grace. "Everyone who calls on the name of the Lord will be saved" (Rom 10:13). Those who believe in Jesus Christ are saved by his unmerited grace. However, believers are not perfect but must live a life of righteousness and good works according to God's will to resemble Jesus Christ. For while salvation is by God's sovereign grace, no one is saved without righteous works. Jesus asks us to be righteous. "Unless your righteousness surpasses that of the Pharisees and the teachers of the law, you will certainly not enter the kingdom of heaven" (Matt 5:20). "Those he predestined, he also called; those he called, he also justified; those he justified, he also glorified" (Rom 8:30). This justification does not save us completely but requires a righteous life of faith in the process of sanctification to imitate Jesus Christ. "Follow peace with all men, and holiness: for without these no man shall see the Lord" (Heb 12:14). No one can see God without being sanctified. The person of faith is holy and glorified.

One cannot be saved and have eternal life without believing in God (Jesus). Salvation means eternal life. The unbeliever dies. However, those who believe have eternal life spiritually. Jesus is the resurrection and the life, and whoever believes in him will never die (John 11:25–26). If you are in Jesus Christ, you are born again and become a new creature (2 Cor 5:17). Salvation is being born again and living a life of eternal life. Jesus is life. In Jesus Christ is life (John 1:4). Jesus said, "I am the way, the truth, and the life; no one comes to the Father except through me" (John 14:6). Faith is the way to life, and without faith it is impossible to please God (Heb 11:6). God says, "Whoever believes in the Son has eternal life" (John 3:36; 6:40). God's gift is eternal life through Jesus (Rom 6:23). Life (eternal life) means salvation, and we are saved only by believing in Jesus (Mark 16:16; Acts 16:31). Jesus said, "Small is the gate and narrow the road that leads to life, and only a few find it" (Matt 7:14). "Make every effort to enter through the narrow door, because many, I tell you, will try to enter and will not be able to" (Luke 13:24). The gate to the kingdom of the God of life is narrow and the road is hard, so salvation is difficult. We must put down the evil things that come from the heart of man, such as sexual immorality, theft, adultery, greed, deceit, envy, slander, pride, etc. (Mark 7:21–23). Jesus said, "Any of you who does not give up everything he has cannot be my disciple" (Luke 14:33). In the Old Testament, the Lord also says, "See, I am setting before you the way of life and the way of death" (Jer 21:8). Salvation is that we go on the hard "road of life" toward the kingdom of God. "No one can enter the kingdom of God unless he is born of water and the Spirit" (John 3:5). "The one who sows to please the Spirit, from the Spirit will reap eternal life" (Gal 6:8). Whoever is baptized with water and the Holy Spirit, the source of life, will be saved (Mark 16:16). All believing Christians are saved by grace and life. "Those who receive God's abundant provision of grace and of the gift of righteousness will reign in life through the one man, Jesus Christ" (Rom 5:17). Those of faith who receive abundantly the grace of God and the gift of righteousness have eternal life through Jesus Christ.

4. THE WORK OF THE HOLY SPIRIT AND SALVATION

When Jesus went to God the Father, he sent us the "Comforter (Counselor)," the Holy Spirit (John 16:7). The Holy Spirit is the Spirit of God and the Spirit of Jesus Christ (Rom 8:9). The Comforter, the Holy Spirit, is with us forever (John 14:16). The Comforter, the Holy Spirit, is God, the Spirit of Truth (John 14:17; 16:13). The Spirit of Truth comes and guides us into all truth (John 16:13), and the Holy Spirit receives the things of Jesus Christ and makes them known to us (John 16:15). The Holy Spirit empowers us, guiding us into God's truth and enabling us to live a life of faith according to God's will. Today is the age of the Holy Spirit. "The Spirit himself testifies with our spirit that we are God's children" (Rom 8:16). The Comforter, the Holy Spirit, convicts the world of sin, righteousness, and judgment (John 16:8). The Holy Spirit, sent by Jesus, works within us to keep us from sin and turn us back to the Lord God. In order for a person to be born again, a change in human nature takes place by the Holy Spirit. Unless a person is born again, he cannot see the kingdom of God (John 3:3). We cannot have eternal life unless we are spiritually born again. The Holy Spirit bears witness to the world and the church about Jesus and salvation. The Holy Spirit descended on the earth on Pentecost (Acts 2:1–21), and "they (the apostles) were all filled with the Holy Spirit" (Acts 2:4). The Holy Spirit came to earth on Pentecost, and Jesus received the Holy Spirit promised by

What Is Salvation

the Father (God) and poured it out on us (Acts 2:33). Our bodies are the temples of the Holy Spirit (1 Cor 6:19). Jesus is the one who baptizes with the Holy Spirit (John 1:33). Pentecost is the beginning of the age of the Holy Spirit and the day the early church proclaimed the gospel. Christians experience the presence and work of the Holy Spirit. The apostle Paul says, "If we live in the Spirit, let us also walk in the Spirit" (Gal 5:25). In this way, we Christians live by the Holy Spirit. It is by the Holy Spirit that we are born again and have life. Those who sow for the Spirit reap eternal life from the Spirit (Gal 6:8).

"Where the Spirit of the Lord is, there is freedom" (2 Cor 3:17). To walk with the Lord is to be set free. Christ set us free so that we might be free (Gal 5:1). The Holy Spirit sets man free from the yoke of sin. If we are led by the Spirit, we are not under the law (Gal 5:18). "Through Christ Jesus the law of the Spirit of life in Christ Jesus set me free from the law of sin and death" (Rom 8:2), so those who are led by the Spirit in Christ Jesus are never condemned (Rom 8:1). The "Spirit of grace" (Heb 10:29) breathes into us not only living, breathing life but also God's love and grace. We receive the promise of the Holy Spirit through faith (Gal 3:14). The Holy Spirit is the truth (1 John 5:6). No one knows the things of God except the Spirit of God (1 Cor 2:11). Human wisdom does not know what the Spirit of God is doing. The unregenerate natural man does not know the things of God's Spirit, but the spiritual man knows everything about the things of God (1 Cor 2:14-15). We must distinguish the Spirit of Truth from the spirit of falsehood (1 John 4:6). We control the spirit of falsehood by relying on the Holy Spirit who dwells in us. The evil "works of the flesh," such as fornication, theft, murder, adultery, greed, lying, debauchery, slander, and pride, which are controlled by the "spirit of falsehood" in the hearts of worldly people, defile people (Mark 7:21-23). In those who belong to God, the Holy Spirit of Truth breaks down these "works of the flesh" (Gal 5:19). The Holy Spirit works to reveal to us the holiness and glory of Jesus Christ. The work of the Holy Spirit is supernatural and invisible to our eyes, but the results of his work are experienced and seen by us. "Do not get drunk on wine, which leads to debauchery. Instead, be filled with the Spirit" (Eph 5:18). As children of God, we are not to be debauched by the worldly "works of the flesh," such as intemperance, corruption, waste, etc. When we obey the Holy Spirit in us, we experience the power and fullness of the Holy Spirit. However, we who live in the world always struggle with the desires of the flesh. "Walk in the Spirit, and ye shall not fulfil the lust of the flesh" (Gal 5:16). Being filled with the Holy Spirit is being free from the desires of the flesh, walking by the Spirit, and living righteously by faith. A person of faith, filled with the Holy Spirit, seeks his righteousness with deep repentance for his sins. Living by the Spirit makes our lives godly and holy, full of joy and vitality. When we are filled with the Holy Spirit, we sing and praise the Lord with our hearts, giving thanks always to God the Father for everything, and submit to one another out of reverence for Christ (Eph 5:18–21). To be filled with the Holy Spirit is to recognize that the Lord is in us and to live boldly in the will of God. Those who are filled with the Holy Spirit let the word of Christ dwell in them richly, teaching and admonishing one another in all wisdom, singing psalms and hymns and spiritual songs, praising God with gratitude in their hearts (Col 3:16).

There are diverse gifts of the Holy Spirit. To some the Holy Spirit gives the word of wisdom, to others the word of knowledge, to others faith, to others the gift of healing, to others the gift of might, to others prophecy, to others the discernment of spirits (1 Cor 12:4–10). However, the gifts of the Holy Spirit cannot be obtained by human power. We must be careful not to be deceived by counterfeit gifts that are the work of Satan, and we must receive the true gifts of the Holy Spirit freely, obeying God's word and being godly in the Spirit. The "fruit of the Spirit" is love, joy, peace, long-suffering, mercy, goodness, faithfulness, gentleness, and self-control (Gal 5:22–23). The fruit of the Spirit is manifested in a life of true faith. The Holy Spirit gives us love. The love of God is poured out into our hearts by the Holy Spirit (Rom 5:5). By the Holy Spirit, we love our brothers and neighbors, passing from death to life (1 John 3:14). Through the Holy Spirit, we wait for the hope of righteousness by faith (Gal 5:5). The apostle Paul said in this way, "May the God of hope fill you with all joy and peace as you trust in him, so that you may overflow with hope by the power of the Holy Spirit" (Rom 15:13). By the power of the Holy Spirit, hope overflows into our lives of faith. By the Spirit of the Lord, we see his glory and are transformed into his image (2 Cor 3:18). "God is spirit, and his worshipers must worship in spirit and in truth" (John 4:24). We worship God truly and faithfully in the Holy Spirit and in truth. We speak the truth in love (Eph 4:15). True love must follow the truth of the Holy Spirit. Christians believe in God and Jesus and are filled with grace by the Holy Spirit to become like the Lord Jesus Christ. God said, "From the beginning God chose you to be saved through the sanctifying work of the Spirit and through belief in the truth" (2 Thess 2:13). We are saved by God's grace through faith in the truth of the Holy Spirit. Not because of our righteous deeds, but only through his mercy (grace), he saved us by the washing of regeneration and renewing of the Holy Spirit (Titus 3:5). Christians in the age of the Holy Spirit rely on the Holy Spirit of Truth to justify them by faith, so that they are saved by the grace of God and Jesus Christ and live in spirit prosperously.

PART II

Understanding Christianity

1

The Origins and History of Christianity

CHRISTIANITY WAS CREATED AROUND the 1st century based on the spread of the gospel, centered on the birth, ministry, and words of Jesus the Messiah in the historical context of Israel in the Old Testament era. For more than two thousand years of Christian history, churches (cathedrals) have accepted the Gospels of the New Testament as historical facts, and the events of Jesus' substitutionary death on the cross and resurrection are at the center of Christianity. At the end of the 4th century, Christianity was designated as the state religion of the Roman Empire. From then until the 16th century, the main Christian denominations were the Roman Catholic Church, Protestantism, and the Eastern Orthodox Church. This chapter 1 covers the emergence of Christianity from the birth of Jesus (ca. 4 BC), his life, ministry, death, resurrection, and ascension to the apostles of Jesus who led the early church (the Apostolic Church). Furthermore, the origins and history of Christianity are outlined, including ancient Christianity, medieval Christianity, the birth of Protestantism and the formation of Christian denominations, and Christianity on the Korean Peninsula.

Part II: Understanding Christianity

1. THE ORIGINS OF CHRISTIANITY AND ANCIENT CHRISTIANITY

Jesus was born around 4 BC in Bethlehem, Judea, as the Son of God incarnated by his mother Mary (Matt 1:18-25; 2:1). He grew up in Nazareth in Galilee (Matt 2:22-23). "After John was put in prison, Jesus went into Galilee, proclaiming the good news of God" (Mark 1:14). Along with his apostles (disciples), Jesus ministered to the people of Israel (Jews) in the region of Palestine (now Israel and the territory of the State of Palestine). He said, "The kingdom of God is near. Repent and believe the good news!" (Mark 1:15). The earliest Christians were Jewish. Jesus Christ came into the world and fulfilled the office of prophet and priest (Heb 5:1-7). However, during his atoning ministry, Jesus lived a life of suffering in soul and body, attacked by Satan and oppressed by an unjust world. He was crucified and died around AD 30 (Mark 15:21-37), resurrected (Matt 28:1-10; Mark 16:9), preached about the things of the kingdom of God for forty days (Acts 1:3), and ascended into heaven (Mark 16:19; Luke 24:51). Jesus is a historical figure in the New Testament who taught his gospel to the apostles. Even after his ascension, he sent the Holy Spirit (the Comforter) into the world to continue his work (John 14:26). Beginning in the 1st century, Jesus' apostles, including Peter, Paul, Barnabas, John, Philip, James, and Jude, performed signs and wonders to Jews and gentiles, preaching the gospel and made them Christians.

Jesus foreshadowed the building of the Christian church, when he said to Peter, "Upon this rock I will build my church" (Matt 16:18). The book of Acts in the New Testament tells the story of Christianity's origins and how the apostles spread the gospel. Jesus' apostles led the early church (Acts 2:1-47), which was born on Pentecost (Pentecost Sunday), and spread the gospel to ancient Greece, Rome, and other countries around the world. The members of the early church were taught by the apostles and fellowshipped together, sharing their property and possessions with one another, gathering daily in the temple to share food and pray with joy and purity of heart (Acts 2:42-46). At this time many wonders and miraculous signs were done through the apostles (Acts 2:43).

The apostle Paul traveled to major cities in the Mediterranean region of the Roman Empire to preach the gospel of Jesus. Paul led early Christianity by preaching the good news of Jesus primarily to gentiles. From the 1st to 3rd centuries, Judaism (Old Testament) and Christianity (New Testament) were in deep conflict, distrusting each other because of their different doctrines. As Christianity spread, Stephen, James, and others were martyred for condemning Judaism (Jews) (Acts 7:54–60; 12:1–2). The Roman Empire persecuted Christianity nationwide, from the time of Emperor Nero (37–68) through the 2nd and 3rd centuries. During this time, Peter and Paul were martyred. Then, in 313, Constantine I of the Roman Empire issued the Edict of Milan, which recognized Christianity. In 325, the First Council of Nicaea was held to adopt the Nicene Creed, which then established Christian doctrine. Finally, the entire Roman Empire adopted Christianity as the state religion in 392.

2. MEDIEVAL CHRISTIANITY

Christianity spread to Western and Northern Europe from the 5th to the 10th centuries. Christianity was first introduced to Ireland in 423, followed by the Frankish Kingdom (481–843) (France, Germany, Austria, Switzerland, Italy, and the three Benelux countries) in Western Europe in the late 5th century. Christianity reached the Anglo-Saxon Seven Kingdoms (England) around 600. In 598, the Roman Catholic Church sent St. Augustine (?–605), born in Rome, to do missionary work for the evangelization of the Anglo-Saxons as Archbishop of Canterbury, England. Christianity spread slowly in northern Europe, on the Scandinavian peninsula. By the year 1000, most of northern Europe had been converted to Christianity. By the 9th century, Christianity had reached the Slavs of Eastern Europe. In the late 11th and early 12th centuries, the Pope of Rome and the emperors of the Holy Roman Empire fought fiercely for the right to appoint clergy. The Holy Roman Empire (800/962–1806) included the Kingdom of Germany, the largest territory, and the Kingdom of Bohemia, Burgundy, and Italy. During the Eastern Roman Empire (Byzantine Empire) (395–1453), there was a doctrinal conflict between the Roman Catholic Church (Western) and the Eastern Orthodox Church of Constantinople (now Istanbul).

The Eastern Orthodox Church has been one church with the Roman Catholic Church (Western) since the early church in the 1st century, but it split in 1054 to become a separate church. After the fall of the Eastern Roman Empire in the late 15th century, the Russian Orthodox Church diverged from the Eastern Orthodox Church. The Eastern Orthodox Church, which upholds the traditions and regulations of the early church from Jesus Christ to the apostles, has played an important role in the history and culture of Greece, Eastern Europe, Russia, and Western Asia. Eastern Orthodoxy has also spread into several other autonomous Orthodox churches around the world, including the Russian Orthodox Church and the Greek Orthodox Church. Together with the Roman Catholic Church, Eastern Orthodoxy is the oldest Christianity in the world and is currently the third largest Christian denomination in the world. The Ecumenical Patriarchate of Constantinople, located in Istanbul, Turkey, currently serves as the world's representative of the Eastern Orthodox Church.

The Crusades (1095–1291) took place on the eastern coast of the Mediterranean Sea in an attempt by the Roman Catholic Church to recapture the holy city of Jerusalem from Islamic forces. During these wars, the Roman Catholic Church sought to secure its supremacy by force of arms, and the Pope was deeply involved in the politics and society of Western Europe. However, the failure of the Crusades undermined the pope's authority, and Western European countries grew into feudal kingdoms centered on monarchs (kings). The English Christian theologian and reformer John Wycliffe (1320–84) attacked the power of the pope and the doctrines of the Roman Catholic Church, and in 1382 he translated the Latin Bible into English. Wycliffe's doctrines later became the basis for the principles of the Reformation movement. From the 14th to the end of the 16th century, the Renaissance, or literary revival, arose in Europe and sought to revive a human-centered spirit by re-recognizing the glorious culture, art, and ideas of ancient Greece and Rome. In the early 16th century, the humanists of the Renaissance became the driving force behind the reform of the Roman Catholic Church and the academic development. From the late 15th century to the mid-18th century, European Catholic countries such as Spain and Portugal explored the world, spreading the Roman Catholic Church to countries in North and South America, Asia, and Oceania.

The Roman Catholic Church, or Catholic Church, is the oldest and largest Christian-centered denomination in the world today. The Catholic Church occupies a huge weight in European history and culture and has had a major influence on Western philosophy, culture, art, science, and more. In East Asia, the Catholic Church is called "Catholicism" (天主教). The Catholic Church has the doctrine of the Trinity, believing that the one God exists in three persons, the Father, the Son, and the Holy Spirit (Matt 28:19). The Catholic Church teaches that it is the one and only church of Jesus Christ and that it comes from the apostles. The Catholic Church emphasizes Jesus' words to the apostles upon his ascension after his resurrection: "And surely I am with you always, to the very end of the age" (Matt

28:20). The Catholic Church operates as a centralized clergy system with the pope and bishops in Rome as the center. All Catholic churches in the world are controlled and managed by the Vatican (Holy See) in Rome.

3. THE REFORMATION AND PROTESTANTISM

In the early 16th century, the Reformation, led by Martin Luther of Germany (1483–1546), broke out against the corruption of the Roman Catholic Church and the authoritarian power of the Roman pope. As a result of Luther's Reformation in 1517, evangelical Protestantism was born in Western Europe and Northern Europe, where the papal Roman Catholic Church dominated. Luther believed that one can be justified and saved by the Bible and faith alone, advocating the five solas: "Scripture alone, faith alone, grace alone, Christ alone, and the glory of God alone." He published his Ninety-Five Theses to refute the doctrines of the Roman Catholic Church and criticize the sale of "indulgences." Luther's Ninety-Five Theses caused a great stir in the dark medieval church and marked the beginning of the European Reformation. While hiding in Wartburg Castle to escape death threats, Luther translated the New Testament from the Greek into German and published the "Septemberbible" in September 1522, making the German Bible freely available to the common people. Thus, the Reformation in Europe began with the Bible, the word of God (gospel).

After Luther, the influence of Calvinism (Reformed), defined by the Reformation movement of Jean Calvin (1509–64) in France, led to the separation of Protestantism from Roman Catholicism, creating the Reformed Church (Puritans) and the Presbyterian Church. "Puritans" refers to both Reformed Christians in the Lutheran Church and the Church of England, as well as traditional Lutheran and Calvinist evangelicals with a thorough biblical stance on the Bible. Calvin's Reformed thought is that the church should always be reformed toward a God-centered church and biblical life based on the word of God. Later, the Church of England was recognized as the state religion of the United Kingdom, and the Presbyterian Church of Scotland became the state religion of Scotland.

Since Luther's Reformation, religious conflicts have led to large and small wars of religion in Europe. The Thirty Years' War (1618–48) between Roman Catholics and Protestants in the Holy Roman Empire resulted in many casualties in Europe. The death toll reached eight million, and Germany suffered the most. After the wars of religion, areas ruled by emperors or monarchs (kings) adopted one religion as their state religion, whether it was Roman Catholic, Lutheran, Anglican, Presbyterian, or Reformed Church. Later, new Christian denominations emerged in Europe, such as the Anabaptist, Baptist, and Methodist churches. In today's world, Protestantism has grown to become the second largest Christian denomination after the Roman Catholic Church.

The Lutheran Church is the first denomination of Protestantism that followed the ideas of Luther of the Five Solas in the 16th century. After the Reformation, the Lutheran Church evolved from the German Lutheran Church to the European Lutheran Church. After 1525, Lutheranism spread to Prussia and the Nordic countries of Sweden, Finland, Denmark, and Norway. Furthermore, Lutheranism spread from Europe to the Americas and Oceania. Many Lutherans immigrated to the United States and other countries during the Thirty Years' War in Europe. Northern European Lutheranism is largely in doctrinal agreement with the Church of England. Anglicanism is a Protestant denomination that originated in England and spread throughout the Commonwealth of Nations. The Anglican Church was called the Church of England after the Reformation, but is now referred to as "the Anglican Communion." The Archbishop of Canterbury is the head of the Church of England and the head of the Anglican Communion. The Episcopal Church in the United States began when members of the Church of England settled in Virginia in 1607. The Episcopal Church is a Protestant denomination that grew after being separated and independent from the Church of England and continues to have a great influence on American society today. Presbyterianism is a Reformed Protestant denomination that follows Calvinism and was formed in Scotland around the reformer John Knox (1513–72), a disciple of Calvin, during the Reformation in the 16th century. Presbyterians are governed by pastors and elders. Baptists are another Protestant denomination. In 1609, John Smith (1570–1612), an Anglican theologian in England, founded the first Baptist church in Amsterdam, the Netherlands. Baptists are the largest Protestant denomination in the United States. Baptists practice the rite of baptism by immersion, reject infant baptism, and pursue evangelicalism. The Methodist Church emerged from the evangelical, social gospel, and revival movements of 18th-century English theologian John Wesley (1703–91). Methodism emphasizes the idea of sanctification, which holds that salvation is not predestined but that people advance toward salvation through a process of sanctification in their lives.

4. CHRISTIANITY ON THE KOREAN PENINSULA

The words of Jesus Christ were spread to the Korean Peninsula via China, and "Christ" was translated into Chinese characters: 基督. Matteo Ricci (1552–1610), a priest of the Roman Catholic Church, came to Macau in 1582 and first preached Christianity (Catholicism) to the Ming Dynasty. In Beijing, he published the Catholic catechetical book *Heavenly Justice* (天主實義) in 1603 and built a Catholic church in 1605, spreading Catholicism to the Chinese mainland. *Heavenly Justice* was also introduced to Chosun (Korea) and Japan. The title of the book is a translation of *De Deo Verax Disputatio*, which literally means "the true debate on God."

The year 1784, when Catholicism (Roman Catholicism) was introduced to Chosun Dynasty (Korea), is considered the first time Christianity spread to the Korean Peninsula. Catholicism developed voluntarily on the Korean Peninsula without the activities of foreign missionaries or clergy. Seung-Hoon Lee (1756–1801), who traveled to China at the urging of Byeok Lee (1754–1786) to learn Catholic doctrine and be baptized, was baptized with the baptismal name "Peter" in January 1784 (lunar calendar) in Beijing, China. He returned to Hanyang (now Seoul) in April of that year with the Bible and Catholic books. Later, in 1785 (the ninth year of King Jeongjo's reign), Lee established the first Korean Catholic Church in the house of Bum-Woo Kim. Together with Byeok Lee, Gah-Hwan Lee, Yak-Jeon Jeong, Yak-Jong Jeong, Yak-Yong Jeong, and others, Seung-Hoon Lee conducted Sunday Mass (worship), translated the Bible into Korean, and distributed it to the Catholics. Together with Il-Shin Kwon, Yak-Jeon Jeong, Chang-Hyeon Choi, and others, Seung-Hoon Lee operated the Catholic Church and led the early church to spread Catholicism. Seung-Hoon Lee was martyred in 1801 during the Sinyu persecution, along with the Chinese priest Jumunmo (1752–1801) and Yak-Jong Jeong. Despite the severe persecution of the early church, Catholicism spread widely among the people because they sympathized with the Catholicism's idea of equality. In 1831, the Chosun's (Korean) diocese was established by the Holy See (Vatican) in Rome and developed independently. Dae-Geon Kim (1821–46), who was sent to Macau Theological Seminary to study theology, became the first Korean to be ordained a priest by the Roman Catholic Church in 1844 and was martyred in 1846 in the Byeongoh persecution. In 1886, Korea and France signed the Korea-France Treaty of Amity and Commerce, which gave Catholics freedom of religion. During the Japanese occupation period, Catholicism was oppressed by the Japanese, but through education

Part II: Understanding Christianity

and the media, the church carried out an enlightenment movement. In 1942, Bishop Gi-Nam Noh was the first Korean to become bishop of Seoul, and in 1969, Archbishop Soo-Hwan Kim was ordained a cardinal. After liberation from Japanese colonial rule on August 15, 1945, and the division of Korea into North and South, Catholicism in South Korea grew rapidly along with Protestantism and continues to grow by leaps and bounds to this day. The Korean Orthodox Church, which belongs to the Eastern Orthodox Church, was introduced from the Russian Orthodox Church in 1897 but has not grown significantly compared to the Catholic Church. Today, the Korean Orthodox Church is an archdiocese under the Patriarchate of Constantinople.

Protestantism was introduced to the Korean Peninsula considerably later than Catholicism. Protestantism began in 1884 when American medical missionary Horace N. Allen (1858-1932) came to the Korean peninsula. In 1885, Allen persuaded King Gojong (1852-1919) of the Chosun Dynasty to establish the first Western hospital (Kwanghyeowon, later renamed Jejungwon), taught Western medicine, and opened the door to medical missions. On April 5, 1885, American Presbyterian missionary Horace G. Underwood (1859-1916) and American Methodist missionary Henry G. Appenzeller (1858-1902) arrived in Jemulpo (now Incheon) to conduct Protestant missions. During the late Korean and Japanese colonial periods, they made significant contributions to the spread of Protestantism by translating the Bible, publishing books, providing education and medical care, and establishing churches. The Presbyterian Church in Korea grew out of the historically active missionary work of the Presbyterian Church in the United States, so its doctrine and operations are largely American-centered, and it has the largest number of Protestant members. Methodism in Korea is the country's leading Reformed Protestant denomination, emphasizing Wesleyan evangelicalism and a practical, experiential faith. During the Japanese occupation, Methodists served as a focal point for the national movement. Nine of the sixteen Christian representatives who signed the March First Movement's Declaration of Independence of Korea in 1919 were Methodists. Baptism in Korea was introduced in 1889 by Canadian missionary Malcom C. Fenwick (1863-1936). Korean Baptists came from the United States and were greatly influenced by American Baptists. Baptists are relatively weaker than Presbyterians and Methodists in Korea. The Korean Anglican Church is a denomination of Protestantism that shares similarities with Catholicism in terms of worship, priests, and cathedrals but is Reformed in doctrine and practice. In 1890, Bishop Charles J. Corfe, who was ordained in the Church of England (UK), began missionary work in Seoul, Gyeonggi, and Chungcheong Province. Since the beginning of its mission, the Korean Anglican Church, unlike other Protestant denominations, has been committed to respecting Korean culture and practicing a variety of social missions and Christian beliefs. The Lutheran Church in Korea began its mission in 1958, later than other Protestant churches, by the Lutheran Church-Missouri Synod in the United States. Currently, the Lutheran Church in Korea is expanding in large cities, but the number of believers is small. Other Protestant denominations in Korea include the Pentecostal Church (Full Gospel Church), the Holiness Church, the Salvation Army, etc.

2

Christian Thought
God, Jesus, and the Holy Spirit

CHRISTIANITY IS A RELIGION that believes in God and the Messiah Jesus Christ. Different denominations of Christianity, such as Catholicism, Protestantism, and Eastern Orthodoxy, have different ideas and doctrines. However, if we properly know God, Jesus, and the Holy Spirit, we can properly know Christian ideas and doctrines. God is "I AM WHO I AM" (Exod 3:14) and a spirit (John 4:24). God is the Creator of all things (Gen 1) and is in control of the providence of the universe and nature. "As for God, his way is perfect; the word of the Lord is flawless" (Ps 18:30). The way of God is the source of all things and the principle by which the universe operates. It is accurate, perfect, and without error. "In the beginning was the Word, and the Word was with God, and the Word was God" (John 1:1). God is Word, life, and love (John 1:1–4; 1 John 4:16). Jesus Christ is the Son of God. The apostle Paul said, "He (Jesus) is the image of the invisible God, the firstborn over all creation" (Col 1:15). All things in heaven and on earth were created by the Son of God and for the Son (Col 1:16). Jesus Christ, whom God sent into the world as the Messiah, is the mediator between God and man (1 Tim 2:5). To know Jesus is to know God (John 8:19), to see Jesus is to see God (John 12:45), and to believe in Jesus is to believe in God (John 12:44; 14:1). The basic ideas of Christianity are based on the life, grace, and love of God and Jesus Christ. Christians believe in and obey God and Jesus Christ and live according to God's Word, doing righteous and good deeds. The word (gospel) of God and Jesus Christ, containing the life, grace, and love that are the basis of Christian thought and doctrine, was preached to all mankind through Jesus' apostles.

Christianity is a religion of life. Christianity begins with the resurrection of Jesus, and resurrection (life) is the central idea of Christianity. Without the resurrection of Jesus, Christianity would have no value to exist. The apostle Paul said, "If Christ be not risen, then is our preaching vain, and your faith is also vain" (1 Cor 15:14). The resurrection of Jesus is the main theme of the preaching of God's gospel. Jesus is the source of life. The resurrection of Jesus reveals God's revelation of human salvation (eternal life) to overcome sin and death. Jesus is life. "In Him was life, and this life was the light of men" (John 1:4), and Jesus is the "Word of life" (1 John 1:1). The resurrection of Jesus is God's saving event that brings life out of lifeless death.

The Bible is the Scripture of Christianity and contains the covenant (word) of God (Old Testament) and Jesus (New Testament). "For the law was given by Moses, but grace and truth came by Jesus Christ" (John 1:17). God's first covenant (the law) was preached by Moses, the "servant of God" (Deut 34:5), and God's new covenant is preached by grace and truth through Jesus Christ, the Son of God (Matt 16:16). The Old Testament records God's covenant (Word) and the history and life of the nation of Israel. In the age of God the Father of the Old Testament, God's word (law) was preached by the prophets such as Moses, Joshua, and others. The laws of the Old Testament God (Moses) are the foundation of Jewish doctrine. The New Testament is God's universal new covenant with all of mankind, from all walks of life, through Jesus Christ. The entire New Testament is a record of God's new covenant (Word) in the words (gospel) of Jesus and the apostles.

The gospel of Jesus Christ is at the center of Christianity. In the age of the Son of God in the New Testament, Jesus preached the word (gospel) of God. Then, during the time of the Holy Spirit, Jesus' apostles and the "Comforter," the Holy Spirit, are preaching the gospel of God (Jesus). We must fully understand the gospel of Jesus Christ and preach the words of new life (Acts 5:20). A person of faith becomes a true Christian when he believes and follows the words of God and Jesus Christ. In particular, in the resurrection of Jesus, humans can believe in salvation and eternal life and wait for the coming of the kingdom of God.

Part II: Understanding Christianity

1. GOD IS A TRINITARIAN GOD OF FATHER, SON, AND HOLY SPIRIT

In the Bible, God is called "Jehovah" (Yahweh). Jehovah is the proper name of God that people use to call God. In English versions of the Old Testament, Jehovah is written as "the Lord." However, in Korean Christianity, instead of calling God by his proper name (Jehovah), he is generally referred to as "God." When the Bible and Christianity speak of God, they usually refer to God the Father.

God created the universe, all things, and mankind (Gen 1). God is the Absolute One who rules the universe and all things and controls time and space. God is one God, the Father of all (Eph 4:6). God exists as the God Father, the Son of God, and the Holy Spirit (Matt 28:19). Christianity holds the doctrine of the Trinity. The Trinitarian God exists in three persons—the Father, the Son, and the Holy Spirit—but in essence, there is only one God. That is, the Father, the Son, and the Holy Spirit are all one God. Faith in God and Jesus Christ is a state of mind in which God's Holy Spirit works in a person's heart to bring about a new birth. "For from him and through him and to him are all things" (Rom 11:36). People of faith are born of God, saved by his grace, and returned to God. This saving faith to return to the Lord God is operated by the Holy Spirit.

2. GOD IS SPIRIT, LIFE, WORD, AND WAY

God said to Moses, "I AM WHO I AM" (Exod 3:14). God exists himself and was not created. God is spirit (John 4:24). Spirit gives life (John 6:63). Because God is a spiritual being, it is impossible to see God with human eyes. God exists beyond time and space and is unchanging and eternal. God is spirit and is omnipotent, ruling and controlling the universe and nature. God is in us as the Holy Spirit, and we are in him. God's Spirit gives life (John 6:63). God is Word, life, and love (John 1:1–4; 1 John 4:16). "In Him (God) was life, and that life was the light of men" (John 1:4). God himself said that he had life in himself (John 5:26), so God exists as life and is the source of life that gives life. God is the God of life. Therefore, God is a spiritual being and is present in living things. However, since idols are dead things, the God of life (the Holy Spirit) cannot be in an idol. Accordingly, we must not worship lifeless idols (Exod 20:4–5; Deut 5:8–9).

In the beginning was the Word, and the Word was with God, and the Word was God (John 1:1). The Logos (Word, Reason) is God. The Word was with God, and all things were made through him. By the Word God created all things (John 1:3). God's Word is eternal and unchanging. God's word is truth (John 17:17). We can only recognize God by reading and hearing his Word in the Bible. God works through his Word. The Word, who is also God, is the light that shines on the people of the world. The Word became flesh and dwelt among us (John 1:14). No one has ever seen God, but we have come to know God through his only Son (Jesus), who is in the bosom of God (John 1:18).

God is the creator of the universe and all things (Gen 1), and as God's "Way," he is in control of the universe, nature, and all things. God (Jesus) is also the Way (John 14:6). The Way of God is the source of all things in the universe and the principle by which the universe operates. The Way of God is the principle of all things in the universe and governs the cycle of the universe. The universe and everything in it operates and exists by God's Way (providence). "As for God, his way is perfect; the word of the Lord is flawless" (Ps 18:30). God's Way is always the same and unchanging. The Way of God is for us to live according to God's will. The laws of the universe established by God (the laws of heaven) are accurate. God is sovereign and perfect. God controls the providence of the universe and nature. Almighty God's actions are perfect, accurate, and right. There is nothing wrong with what God does.

3. GOD IS A GOD OF JUSTICE AND LOVE

Christians are not obligated to keep all of God's laws. However, Christians should not neglect to keep God's law. God gave his law through Moses (John 1:17). In the Old Testament, the law is God's covenant with the nation of Israel (Jews). When there was no law, sin was not considered sin (Rom 5:13). Without the law, sin is not recognized. Jesus did not come to abolish the law or the words of the prophets but to fulfill them (Matt 5:17). The Son of God (Jesus) is the image of the invisible God (Col 1:15). Jesus Christ is the mediator between God and man (1 Tim 2:5). Jesus Christ preached the word of God and mediated the relationship between God and man. Since Jesus' resurrection and ascension, the Holy Spirit has been preaching the word (gospel) of God in the present age of the Holy Spirit. This indicates that God's law in the Old Testament and Jesus' word of grace and truth in the New Testament are in continuity and complementary to each other.

God has both justice and love. God is a God of justice and love. God has both the whip of the law and the carrot of grace. God harmoniously shows us justice through law and love through grace. God's justice is revealed through the law. God is a God of justice (Ps 89:14). God is just and righteous (Deut 32:4). God walks in the paths of justice and walks in the midst of righteousness (Prov 8:20). God judges with justice (1 Pet 2:23). God is fair and righteous, allowing people to be punished when they break the law and commit sin. God is a righteous judge and a God who is angry every day (Ps 7:11). God has set a day when he will judge the world with justice through his Son, Jesus (Acts 17:31). God's love is shown through grace. Love is giving without expecting anything in return. The apostle John says, "Whoever does not love does not know God, because God is love" (1 John 4:8). God's love, which is rich in mercy and grace, is infinite (Eph 2:4). God so loved us that he sent his Son, Jesus, to forgive us our sins (1 John 4:10). God loves us as he has loved his Son, Jesus Christ (John 17:23). Those who love Jesus are loved by God (John 14:21). God's love is fully realized when we love one another (1 John 4:12). If we love Jesus, we will keep his commandments (John 14:15). In this way, God's justice and love are demonstrated to humans through Jesus, as justice by law and love by grace harmonize with each other. However, God's love is greater than God's justice. We are to love our neighbors (others) (Matt 22:39). Because God so loved us, we are to love one another (1 John 4:11). He who loves God must also love his brother (1 John 4:21). If you love God, you will love your neighbor, your brother, and even your enemy. A person of true faith lives by God's agape love but not by the erotic self-love.

4. GOD IS A GOD OF COMFORT, PEACE, AND HOPE

The most valuable thing that the people of the world can obtain from the Christian faith is their own comfort and peace through faith in God (Jesus). God is a God of mercy and comfort, and he comforts us in all our tribulations (2 Cor 1:3–4). God says, "Comfort my people" (Isa 40:1), and God wipes away all tears (Rev 21:4). And God is the God of peace (1 Thess 5:23). Jesus preached the gospel of peace in his public life and ministry. "Peace I leave with you; my peace I give you. I do not give to you as the world gives. Do not let your hearts be troubled and do not be afraid" (John 14:27). Even after his resurrection, Jesus continued to tell his disciples, "Peace be with you" (Matt 28:9; Luke 24:36; John 20:19, 21, 26). Peter and the apostle Paul also told the churches, "Grace to you and peace from God our Father and the Lord Jesus Christ" (Rom 1:7; 1 Cor 1:3; Gal 1:3; Eph 1:2; 1 Pet 1:2). Christians who believe in and obey God (Jesus) and live a life of grace are comforted by God so that they have no anxiety, no worries, and are always at peace. Our faith and love come from the hope we have stored up in heavenly places (Col 1:5). The God of hope fills our life of faith with all joy and peace, so that we may abound in hope by the power of the Holy Spirit (Rom 15:13).

5. JESUS IS LIFE, GRACE, AND LOVE

The New Testament contains the words of Jesus Christ, the preaching of the gospel, and the Christian ideas of life, grace, and love based on Jesus' death on the cross and resurrection. God sent Jesus Christ into the world as the Messiah and established him as a mediator between God and us (1 Tim 2:5). God gave Jesus life. Jesus is life. Jesus is the source of life. In Jesus Christ is life (John 1:4), and Jesus is the "Word of life" (1 John 1:1). From the beginning was the Word of life, and the life appeared; we have seen the eternal life (Jesus) (1 John 1:1–2). And the Word became flesh (Jesus), and we have seen the glory of Jesus, who was full of grace and truth (John 1:14). Jesus is the Way, the truth, the life, and the grace (John 1:17; 14:6). Jesus' words are truth, unchanging and eternal. Jesus' resurrection demonstrated that Jesus is the source of life. In the New Testament, the apostle Paul makes the following powerful statement about the preaching of God's gospel: "And if Christ be not risen, then is our preaching vain, and your faith is also vain" (1 Cor 15:14). Jesus is the resurrection and the life; whoever believes in him will never die (John 11:25–26). Life (eternal life) means salvation, and it is only by believing in Jesus that one is saved (Mark 16:16; Acts 16:31). Those who believe are saved by God. This idea of life, derived from the resurrection of Jesus, is a central idea of Christianity that is not found in any other religion. Christianity is a religion of life.

God's grace came through Jesus Christ (John 1:17). Grace is a gift from God. God forgives sins by grace through faith and gives salvation (eternal life) as a gift without merit (Eph 2:8). God gives grace to sinners, even those who have done evil, because he loves them unconditionally. Furthermore, the apostle Paul says in his New Testament Epistles that the Christian faith is all about "grace." Since grace came through Jesus (John 1:17), the Lord

Jesus Christ is the God of grace. Martin Luther's Reformation idea, or the Christian doctrine of "being justified by faith" (Rom 5:1), is based on God's grace. Grace reigns through righteousness to bring eternal life through Jesus Christ our Lord (Rom 5:21). A person of true faith is a righteous person. Christians are saved by "sola fide" (faith alone) and "sola gratia" (grace alone) in Jesus Christ. God saves us according to his will and by the grace given to us in Christ Jesus our Lord (2 Tim 1:9).

Christians reach out to people in Christ with love and mercy. Jesus gives us love through grace. Jesus said, "Love the Lord your God with all your heart and with all your soul and with all your mind. This is the first and greatest commandment. And the second is like it: Love your neighbor as yourself" (Matt 22:37–39). God loves us as he loved Jesus Christ (John 17:23). Those who love Jesus keep his commandments and are loved by God (John 14:21). The love of God that loved Jesus is in us, and Jesus is in us (John 17:26). The apostle Paul tells us, "Do everything in love" (1 Cor 16:14). "Live a life of love, just as Christ loved us" (Eph 5:2). "Now these three remain: faith, hope and love. But the greatest of these is love" (1 Cor 13:13). Even if we have the faith to move mountains, we are nothing without love (1 Cor 13:2). Love is supreme. "Love is patient, love is kind. It does not envy, it does not boast, it is not proud. It is not rude, it is not self-seeking, it is not easily angered, it keeps no record of wrongs. Love does not delight in evil but rejoices with the truth" (1 Cor 13:4–6). Christianity is a religion of love.

6. THE HOLY SPIRIT IS THE SPIRIT OF CHRIST AND THE GOD OF TRUTH

When you believe in God and Jesus Christ, you are forgiven of your sins, freed from them, reconciled to God through the Holy Spirit, and given joy and peace through the fellowship of love. The Holy Spirit (the Comforter or the Counselor) is God, the Spirit of Truth that guides Christians to the path of truth on behalf of Jesus (John 14:17; 16:13). This is the age of the Holy Spirit. "God sent the Spirit of his Son into our hearts" (Gal 4:6). After Jesus ascended into heaven, he sent the Comforter, the Holy Spirit, to us (John 16:7). We are baptized with the Holy Spirit (Acts 1:5). "We live in him and he in us, because he has given us of his Spirit (the Holy Spirit)" (1 John 4:13). The Comforter, the Holy Spirit, lives and works with us forever (John 14:16). When we repent and are baptized in the name of Jesus Christ for the forgiveness of sins, we receive the gift of the Holy Spirit (Acts 2:38). Therefore, the Holy Spirit dwells in Christians. The Holy Spirit is the Spirit of God and the Spirit of Jesus Christ (Rom 8:9). "If anyone does not have the Spirit of Christ, he does not belong to Christ" (Rom 8:9). The Holy Spirit himself testifies with our spirit that we are God's children (Rom 8:16). The Holy Spirit guides us into God's truth and enables people of faith to live righteously and good according to God's will.

Our bodies are temples of the Holy Spirit (1 Cor 6:19). "Be filled with the Spirit" (Eph 5:18). As a child of God, a Christian is filled with the Holy Spirit. Christians live by the Spirit. By the Holy Spirit, we are born again and have life. The Holy Spirit gives us love. By the Holy Spirit, God's love is poured out into our hearts (Rom 5:5). By the Holy Spirit, we love our brothers and neighbors, passing from death to life (1 John 3:14). Through the Holy Spirit, we wait for the hope of righteousness by faith (Gal 5:5). By the power of the Holy Spirit, hope overflows into our lives of faith. There are different gifts of the Holy Spirit, but the Spirit is the same (1 Cor 12:4). To some, the Holy Spirit gives words of wisdom, to others words of knowledge (1 Cor 12:8). To others the same Spirit gives faith, to others the gift of healing, to others the gift of might, to others prophecy, to others various kinds of tongues, as the Spirit wills, he gives to each person differently (1 Cor 12:9–11). However, the gifts of the Holy Spirit cannot be obtained through human ability and effort. "Walk in the Spirit, and you shall not fulfill the lust of the flesh" (Gal 5:16). Christians are to walk in faith and righteousness by following the Holy Spirit, free from the lusts of the flesh. If we live by the Spirit, we walk by the Spirit (Gal 5:25). The Holy Spirit works in the human heart to cause a person to be born again and awakened. The "fruit of the Spirit" is love, joy, peace, long-suffering, mercy, goodness, faithfulness, gentleness, and self-control (Gal 5:22–23). The fruit of the Spirit is produced in a life of godly faith. We are filled with the Holy Spirit, singing and praising the Lord, giving thanks to God for everything, and submitting to one another in the fear of Christ (Eph 5:18–21). Christians are filled with grace by the Spirit of Truth so that they may live spiritually abundantly and become more like the Lord Jesus Christ.

3

The Main Points of the Christian Faith

THE CORE OF THE Christian faith is true faith in God and Jesus Christ. Christians who believe in God and Jesus Christ believe that Jesus saves them from their sins, leading to the kingdom of God. Christians practice their faith in their daily lives by attending church, reciting the Lord's Prayer and the Apostles' Creed in worship, listening to their pastor preach, singing hymns, and praying. We are baptized to become Christians. During the worship service of the church, Christians regularly celebrate the Lord's Supper in commemoration of Jesus Christ. Praying daily is the Christian life. The Lord's Prayer, the Apostles' Creed, baptism, the Lord's Supper, prayer, and the right view of salvation that Christians need to know correctly while living their life of faith are analyzed and explained below in an easy-to-understand way.

1. THE LORD'S PRAYER

The Lord's Prayer is a prayer taught by Jesus Christ himself. The Lord's Prayer is the most read and recited passage of Scripture by humans today, and it is the primary prayer used by all Christians in both group and family worship. In the New Testament, the Lord's Prayer is recorded in Matt 6:9–13 and Luke 11:2–4 and is usually adopted from Matthew's version and used in worship. The Lord's Prayer, which forms the framework of Jesus' Sermon on the Mount (Matt 5–7), is the example for all prayers in the Bible.

Lord's Prayer

> Our Father in heaven,
> hallowed be your name, your kingdom come,
> your will be done on earth, as it is in heaven.
> Give us today our daily bread.
> And forgive us our debts, as we also have forgiven our debtors.
> And lead us not into temptation, but deliver us from the evil one.
> For yours is the kingdom and the power
> and the glory forever. Amen.
> (Matt 6:9–13)
>
> Source: Color The New International Version (NIV) Korean-English Commentary Bible. . Agape

The first part of the Lord's Prayer states our praise and worship of God. This part is about God. "Our Father in heaven, hallowed be your name, your kingdom come" (Matt 6:9–10). Christians offer praise and thanksgiving to God in heaven, praying that his name be hallowed and that his kingdom come. As we believe and obey God, the kingdom of God will come, with righteousness, peace, and joy that is not of this world (Rom 14:17). The next supplication prayer says, "Your kingdom come, your will be done on earth, as it is in heaven" (Matt 6:10). This is not a prayer for what we want but for all things to be done according to God's will. It's not a prayer for our own desires and blessings but a God-centered prayer for God's wisdom. If what we do is done in the right way, according to God's will, we will always be happy and at peace.

The middle part of the Lord's Prayer contains a number of supplications that we make to God (the Lord). This part is about ourselves and our lives. "Give us this day our daily bread, and forgive us our debts, as we also have forgiven our debtors; and do not lead us into temptation, but deliver us from evil" (Matt 6:11–13). We ask God to give us only our daily bread, and we confess that this is enough. We ask God to give us only the minimum necessary for human life. It is because of our trust and faith that God will provide tomorrow's food for us as well. In the next prayer, we ask God to forgive us our sins as we forgive the sins of others. God forgives our sins with great mercy and without payment. However, because of our own greed and lust, we fall into temptation and live in the midst of many satanic tests. "Every man is tempted, when he is drawn away of his own lust, and enticed"

Part II: Understanding Christianity

(Jas 1:14). But God does not tempt us. We are tempted by our fleshly desires and pride, and we ask God to keep us from these evils and temptations.

At the end of the Lord's Prayer, we pray that the kingdom, power, and glory of God be with God forever. "For yours is the kingdom and the power and the glory forever, Amen" (Matt 6:13). Because the kingdom, power, and glory belong to God forever, Christians believe in God, obey God, and live a life of faith. If you pray on the basis of the Lord's Prayer, you will give praise, thanks, and glory to God, receive forgiveness of sins through repentance, and find comfort and peace, asking for your own wishes.

2. APOSTLES' CREED

The Apostles' Creed is a prayer used as an official confession of faith in Christianity. However, the Apostles' Creed is not found in the Bible. The Apostles' Creed summarizes the belief in God and Jesus Christ, the Holy Spirit, the Church, the saints, the forgiveness of sins, the resurrection, and eternal life (salvation). It contains the core content of the Christian faith. The Apostles' Creed also provides a concise and clear statement of the Christian faith. The form of the confession of faith practiced at baptism in the early church in the first and second centuries was submitted to the Council of Milan in AD 390 and became the basis for the Apostles' Creed. The Apostles' Creed began to be used by the western churches in the 10th century. It is still used today as a standard of faith by both Catholic and Protestant churches in worship services (Mass) and other confessions of faith.

Korean-English Apostles' Creed

전능하사 천지를 만드신 하나님 아버지를 내가 믿사오며,
그 외아들 우리 주 예수 그리스도를 믿사오니,
이는 성령으로 잉태하사 동정녀 마리아에게 나시고,
'본디오 빌라도'에게 고난을 받으사, 십자가에 못 박혀 죽으시고,
장사한 지 사흘 만에 죽은 자 가운데서 다시 살아나시며,
하늘에 오르사, 전능하신 하나님 우편에 앉아 계시다가,
저리로서 산 자와 죽은 자를 심판하러 오시리라,
성령을 믿사오며, 거룩한 공회와, 성도가 서로 교통하는 것과,
죄를 사하여 주시는 것과, 몸이 다시 사는 것과,
영원히 사는 것을 믿사옵나이다. 아멘.

The Main Points of the Christian Faith

I believe in God the Father Almighty, Maker of heaven and earth,
and in Jesus Christ, His only Son our Lord,
who was conceived by the Holy Spirit, born of the Virgin Mary,
suffered under Pontius Pilate, was crucified, dead, and buried;
He descended into hell; The third day He rose again from the dead;
He ascended into heaven,
and sitteth on the right hand of God the Father Almighty;
from thence He shall come to judge the quick and the dead.
I believe in the Holy Spirit, the holy universal church,
the communion of saints, the forgiveness of sins,
the resurrection of the body, and the life everlasting. Amen.

Source: Color The New International Version (NIV) Korean-English Commentary Bible. Agape

First Part: I Believe in God the Father Almighty, Maker of heaven and earth.

The first part of the Apostles' Creed is a confession of faith (belief) in God the Father. We thank, praise, and worship God for his grace and mercy through our confession of faith in Almighty God, who created the heavens and the earth.

Middle Part: I believe in Jesus Christ, His only Son our Lord, who was conceived by the Holy Spirit, born of the Virgin Mary, suffered under Pontius Pilate, was crucified, dead, and buried; He descended into hell; The third day He rose again from the dead; He ascended into heaven, and sitteth on the right hand of God the Father Almighty; from thence He shall come to judge the quick and the dead.

The middle part of the Apostles' Creed is a confession of faith in the Son of God, Jesus Christ. Born as the Son of God, Jesus exhibits both divinity and humanity. In his divinity as the Son of God, Jesus' humanity is manifested in his person. After his birth, suffering ministry, and death by crucifixion (Mark 15:21–37), Jesus descended into Hades (hell) (Apostles' Creed) and entered the lowest place (Eph 4:9). He rose again from the dead in a spiritual and physical body, free from the curse and exalted (Matt 28:1–10; Mark 16:9; 1 Cor 15:44–46). By the Spirit of holiness, Jesus was resurrected from the dead and declared with power to be the Son of God (Rom 1:4). Jesus ascended into heaven and sits at the right hand of God (Mark 16:19). All dominion, authority, power, and sovereignty were given to Jesus to participate in the work of God's government (Eph 1:21; 1 Pet 3:22). In due time, Jesus Christ will descend from heaven back into this world to judge the living and the dead (John 5:21–22; Acts 1:11; 1 Cor 4:4–5; 1 Thess 4:13–17; Rev 1:7–8). No one, living or dead, will escape the judgment of Jesus. Here in the Apostles' Creed, we confess our faith in the Lord Jesus Christ; tell of his birth, suffering, death, resurrection, and ascension; and foresee the return of Jesus.

End Part: I believe in the Holy Spirit, the holy universal church, the communion of saints, the forgiveness of sins, the resurrection of the body, and the life everlasting. Amen.

The end of the Apostles' Creed is a confession of faith in the Holy Spirit and the church. Jesus ascended into heaven, and the Holy Spirit (the Comforter) was sent from God and Jesus (John 16:7). The Holy Spirit, the Counselor, is the Spirit of Truth who, on behalf of Jesus, guides Christians in the way of truth (John 14:17). After Jesus' resurrection and ascension, the Holy Spirit is spreading the word of God (Jesus) (the gospel). This is the age of the Holy Spirit. It is through the Holy Spirit that we can receive God's grace and be saved. We believe in the holy church built on faith, hope, and love. We believe in believers' fellowship and communication with one another. Jesus Christ is the head of the church (Eph 1:22–23), and believers are his body and members (1 Cor 12:27; Eph 5:30). In the church, believers fellowship with one another and participate in what God is giving. We believe in the "forgiveness of sins." The believer's life is a life of repentance where sins are confessed and forgiven. We believe in the resurrection of the body and in eternal life. That is, we believe in being born anew in God (Jesus) and having eternal life. If we believe in and obey God (Jesus), we believe in the coming of the kingdom of God, where there will be no death and where it will be overflowing with righteousness, peace, and joy. As Jesus ascended into heaven, he promised to be with us always, even to the end of the world (Matt 28:20). Christians are saved by faith and grace in Jesus and will live forever.

The Main Points of the Christian Faith

(1) "그(예수)가 지옥에 내려가셨다. He descended into hell." (The phrase is missing from the Apostles' Creed in the Korean Version of the Bible.)

The original English version of the Apostles' Creed contains the following phrase: "He descended into hell." However, the deletion of this part in the Korean version of the Apostles' Creed is controversial among Korean Catholics, Anglicans, and Protestants. The Korean Catholic and Anglican versions of the Apostles' Creed translate the phrase into Korean "저승에 가시어 (descended into hell)" and "죽음의 세계에 내려가시어 (descended into the world of the dead)," respectively. In contrast, the Korean version of the Apostles' Creed, used by Protestants in Korea, omits the phrase "he descended into hell." By not including "Jesus descended into hell" in the Apostles' Creed, Korean Protestants have completely erased the human side of Jesus. In particular, most Korean Protestants are not aware of the fact that the Apostles' Creed in the Korean version of the Bible does not include "저승에 가시어 (Jesus descended into hell)," even after attending church for thirty to fifty years. And the reality is that they blindly recite the flawed Apostles' Creed and lead a life of faith in Korea.

Why would not even English-speaking Western clergy and believers want to portray Jesus Christ as holy as God in the Apostles' Creed? The fact that Jesus was in the tomb for three days after his death on the cross and burial is recorded in the English Apostles' Creed as the phrase "he descended into hell." The Bible makes a similar analogy when it says, "He (Jesus) was assigned a grave with the wicked, and with the rich in his death, though he had done no violence, nor was any deceit in his mouth" (Isa 53:9). This shows the terrible spiritual suffering of Jesus, who lived a lowly life like a normal human being in the world before his resurrection. It also tells us that Jesus went down to hell and overcame death to atone for the sins of mankind. However, without the descent into hell, which represents Jesus' spiritual suffering, the holiness of Jesus and the power of grace symbolized in his substitutionary death would be greatly diminished. Likewise, as Jesus was dying on the cross, he cried out, "My God, my God, why have you forsaken me" (Matt 27:46). In his desperation, we see a glimpse of Jesus' deep human anguish and pain. Jesus has a human physical nature or "humanity" (Luke 24:39). As the Son of God, Jesus came to earth; however, as the Son of Man, he was baptized by John the Baptist (Matt 3:13–17; Mark 1:9). "Jesus has been tempted in every way, just as we are, yet was without sin" (Heb 4:15). Jesus was also tempted by Satan. Christ Jesus emptied himself, taking the form of a servant, being born in the likeness of men, and humbled himself, becoming obedient to the point of death, even death on a cross (Phil 2:7–8). We should recognize that Jesus lived a life like a normal human being until his crucifixion and resurrection. Based on this scientific (logical) analysis, it is reasonable to include the phrase "저승에 가시어 (he descended into hell)" in the Apostles' Creed of the Korean version of the Bible, which shows the humanity of Jesus. The Bible and Christianity could not have been created, if Jesus had only been deified as the Son of God, hiding his humanity of pain and suffering in all the events that occurred in his life from birth to resurrection. Christians who live according to the Bible are truthful and honest. Korean Christianity should not hide facts and truths about Jesus and distort the Bible. Christians in Western European countries that were founded on Christianity live rationally without lies because of their correct perception and understanding of the Bible based on facts and truth. By and large, they see, think, and speak as they are, and are straightforward and without pretense. This is because people in the West read the Bible as it really is and live by it. If we Korean Christians recite the Apostles' Creed in the Korean version of the Bible with the phrase "저승에 가시어 (he descended into hell)," we will see the true picture of the person of Jesus Christ as the Son of Man. Furthermore, we will live a biblical life that brings us closer to Jesus. This is because we Christians can get closer to "Jesus who descended into hell." Now, we Korean Christians must live a life of faith, recognizing God (Jesus) as a God of love, grace, and life who is perfect and worthy of holy worship but who is always approachable, like a warm, loving parent.

3. BAPTISM AND THE SACRAMENTS

(1) Baptism

Baptism is the ceremony by which a person joins God and becomes a believer (Christian) in God. It signifies that you receive God's spirit, the Holy Spirit, and begin your life of faith by God's grace. Today, baptism is performed in the name of the Triune God by pastors and priests in churches and Catholic cathedrals. Those who are baptized are united with Christ and become God's people, clothed in Christ (Gal 3:26–27). Baptism is a public recognition that we have become God's people (children) in Christ. When we are baptized, we are enrolled in a church and become Christian

The Main Points of the Christian Faith

believers. We are baptized only once in our lifetime. Baptism is the beginning of the Christian faith. When analyzed scientifically, baptism is a ritual that puts the Spirit of God into a person's heart. A Christian believer shares God's spirit and becomes one with God. Baptism is not the removal of dirt from the body but the pledge of a good conscience toward God (1 Pet 3:21). The word "baptize" means "to immerse in water." Baptism is a ritual of immersion or wetting with water to signify the forgiveness of sins and spiritual renewal through regeneration of life. In baptism, God promises to accompany the Christian believer with his favor (grace) and goodness.

In Old Testament times, all Jews were circumcised in order to be chosen as God's people and become Jewish. The Bible records that all males were circumcised on the eighth day after birth as a covenant that God would keep with Abraham, his family, and their descendants (Gen 17:9–14). God said, "This is my covenant with you and your descendants after you, the covenant you are to keep: Every male among you shall be circumcised" (Gen 17:10). Accordingly, Abraham circumcised Isaac on the eighth day after his birth (Gen 21:4). In Judaism, this tradition of circumcision continues. However, in New Testament times, the apostle Paul emphasized that it doesn't matter whether a person is circumcised or not, only that they keep God's commandments (1 Cor 7:19).

After his resurrection, Jesus appeared to his disciples and asked them to "go and make disciples of all nations, baptizing them in the name of the Father and of the Son and of the Holy Spirit" (Matt 28:19). We are baptized in the name of God. We are Christ's people, because we have the Spirit of God (Jesus) in us (John 8:9). If we want to receive the Spirit of God, we must be baptized. Today, all Christians in the age of the Holy Spirit are baptized to become believers. When we are baptized, we are united to God (Jesus) and live a life of faith with God. In the New Testament era, baptism is a ritual that puts the Spirit of God into the hearts of believers. Jesus was also baptized by John the Baptist (Matt 3:13–17; Mark 1:9). When Jesus was baptized by John in the Jordan (Mark 1:9), he heard a voice from heaven saying, "You are my Son, whom I love; with you I am well pleased" (Mark 1:11), and he was recognized as God's Son. "For we were all baptized by one Spirit into one body, whether Jews or Greeks, slave or free, and we were all given the one Spirit to drink" (1 Cor 12:13). We are the body of Christ and each member of it (1 Cor 12:14). In the Holy Spirit age, we are baptized with the Holy Spirit and led to Jesus Christ.

Part II: Understanding Christianity

To become a Christian, a person must be baptized. A baptized person is a Christian. You are baptized with water and the Holy Spirit (Acts 1:5). Jesus is the one who baptizes with the Holy Spirit (John 1:33). "This water symbolizes baptism that now saves you" (1 Pet 3:21). Water signifies baptism, a symbol of our salvation. Scientifically speaking, being baptized with water is because the Spirit of God is in the water. Therefore, water baptism makes one a true believer, and the Spirit of God is indwelling in the body of a Christian believer. The Bible records in Genesis that the Spirit of God entered and existed in the waters before God created all things. "The Spirit of God was hovering over the waters" (Gen 1:2). The Bible also says, "There are three that testify: the Spirit, the water, and the blood; and these three are one" (1 John 5:7–8). All living things have water. Water is the source of life and is the primary substance absolutely essential for the creation of living things. Water is life. Without water, life cannot exist. To be baptized in water is to put the Spirit of God into the body and mind of the believer and by extension, to put the "life of Jesus." When Jesus offered the Samaritan woman the water of life as a gift of salvation, he said, "Whoever drinks the water I give him will never thirst. Indeed, the water I give him will become in him a spring of water welling up to eternal life" (John 4:14). Jesus made the Samaritan woman drink of the spiritual water of life, and she worshiped God in spirit and truth (John 4:23–24). Scientifically analyzed, this is why believers who are baptized with water and the Holy Spirit (Acts 1:5) worship God and live a life with God (Jesus).

John the Baptist baptized people to confess and repent of their sins (Matt 3:6, 11). "Repent and be baptized, every one of you, in the name of Jesus Christ for the forgiveness of your sins. And you will receive the gift of the Holy Spirit" (Acts 2:38). We receive the forgiveness of sins through a baptism of repentance. John the Baptist preached a baptism of repentance for the forgiveness of sins (Luke 3:3). We are baptized to become believers, to be forgiven of our sins, and to receive the gift of the Holy Spirit, that is, faith. We receive forgiveness of sins through baptism. Even after being baptized, Christians are born again for the forgiveness of sins through repentance in Jesus Christ by the power of the Holy Spirit at every moment of their lives. The Christian is a temple (house) in which the Holy Spirit dwells (1 Cor 6:19–20). "Whoever believes and is baptized will be saved" (Mark 16:16), so only those who are baptized are saved. "No one can enter the kingdom of God unless he is born of water and the Spirit" (John 3:5). A person can enter the kingdom of God by God's grace through baptism and faith.

(2) Sacraments

Holy Communion is a sacrament celebrated according to the Gospels, where it is written that Jesus shared bread and wine with his disciples to commemorate his death at the Last Supper on the Passover before he died on the cross (Matt 26:26–29; Mark 14:22–25; 1 Cor 11:23–25). Indeed, bread and wine are the food and drink that sustain physical life. Jesus is the bread of life (John 6:48). Jesus is the living bread that came down from heaven; if anyone eats of this bread, he will live forever (John 6:51). Jesus said, "Unless you eat the flesh of the Son of Man and drink his blood, you have no life in you" (John 6:53). Those who eat the bread and drink the wine, which symbolize Jesus' flesh and blood, respectively, have life (eternal life) (John 6:54–55). The symbolic bread and wine are the food and drink for our spiritual life. At the Last Supper, Jesus said to his disciples, "This bread, which is broken, is my body given for you. Do this in remembrance of me. This cup, which contains the wine, is the new covenant in my blood, which is poured out for you" (Luke 22:19–20). Thus, in today's sacraments, pastors and Christian worshipers share the bread, which symbolizes the flesh of Jesus, and the wine, which symbolizes the blood of Jesus. By sharing Jesus' body (flesh) and blood, Jesus is spiritually with the believers. "Whoever eats my flesh and drinks my blood remains in me, and I in him" (John 6:56). The sacraments are by which we become fully one with Jesus Christ. The sacraments awaken and nourish our faith. Through the sacraments, we receive the vitality of faith and life, so that we can grow spiritually and reach eternal life.

The sacraments, along with the sermon, are central to Christian worship. The Eucharist is a sacrament that commemorates Jesus Christ, reminding us of his death until his return (1 Cor 11:25–26). Through the sacrament, we remember the events of Jesus' substitutionary death on the cross and resurrection and give thanks for his grace. Unbaptized people, or even faithful believers, who are spiritually unstable because they have sinned, cannot participate in the sacrament (1 Cor 11:27–32). The sacrament is valid for spiritually faithful Christian believers. In the Christian church, the sacraments are a way of giving thanks and praise to God, commemorating the substitutionary death and resurrection of Jesus Christ, and being with the Holy Spirit (Jesus) and in fellowship with believers in Christ. The sacraments are celebrated in churches several times a year by the pastor with the congregation. Frequent communion reminds us to keep the new covenant that Jesus Christ established for us with his flesh and blood (Mark

14:24) and to remember that Jesus is the bread of life (John 6:48). Through the sacrament, Jesus Christ fills our souls with himself, uniting us spiritually with him. "In Christ all the fullness of the Deity lives in bodily form" (Col 2:9). In Jesus Christ, who is both divine and human, the Holy Spirit fills us to inspire faith and love, and we receive eternal life by his grace.

4. PRAYER

Prayer allows Christians to communicate and fellowship with God and become one with God (the Lord). Prayer is the link between Almighty God and sinful humans. Prayer is the way to become self-aware, to know God, to glorify God, and to serve God. In prayer, we confess our sins to God and ask for forgiveness, ask for hopes to be fulfilled, and offer praise and thanksgiving to God. Jesus said, "If you believe, you will receive whatever you ask for in prayer" (Matt 21:22). Whatever we ask in faith, God will give us. We pray that God will forgive our sins and give us rest.

When our life brings us financial hardship or a crisis in our social status, we pray earnestly, but when life is going well, we neglect prayer. However, prayer should be the life of a Christian. Rather than being a Christian duty, prayer is a path to joy and peace. Through prayer, Christians feel God's love, passion, and warmth in the communion they share with God in their lives. The goal of human life is peace. Those who have received grace are at peace with God (Luke 1:28). After his resurrection, Jesus said to his disciples several times, "Peace be with you" (Luke 24:36; John 20:19). Peace comes into our lives when we pray. "So do not fear, for I am with you" (Isa 41:10). "Whatever you ask for in prayer, believe that you have received it, and it will be yours" (Mark 11:24). If you pray, God will eventually hear you and make it happen in the right way. "In everything, by prayer and petition, with thanksgiving, present your requests to God. And the peace of God will guard your hearts and your minds in Christ Jesus" (Phil 4:6–7). We should pray to God with a humble attitude, so that God's will may be done. "Father, yet not my will, but yours be done" (Luke 22:42). "God opposes the proud but gives grace to the humble" (Jas 4:6).

(1) The Meaning of Prayer

In Christianity, prayer is a spiritual encounter with God, a conversation and communion with God in a personal way. Prayer is a conversation with

God. Prayer is getting to know God (the Lord) fully. Prayer is knowing God and getting to know yourself. Prayer is singing the songs of the heart to God. Prayer transcends time to experience eternity. Through prayer, we feel and experience God's love and the power of the gospel. In prayer, Christians rely on God's Word and grace. We hear the Lord's voice in God's Word and answer it in prayer. God speaks through the Bible, and Christians respond through prayer. The more we know about God, the more faithful our prayers will be, so reading the Bible is important. God's Word evokes hope and inspiration in prayer. Speaking honestly to God, not hiding anything from him, leads to a dialog and communication with him. Prayer should be honest and straightforward. God hears and answers prayer in the Holy Spirit. Prayer transforms people, causing them to be born again. The world looks beautiful when we pray and let the kingdom of God into our daily lives. Prayer gives us spiritual strength and confidence in our lives and makes us strong in the Lord. The Holy Spirit empowers our prayers. Prayer brings us to know God and overflows with love and joy. When we pray, our anxieties and worries disappear, our sorrows fade away, we have peace, and we are energized.

(2) The Center of Prayer

Prayer is the act of human beings recognizing their weakness and relying on God. Prayer should be sincere, out of reverence for God. True prayer is not praying for what we want, but for what God wants us to do. It is not a self-centered prayer but a God-centered prayer that seeks only God's glory. This is because God is sovereign and works things out according to his will and plan. Jesus prayed in the garden of Gethsemane and said, "Yet not as I will, but as you (God) will" (Matt 26:39; Mark 14:36; Luke 22:42). Jesus' prayer in Gethsemane is a prime example of a "God-centered prayer" that balances human hope with obedience to God. If prayer is solely focused on our desires, it becomes self-centered. Prayer should not be a pretentious prayer, asking for our worldly desires and wishing for blessings. God only hears and answers the prayers of those who do his will.

No human prayer is perfect. This is why we should earnestly pray to God with confidence, not with fear. When Christians pray with a firm hope, God listens and answers. "You do not have, because you do not ask God" (Jas 4:2). If you ask in the name of Jesus Christ, it will be done, and you will be filled with joy (John 16:24). However, man's own works are not perfect in God's sight, so it is only by God's grace that what he asks for is done. Prayer is seeking God's timing and wisdom in all human affairs. A good prayer renews oneself before the Lord. God is a spirit, and he seeks worshipers as they worship in spirit and truth (John 4:23–24). If you make an effort and ask God in prayer, he will work in the right direction. When you pray passionately in times of adversity, God will open a way for you to get through and find peace. God may not give you what you want right away, but by his grace, he will give it to you in the right direction and at the right time. "Ask and it will be given to you; seek and you will find" (Luke 11:9). A prayer that asks God earnestly for what you want, but is willing to obey God's will, is preferable. If you don't receive God's answer for your prayer for a long time, you need to find your faults, ask for forgiveness, and move toward God's will. "When you ask, you do not receive, because you ask with wrong motives, that you may spend what you get on your pleasures" (Jas 4:3). Humans should not ask God for things they should not possess out of greed. No matter how earnestly you pray for any hope, you cannot change the will of God. Instead, the will of the praying person must be changed and aligned with the will of God. We wait for God to work in the right direction by praying for what we should try to do but cannot do on our own.

(3) Forms of Prayer

The general forms of prayer include praise, thanksgiving, confession, intercession, and supplication. With a heart full of reverence toward God, we praise his glory, thank him for his grace, confess our sins, ask for forgiveness, and ask for his help. The Word was Jesus Christ, and he made his dwelling among us (John 1:14). We pray "in the name of Jesus Christ," seeing the glory of God through Jesus Christ. Praying in Jesus' name makes it easy to approach God. Praise and thanksgiving to God take precedence in prayer. The Lord's Prayer taught by Jesus includes praise and worship of God at the beginning and end. "Our Father in heaven, hallowed be your name, your kingdom come" (Matt 6:9–10). "For yours is the kingdom and the power and the glory forever" (Matt 6:13). Then there is the apostle Paul's prayer of thanksgiving in the Bible. "Always giving thanks to God the Father for everything, in the name of our Lord Jesus Christ" (Eph 5:20). When you make praising God and giving thanks in all things as a part of your life, it changes your life. Sincere prayer is honestly confessing your sins to God, thanking and praising him, interceding for others, and asking for what you want. When we confess our sins in prayer and ask for forgiveness, we will feel overwhelmed with gratitude for God's grace.

Jesus earnestly interceded for humanity. Jesus Christ is the mediator between God and man (1 Tim 2:5). We pray to God in thanksgiving for the intercession of Jesus and the empowerment of the Holy Spirit. Intercessory prayer refers to praying toward others and the world. You pray for the world and the church, as well as for family, friends, and acquaintances. Finally, supplication prayer is asking God for what you want for yourself and the world. "Your heavenly Father gives the Holy Spirit to those who ask him" (Luke 11:13). Since we do not know what to pray for, the Holy Spirit intercedes for the saints according to the will of God (Rom 8:27). "In everything by prayer and supplication with thanksgiving let your requests be made known unto God" (Phil 4:6). The earnest supplication prayer makes a huge difference in the Christian life. "Ask and it will be given to you; seek and you will find" (Matt 7:7). The Lord's Prayer also contains many of our requests to God (the Lord). "Give us this day our daily bread, and forgive us our debts, but do not lead us into temptation, but deliver us from evil" (Matt 6:11–13). "Watch and pray so that you will not fall into temptation" (Matt 26:41). The apostle Paul spoke to the saints about prayer and supplication. "Strive together with me in your prayers to God for me" (Rom 15:30). "And pray in the Spirit on all occasions with all kinds of prayers and requests. With this in mind, be alert and always keep on praying for all the saints" (Eph 6:18). James spoke of the Lord's work in supplication. "Pray for each other so that you may be healed. The prayer of a righteous man is powerful and effective" (Jas 5:16). God is able to do exceedingly abundantly above all that we ask or think (Eph 3:20).

(4) Jesus' Prayers and How to Pray

Jesus taught his disciples how to pray. "When you pray, do not be like the hypocrites to be seen by men, but go into your room, close the door and pray to your Father, who is unseen. And when you pray, do not keep on babbling like pagans, for your Father knows what you need before you ask him" (Matt 6:5–8). Jesus often prayed in secluded places (Luke 5:16), and when he went to the mountain to pray, he prayed to God all night long (Luke 6:12). Like Jesus, it is desirable for Christians to pray privately in secret. We should pray from the depths of our hearts. In church services or Bible studies, we pray in silent contemplation. However, it is to be careful not to pray in a loud voice only to be seen by others. The apostle Paul said to his brothers, "Always seek after that which is good. Rejoice always; pray without ceasing; in everything give thanks; for this is God's will for you in Christ Jesus" (1 Thess 5:15–18). In Paul's early church, prayer was at the center of life.

We meditate on the Ten Commandments (Exod 20:1–17), the Sermon on the Mount (Matt 5–7), the Lord's Prayer (Matt 6:9–13), and the Apostles' Creed, and we incorporate stories about ourselves and the world into our prayers. It is beneficial to base your prayers on the Lord's Prayer so that the prayer is not distracted. When we pray with the Lord's Prayer, we give praise, thanks, and glory to God, ask for forgiveness of sins through repentance, and ask for hope. Praying according to the Lord's Prayer brings comfort and peace by asking for your own hope. As you focus on God (the Holy Spirit) while petitioning the Lord in prayer, God's Word, the spiritual teaching of good enlightenment, comes to you. In this way, Christians hear God's voice (revelation, instruction, etc.) through prayer. These are the wonderful spiritual teachings of God that cannot be obtained from the words of the Bible but only from prayer.

Christians today make prayer a way of life by praying regularly and consistently. We voluntarily pray twice a day, when we wake up in the morning and before we go to bed every night. God's voice is heard primarily through his Word. Prayer is based on reading God's word in the Bible. To learn how to pray, we immerse ourselves in the individual words of God recorded in the Bible. Christians encounter God through the Word. Jesus Christ himself is an object of contemplation, and the words of the Bible are meditated on or recited. We read and meditate on the psalms of the Old Testament, as they have much to offer for prayer. It is important to meditate deeply on the Bible and listen to God's voice. Prayer without meditation on the Word is a poor communion with God. Meditating on the Bible gives Christians stability, joy, peace, and blessing. The blessed meditate on the law of the Lord day and night (Ps 1:1–2). Christian meditation on the Word is not "emptying the mind" but rather an analytical and spiritual savoring of the Word, focused on the glory of God. We think about the true meaning of the Bible's words, give thanks and praise to God, confess our sins and ask for forgiveness, and ask the Lord what to do. Rather than saying the same thing every time we pray, we pray differently today and tomorrow. Even if we do not get what we want, we should not stop praying.

The Main Points of the Christian Faith

5. THE CHRISTIAN'S RIGHT VIEW OF SALVATION

Salvation requires the carnal man to be born anew by the Spirit. Jesus said, "No one can see the kingdom of God unless he is born again" (John 3:3). We cannot be saved and enter the kingdom of God unless we are born again of true faith and made completely new. Christians are saved when they are born again, believe in God and Jesus Christ, and live according to God's will in obedience. God sovereignly determines who is saved and who goes to the kingdom of heaven. One is saved and enters the kingdom of God through faith in Jesus Christ and God's grace alone. One is saved by grace through faith, and salvation is the gift of God (Eph 2:8). Jesus said this about salvation and the kingdom of God: "Not everyone who says to me, 'Lord, Lord,' will enter the kingdom of heaven, but only he who does the will of my Father who is in heaven" (Matt 7:21). Only those who do God's will go to the kingdom of God. Salvation is not the goal of the gospel but rather the result of believing the gospel and obeying God. Salvation is the fruit that comes from believing the gospel but not the core of the gospel itself. Without a life of obedience to God, free from sin and evil, we are not saved. The events of Jesus' ministry, crucifixion, and resurrection are the way to salvation (eternal life) for the people of the world to imitate and follow. Jesus is the image that Christians are to imitate (Rom 8:29).

In the 16th century, the Reformers Martin Luther (1483–1546) and Jean Calvin (1509–64) developed "salvation theory" (soteriology) as a Christian doctrine. Human beings are saved by the concrete works of justification (Luther: justified by faith) and sanctification (Calvin: justified, obedient, and holy by faith). True salvation does not end with justification by faith. Soteriology was refined by Luther and then by Calvin to make it more understandable to the ordinary Christian. If one properly obeys and believes, there are works, and one is justified, sanctified to be holy like Jesus Christ, and saved (eternal life). In order to be justified and saved through faith, there must be a life of sanctification. Faith without works cannot be called true faith (Jas 2:26), because faith presupposes righteous and good works (practice). You cannot be saved by faith without works (Jas 2:14). True faith makes good works visible. However, salvation does not deny works, but it is not earned by human will and effort. God saves us, not according to our works, but according to his will and the grace he has given us in Christ Jesus (2 Tim 1:9). It is not by works of man that salvation is earned, but by God's grace, after judgment, we are saved to eternal life. The apostle Paul said that salvation is "not by works, so that no one can boast"

(Eph 2:9). This means that no human work to be saved is perfect in God's sight. However, God never denies human works for salvation. We cannot separate works from faith, because the Christians of true faith do righteous and good works.

When we analyze the Bible scientifically, we can find profound meanings hidden in each word. In church (cathedral) sermons, pastors often say to Christian believers, "Saints, you have been saved." However, salvation is not a past fact that has already happened. It is a future event. Indeed, every human being in the world will die someday. However, the Christians of true faith will be judged by God after death and will be saved by God's grace and live forever. Jesus himself was crucified, buried, and descended into hell (see the Apostles' Creed in English versions of the Bible), and on the third day he rose from the dead and ascended into heaven. If Christians are already saved now, they should not actually die because they have eternal life. When analyzed logically, salvation and eternal life occur simultaneously and have a synonymous meaning.

It is necessary to analyze the true meaning of the name "Jesus" given by God through the angel of the Lord in the Bible. In the Korean and English Bibles, it is written, "그(예수)가 자기 백성을 그들의 죄에서 구원할 자 이심이라" (마태복음 1:21); "He will save his people from their sins" (Matt 1:21). However, the translation "그(예수)가 자기 백성을 그들의 죄에서 지켜줄 자 이심이라" (마태복음 1:21), which is used in the Korean version of the Bible, may be the correct translation. The English word "save" is better translated into Korean as "keep" (지키다) or "protect" (보호하다) than "save" (구원하다). If Korean Christians were to read a Korean Bible that translated "save" as "protect" (보호하다) or "keep" (지키다), their view of salvation would drastically different. Jesus healed the woman with the hemorrhage through wonder (Mark 5:25–34). "내가 그의 옷에만 손을 대어도 구원 (save) 을 받으리라" (Mark 5:28); "If I just touch his clothes, I will be healed" (Mark 5:28)]. In this way, the English translation of "I will be healed(치료받는다)" is mistakenly translated as "I will be saved (구원받는다)" in the Korean Bible. As another example, "God save the Queen" is the name of the national anthem of the United Kingdom, which originated from the hymn and is used by many countries in the British Commonwealth, including the United Kingdom. The word "save" in the title and lyrics of the British national anthem is translated into Korean as "protect" (보호하다) rather than "save" (구원하다).

The Main Points of the Christian Faith

The English word "save" has many different meanings in Korean, including "to save" (구원하다), "to rescue" (구출하다), "to protect" (보호하다), "to keep safe" (안전하게 지키다), "to keep money" (저축하다), "to use less money" (절약하다), etc. However, in the Korean version of the Bible, the word "save" is translated as "to save" (구원하다) only, and the entire Bible is described as a story of salvation. Korean pastors use the word "salvation" (구원) countless times in their sermons, and most of their congregants believe this and practice their faith accordingly. A sermon that talks less about salvation is a good sermon. No one in the world is "saved" at this time. Even Christians living in the world will die someday. However, just like Jesus, we will be judged by God after we die and saved by God's grace so that we can go to the kingdom of God. The word "save" in the English Bible is preferably translated into Korean as "to save" (구원하다), "to rescue" (구출하다), "to protect" (보호하다), or "to keep" (지키다), depending on the content of the Bible. Then, Korean Christianity will be able to move away from the current "religion of salvation" that prays only for blessings.

A pastor in a church or a priest in a Catholic cathedral cannot act as a mediator to bring Christians to salvation. They are not saviors; they can only communicate God's word and will to Christians and lead them to God (Jesus). This is because there is only one mediator between God and man, Jesus Christ (Heb 12:24). We are saved by the work of the Holy Spirit through God's grace and love but not as a result of any human work or merit (Titus 3:4-5). Many Korean pastors today say that when a person is baptized and becomes a Christian, he will go to the kingdom of God, because he has been saved. However, salvation cannot be judged by a human pastor and cannot be given to believers. The only way to be saved is through true faith in Jesus Christ. It is only through Jesus Christ, the Mediator, that we can be saved.

To say, "If you become a Christian, you will all go to the kingdom of God because you have been saved" is not logical, and this is an incorrect view of salvation that is not found in the Bible. In Korean Christianity, pastors often tell their congregations in church sermons, "Dear saints, you have been saved." This is to mislead the congregations with a distorted view of salvation in the name of God (Jesus). However, it is unlikely that Korean pastors preach a distorted view of salvation because they are not familiar with the true view of salvation. While these pastors know the correct soteriology, they neglect or ignore to teach it to their congregations.

Part II: Understanding Christianity

This is because the biblical view of salvation is an obstacle to the expansion of Christianity (church) among Koreans who want a life of worldly desires, success, and blessings. To put it more simply, one must preach and evangelize with the "Korean Christian doctrine" (salvation view), which is a salvation faith that wishes only to be blessed, in order to gather believers and expand one's church. However, a sermon that talks a lot about "salvation and the kingdom of God" is not a good sermon. No matter how devout Christians Korean pastors and laypeople are, traditional Confucian and Buddhist culture is deeply rooted in the background of their lives. Just as people in Western Europe may have become devout Buddhists but their lives are still infused with Christian culture. Now, before Korean Christianity is indigenized as a "religion of salvation," all Korean Christians should strive to be reborn as a Christianity of life, grace, and love. Salvation cannot be achieved through religious activities that pray for hope and blessings, including dawn prayers, physical and spiritual training in monasteries and prayer houses, etc. To be saved, one must be born again of true faith and live a practical and godly life of faith with good and righteous deeds. Christianity is a religion of life and love, and it is also a religion of practice.

Christians of faith have spiritual comfort and peace through God's grace by controlling worldly (secular, physical) lusts and desires (appetite, lust, covetousness, power, honor, etc.) with the agape love of God while living in this world. However, God and Jesus Christ are always with Christians, seeing their deeds (good, evil, and sin), so we must live according to God's will (Word) in the Bible. Only by believing God's Word correctly, living an obedient life, being honest, giving to others, and living good and righteous lives, can we be judged by God when we die and be saved and have eternal life. The distorted view of salvation, which says that even if you lie, cheat, and do evil things in your life, God will always forgive and save you as long as you repent, is very wrong. If you are hypocritical and say you believe only with your mouth, you will not enter the kingdom of God. After his resurrection, Jesus said to his disciples, "Are you in peace?" (Matt 28:9); "Peace be with you" (Luke 24:36; John 20:19, 21, 26); "I am with you always, to the very end of the age" (Matt 28:20); "Whoever believes and is baptized will be saved" (Mark 16:16); "I am sending you the Holy Spirit" (John 20:21–22); and "Go into all the world and preach the good news (gospel) to all creation" (Mark 16:15). As such, while ascending to heaven after the resurrection, Jesus spoke mostly about "peace," "the descent of the

Holy Spirit," and "the preaching of the gospel." However, Jesus Christ never said to us, "Come all into the kingdom of God, for you have been saved."

God is a God of justice (Ps 89:14) and a God of love (grace) (1 John 4:16). God gives grace and blessings for good and righteous deeds, but he always punishes evil deeds with the punishment they deserve. Neither Christian ministers nor believers can earn "salvation to the kingdom of God" while they are alive in the world. No priest or pastor can also grant salvation to Christian believers. This is because salvation (eternal life) is determined by the sovereignty of God, not by human will or ability. Only God judges whether a person is saved or not. True Christians must have a correct view of salvation, be born again, faithfully believe in and obey God (Jesus). And, we must live a life that resembles Jesus Christ according to God's will (the Word) in order to be judged by God after death and saved, and to have eternal life in the kingdom of God.

4

The Bible, Christianity, and Science

WHEN WE KNOW SCIENCE in depth, we encounter God's providence that governs the universe, nature, and all things. The Bible was written between 3,500 years ago (Old Testament) and 2,000 years ago (New Testament), before the systematic study of natural science began. The Bible exemplifies various scientific facts. Today's scientists can access unknown scientific facts from the illustrative content of the Bible. In modern science, with a short history of about 200 years, what scientists have so far uncovered about the universe, nature, and life phenomena is only the tip of the iceberg. It is unreasonable to analyze and interpret the profoundly illustrative content of the Bible through these insignificant scientific facts that have been revealed. However, it is desirable to understand the Bible and Christianity in relation to scientific facts and the discovery of cosmic (natural) laws.

The Bible is written in a very logical and scientific manner. It contains many metaphorical examples that have not yet been proven to be facts but are likely to be scientifically discovered in the future. Some things written in the Bible have been proven to be true by scientists. It is worth noting that with the rapid development of natural sciences such as mathematics, physics, chemistry, and biology, based on the principles of the universe since the 17th century, many scientists have been inspired to discover new facts while reading the Bible. Nicolaus Copernicus (1473–1543), Galileo Galilei (1564–1642), Isaac Newton (1642–1726), Charles R. Darwin (1809–82), Gregor Mendel (1822–84), Louis Pasteur (1822–95), Albert Einstein

(1879–1955), and others pioneered modern sciences and led the science and technology of modern civilization. Interestingly, we can see that many world-renowned scientists, like these world-leading scientists, drew their creative intuition and inspiration from their daily lives steeped in the Bible and deeply committed to Christianity.

Science is the search for facts and truth based on empirical, theoretical, and experimental knowledge gained from observing the universe and natural phenomena. In science, only those universal, objective facts that have been thoroughly tested are true. The Bible is not a scientific book, but it is written in a very scientific (logical) manner. Christians sometimes interpret the Bible literally and deny already known scientific facts on the grounds that they contradict Christian doctrine. This is a blind faith in the Christian faith, and it is wrong. However, scientists also tend to believe only in the scientific facts known to date and underestimate the accounts implicit in the Bible to be unscientific or classical because they were written without scientific argument. This, too, is a blind faith in the self-fulfillment of scientists and is wrong. In addition, people with strong religious beliefs tend to believe in the power of faith and view the universe and natural phenomena through biblical standards of judgment. As a result, they tend to judge scientific facts theologically rather than objectively. Likewise, scientists who seek only objective facts try to justify their findings as if they are the only unchanging facts and truth.

Natural scientists work with the universe and nature, drawing inspiration from nature to formulate hypotheses, discover new facts through experimental evidence, and establish principles and theories. These principles and theories are useful in the present, and if new facts are discovered in the future, new principles can be redefined. Today, in the era of the Fourth Industrial Revolution, science and technology are highly advanced. However, there is still too much that modern science does not know to reach absolute and universal principles of the complex universe and life. In the following, scientific examples of cosmic principles and life phenomena that are recorded in the Bible or mentioned in Christianity, but are viewed differently by scientists, are explained and analyzed from biblical and scientific perspectives.

Part II: Understanding Christianity

1. GEOCENTRIC AND HELIOCENTRIC THEORIES AND COSMOLOGY

God created the laws of the universe and the universe operates according to God's laws. Geocentrism (the sun revolves around the earth), a cosmological view that the earth is the center of the universe, is a prime example of an erroneous scientific view that dominated Christianity in the Middle Ages. At the time, the church and clergy, including the pope, were advocating geocentrism, but the astronomer Nicolaus Copernicus (1473–1543) advocated heliocentrism (the earth revolves around the sun). When Italian astrophysicist Galileo Galilei (1564–1642) also claimed heliocentrism, the pope forced him to withdraw his assertion, accused him of heresy, and sent him to prison. In another example, in the 17th century, the English physicist, mathematician, and astronomer Isaac Newton (1642–1726), a devout Puritan, discovered the law of universal gravitation, which became the basis for the laws of motion and basic theories of gravity. On this basis, he established the scientific law of the universe, which states that the universe moves according to mathematical laws. In the early 20th century, Albert Einstein (1879–1955) advocated the theory of relativity and proposed that time and space are intimately connected and interdependent, thus breaking down Newton's concept of time and space, which was thought to be an eternal truth. Since then, with the development of astrophysics, a new cosmic principle that can explain the creation of the universe more accurately than Einstein's theory of relativity has been established and recognized by the general public.

Since Einstein, many astrophysicists have studied the expansion of the universe and proposed the Big Bang Theory to explain the origin of the universe. Today, the Big Bang Theory is accepted by most astrophysicists. The theory is the hypothesis that the universe came into being 13.7 billion years ago when a tiny piece of extremely energetic matter exploded from a single point and expanded far away, forming celestial bodies and galaxies. The Milky Way galaxy, of which our solar system is a part, contains more than 200 billion stars. Immediately after the Big Bang, elementary particles and photons were created, photons spread out into space as light, elementary particles combined to form atoms and hydrogen molecules, and stars and galaxies were created. About 4.6 billion years ago, a cloud-like nebula of gas (hydrogen) and dust (interstellar matter) spread among the stars of the Milky Way, giving rise to the Sun and Earth. As such, the universe and natural phenomena are governed by mysterious cosmic laws. However, although human knowledge of the universe and nature is still insignificant, the vast and unknown mysteries of the universe and nature continue to be uncovered.

2. CREATION AND EVOLUTION

Creationism and evolutionism are hypotheses, not absolute facts or truths that have been fully scientifically proven. The Bible says, "In the beginning God created the heavens and the earth and all that is in them in six days" (Gen 1). "You (God) created all things, and by your will they were created and have their being" (Rev 4:11). Creationism is the belief that the universe and all things were created and governed by God, the creator beyond time and space. However, biblical creationism is not an absolute fact that has been scientifically proven. Creationism is largely religious. Scientists explain the theory of evolution by studying biological evolution using well-established scientific research methods. According to evolutionary theory, all living things have evolved over long periods of time through random mutation and natural selection. However, the theory of evolution is difficult to establish as an absolute fact, because it is an inference of the evolutionary process of biological traits based on fossils and genetic variations in various living things.

"In his (Jehovah's) hand is the life of every creature and the breath of all mankind" (Job 12:10). Creationists religiously believe that the creation of God Almighty is true. Evolutionists believe in the evolution of life based on scientific and experimental evidence accumulated by modern science and technology. However, the theory of evolution is not an absolute fact, like heliocentric theory, which states that the earth revolves around the sun. There is no scientifically studied experimental evidence to explain creationism other than the literal account of God Almighty's creation of the heavens and the earth and all things in Gen 1 of the Old Testament. In contrast, the development of evolutionary biology and molecular biology today has radicalized phylogenetic research through the study of the structure and function of the genome of living organisms and the analysis of genetic variation and molecular clock technology. As a result, we are rapidly unraveling the mysteries of how organisms evolved. For example, the genetic code (base) sequences of the genomes of humans and mice are 80 percent identical, while humans and chimpanzees are 98 percent to 99 percent identical. Therefore, it is assumed that humans and chimpanzees share a common ancestor. However, with modern life science and biotechnology, there is still insufficient scientific evidence to explain the origin of any organism by evolution. On the other hand, Big Bang Theory is considered the most reliable cosmological theory to explain the origin and evolution of the universe. According to this theory, the universe began 13.7 billion years ago at a certain point in space and time, and then a giant explosion occurred and continued to expand, creating our current universe. It is a hypothesis that the universe was created by the explosion of matter and energy at a small point at the moment of the big bang, forming galaxies and celestial bodies within the galaxy.

British biologist Charles R. Darwin (1809–82) published *On the Origin of Species* in 1859, presenting the facts of biological evolution and establishing the theory of natural selection. The theory states that as single-celled organisms evolve into multicellular higher organisms, natural selection creates a variety of organisms that are different from their ancestors. After Darwin, a fierce debate ensued over the pros and cons of evolutionary theory. There was a huge backlash in Christian circles that Darwin's theory of evolution was a blasphemy against God. Churches and clergy at the time rejected Darwin's theory of evolution. They believed that all life was created by God. However, over the past 160 years, a great deal of scientific research has been accumulated on the evolution of the universe and living things, and the theory of evolution is now accepted by scientists and laypeople alike. Over the 4.6 billion years of Earth's history, science has shown that life has evolved, creating and destroying countless species. In 1996, Pope John Paul II (Ioannes Paulus II, 1920–2005), in his encyclical "On the Origin and Evolution of Life," recognized a "theistic evolutionary theory," in which the process of evolution itself is a process of God's creation, meaning that God's power is involved in evolution.

In Lao Tzu's *Tao Te Ching* (老子 道德經), there is an aphorism that states, "The Coexistence of Existence and Non-Existence (有無相生)." It means that "what is and what is not" coexist with each other. Although existence and non-existence appear to be in opposition, they coexist and harmonize to fulfill the laws of nature. Creation and evolution coexist and work together. Creation and evolution seem to be in opposition to each other, but they are complementary. Creationism is fundamentally about the origin of life (living organisms), and evolutionism is about how living things have changed and evolved over time. Creation and evolution coexist and complement each other in a harmonious relationship. If life were not created, evolution would not occur and would not be recognized. Also, if evolution did not occur in existing life, new life would not be created in the future. God is involved in both of these processes, creation and evolution. Without changes in the structure of DNA (genetic information) in a cell, there is no evolution of life. At the 2014 meeting of the Pontifical Academy of Sciences, Pope Francis (Papa Francesco, 1936–2025) said, "Evolution takes place after the creation of the beings that will evolve. Evolution comes after creation." The Pope is saying that both creationism and evolutionism are correct and compatible. Therefore, it is necessary to establish a harmonious and complementary relationship between creationism and evolutionism. The creation and evolution of the human race is beyond our ability (knowledge) to know perfectly. Creationists and evolutionists need to recognize each other's views. Life scientists are studying and experiencing the origin of life and the phenomena of life within the cells of living organisms. However, it is worth pondering whether it is possible for humans to create life with such intricate structures. It's not possible for humans to create life. There is still no human-created life that exists forever. This is because creation is the sovereign work of God. Life scientists read the book of Genesis in the Bible and marvel at the wonders of God's creation of all life. But as long as humanity exists, the evolution of life will continue, and the scientific study of evolution will continue. Also, all things in the universe will continue to be created and evolve.

3. GOD AND DNA; JESUS AND MESSENGER RNA

In the beginning, God created the universe, the earth, all things, and man (Gen 1). God created man in the image of God (Gen 1:27). This biblical statement suggests that God and man are similar in nature. God is sovereign and perfect. The cells that make up living things, including humans, are called a "microcosmos." Every cell has a nucleus, which contains molecules of deoxyribonucleic acid (DNA). As a living substance, DNA is sovereign and perfect, creating everything in the cell and governing life phenomena with perfect machineries (laws). DNA is like God in the cell. DNA is the source of life in the cell. The essence of God is spirit (Isa 42:1; John 4:24). Spirit gives life (John 6:63). If scientifically analyzed, the essence of the Trinity (Father, Son, and Holy Spirit) is the Spirit of God. God the Father is the Creator of all creation and the Father of God the Son, Jesus. The Son of God (Jesus) is the image of the invisible God (Col 1:15). Jesus Christ is the mediator between God and man (1 Tim 2:5). Jesus, the only

Part II: Understanding Christianity

Son, came from God the Father as the Messiah, and God sent the Holy Spirit into the world in Jesus' name (John 14:26). God, Jesus, and the Holy Spirit are in a vertical relationship with each other. After Jesus' resurrection and ascension, the Holy Spirit has been preaching the word (the gospel) of God (Jesus). Today is the age of the Holy Spirit. The Holy Spirit is witnessing to the world and the church about Jesus Christ. Messiah (any expected deliverer) has the meaning of savior, deliverer, or messenger. The Messiah, Jesus Christ, is the Son of God with God's DNA (genetic information), who delivers God's revelation, covenant, word, and gospel. The gospel delivery and ministry of the Messiah Jesus Christ for God is very similar to the cellular function of messenger RNA (mRNA), which transmits the genetic information contained in DNA (genes) in cells. When life scientists first discovered and named messenger RNA, which is made from DNA in cells, they may have been inspired by Jesus Christ's other name, Messiah.

A cell is the basic unit of structure and function of a living organism. The DNA in the nucleus of an organism's cell is responsible for creating identical cells. Cells continue to divide and multiply, eventually forming an organism. DNA (genes), messenger RNA (mRNA), and protein molecules are present in the cell to control all metabolic processes in the cell. DNA (genes) is transcribed to make messenger RNA, and messenger RNA is translated into amino acids to make proteins. These living substances (molecules) are in a vertical relationship with each other. The essence of DNA, messenger RNA, and proteins is the same: genetic information. The essence of DNA is genetic information. Messenger RNA acts as a messenger that transmits the genetic information of DNA within the cell. These three living substances (molecules) derived from the nucleic acids exist in different forms; however, they have the same essence: the same genetic information, the genetic code, in a certain sequence of bases. DNA has a double-stranded structure with the genetic code of four bases: adenine (A), cytosine (C), guanine (G), and thymine (T). In 1953, James D. Watson (1928–) and Francis H. C. Crick (1916–2004) discovered the double helix structure of DNA and were awarded the Nobel Prize in 1962. When DNA (genes) are transcribed, messenger RNA is produced. The structure of messenger RNA is also composed of four bases. The messenger RNA has uracil (U) in place of guanine (G) in its DNA structure, and the other bases are identical to the other bases in DNA. Messenger RNA is the transcript of DNA that is made from DNA (genes). In 1961, François Jacob (1920–2013) and others discovered the existence and function of messenger RNA and were awarded the Nobel Prize in 1965 for their work. In the cell, messenger RNA is translated into amino acids to make proteins with the same genetic information, which participate in all metabolic processes in the cell. While we cannot see the function of DNA in the cell, we can observe the expression of messenger RNA and proteins. However, if the DNA (gene) that contains the genetic information is different from the original, a mutation occurs, and the messenger RNA and protein made from the modified DNA cannot function normally.

God (the Father) and DNA are intricate, perfect, and similar to each other. Also, Jesus Christ, the Messiah, the Son of God, and messenger RNA are similar in what they do. It can be inferred that DNA plays a God-like role in the cell, and messenger RNA, which is derived from DNA, plays a Messiah-like role by carrying the genetic information of DNA. The Messiah Jesus Christ was God's mediator (messenger), who preached God's will and word (gospel) to the apostles and people. The structure of DNA, the base sequence, is perfect. If any of the bases in the sequence are defective, mutations occur, causing dysfunction in the cell. Therefore, the perfection of God and the perfection of DNA exhibit the same characteristics. The Bible says, "I (God) am who I am" (Exod 3:14). As a spiritual being, God cannot be seen with human eyes. Just as we cannot see the image of God, we cannot see the image of DNA, except for the base sequence of double helixes. However, we can see the function of DNA (genes) only when they are transcribed into messenger RNA, which is then translated into amino acids to make proteins, which are then expressed. Just as we can see God, the Messiah Jesus, his works (deeds), and the Holy Spirit in the Bible, we can see the functions of DNA, messenger RNA, and proteins in a cell, which is called a microcosm. Just as in the Gospels of the Bible, Jesus performed signs and wonders to reveal the invisible work of God, messenger RNA is also expressed in cells to perform various functions to show the invisible work of DNA. God, Jesus, the Holy Spirit, as well as DNA, messenger RNA, and proteins are all alive and give us life. However, the leap of logic that "God is DNA" does not hold. Since God is an invisible spiritual image (spirit), we cannot say that God is DNA because DNA is a nuclear product that we can see. However, just as in the universe and the world God is in control of life, creation, universal laws, and the spiritual world, it is interesting to note that in the microcosm, the cell, DNA is in control of the creation of life and the phenomena of life.

Part II: Understanding Christianity

4. SPIRIT, WATER, AND LIFE

In the universe and the world, there was spirit before all things existed. "The Spirit gives life" (John 6:63). The Spirit of God is a spirit that gives life (Rom 8:11). In the book of Genesis in the Bible, it is recorded that the "Spirit of God" existed in the waters before God created all things. "The Spirit of God was hovering over the waters" (Gen 1:2). The biblical book of Genesis, written around 1450 BC, tells us that water exists on Earth and suggests that water is a reservoir of the Spirit. The Spirit of God is in the water. The Bible (God) is the first to illustrate this marvelous biological fact. "For there are three that testify: the Spirit, the water and the blood; and these three are one" (1 John 5:7–8). A life science analysis of the true meaning of these records about "spirit, water, and life" hidden in the Bible reveals that all living things have water with spirit. Water is life. "Come, all you who are thirsty, come to the waters" (Isa 55:1). In the Old Testament, Jehovah God made sure that everyone who was thirsty would drink of the water of life. Whoever drinks of the water that Jesus gives will never thirst again, and the water that Jesus gives becomes a well of water springing up in people to eternal life (John 4:13–14). Thus, in the New Testament, Jesus promises to give the Samaritan woman the water of life that will never thirst as a gift of salvation. God and Jesus reveal that the water they offer to people contains the Spirit that gives life. The Holy Spirit gives the water of life without cost to those who thirst and want it (Rev 22:17).

Among the numerous stars in the universe, only Earth has 70 percent of its surface covered by water and is inhabited by living organisms. Water (H_2O) is an essential chemical that sustains life. Without water, life cannot live. And life cannot survive without spirit. Spirit (soul) is in water. Living things are alive because they drink or absorb water that contains life-giving spirit. Plants utilize the energy of the sun (light) to generate chemical energy, called photosynthesis. This absolutely requires water and carbon dioxide (CO_2). The electrons generated by the photodissociation of water are used to generate the energy-storing compounds nicotinamide adenine dinucleotide phosphate (NADPH) and adenosine triphosphate (ATP). The chemical energy converted from light energy is stored in carbohydrate molecules, such as sugar, and utilized by living organisms. All animals, including humans, cannot live without absorbing and utilizing water, meaning that all living organisms have water and require it for their cellular metabolism. This is because water, which contains spirit, is the source of life. All living things cannot survive without water.

The Bible, Christianity, and Science

To become a Christian, you must be baptized. "John baptized with water, but in a few days you will be baptized with the Holy Spirit" (Acts 1:5). You are baptized with water and the Holy Spirit. Christ Jesus himself was also baptized in water by John the Baptist (Matt 3:16; Mark 1:9; Luke 3:21). A Christian becomes a true Christian by being baptized in water. This is because the Spirit of God is immanent in the water. "No one can enter the kingdom of God unless he is born of water and the Spirit" (John 3:5). This Bible verse tells us that only Christian believers who are baptized in water can enter the kingdom of God. Every Christian's body is indwelt by God, that is, the spirit of God and the spirit of Christ. In Christianity, God's commandment "you shall not worship or serve idols" (Exod 20:1-6) is very important. A biological analysis of the Christian commandment against idolatry is that an idol is a dead object without water, so an idol cannot have the life-giving spirit of God (the Holy Spirit). Idols are lifeless and dead, so Christianity, the religion of life, cannot worship idols.

5. THE BIBLE AND MENDEL'S LAWS OF INHERITANCE

In the life sciences, Gregor Mendel (1822-84; botanist, Catholic monk) opened the first chapter of genetics with his formulation of Mendel's laws of inheritance. Between 1856 and 1863, Mendel planted several varieties of peas (*Pisum sativum*) in a small monastery garden and crossed them with each other, obtaining twelve thousand hybrids to test the inheritance of different traits. He theorized that the peas had alleles for traits such as flower color and pod shape and that the continued appearance of these traits in their offspring is due to the basic unit of inheritance. This basic unit of inheritance turned out to be the gene, which is made up of DNA. The basic principle of Mendel's law of inheritance is that the germ cells of hybrids contain half genetic material from one parent (maternal line) and half genetic material from the other parent (paternal line). This is the fact that alleles (genes) in germ cells are passed on (inherited) to offspring according to the laws of dominance, segregation, and independence. Mendel discovered that he could predict in advance which traits would be passed on to offspring. Mendel's laws of inheritance did not receive much attention when they were first published (1865-66). However, their rediscovery in the early 20th century established modern genetics. In 1910, American geneticist Thoma H. Morgan (1866-1945) proved that Mendel's laws of

Part II: Understanding Christianity

inheritance hold true even in animals through fruit fly (*Drosophila*) hybridization experiments.

Mendel's laws of inheritance are a major breakthrough in interpreting the heredity of diversity and variation in living organisms. Mendel is the founder of modern genetics. Mendel's laws of inheritance are the basis for explaining the inheritance of all living things, including humans. Peas are not a crop that is widely grown by European farmers for commercial use, so it is remarkable that Mendel chose peas as his experimental material for hybridizing plants. Mendel may have chosen peas for his experiments after receiving a revelation from God. Peas are very suitable for genetic research because the expression of genetic traits is simple and clear—and easy to distinguish by appearance. In the world, some things happen by chance, but when we analyze them closely, they are often not coincidental but inevitable based on intuition and inspiration. This is because here is the revelation of God. If Mendel had not chosen peas as his experimental material, we wonder if he would have discovered the great laws of inheritance. In fact, Mendel's work on the laws of inheritance is one of the greatest achievements in the history of life sciences, because of the sophistication of his experimental design, the accuracy of his experiments, the excellence of his data analysis, and the sophistication and clarity of his logic. Given the underdeveloped state of natural science in the 19th century, Mendel's groundbreaking discovery of the laws of inheritance, which was difficult for humans to accomplish, was characterized by prophetic superhumanity. As a Catholic monk, Mendel read the Bible daily and could have drawn inspiration for his genetic laws from the Bible. This is because the Bible is not a science book; it is a Scripture book that contains many scientific examples.

It is interesting to note that there is a biblical account of the genetic traits of an animal (sheep) that can be foreshadowed for the discovery of Mendel's laws of inheritance. In the Bible's book of Genesis, God made it possible for Laban, as well as his maternal uncle and father-in-law, to identify the sheep he promised to give to Jacob by their color. "In breeding season I once had a dream in which I looked up and saw that the male goats mating with the flock were streaked, speckled or spotted" (Gen 31:10). "And he said, 'Look up and see that all the male goats mating with the flock are streaked, speckled or spotted, for I have seen all that Laban has been doing to you'" (Gen 31:12). Laban had promised Jacob ten times that he would provide sheep as wages, but he broke his promise. However, God took away the sheep from Laban and gave them to Jacob by sorting them according to the color of the sheep. This was revealed to Jacob through an angel in a dream (Gen 30:32; 31:7–12). In another example, God knew the traits that make up living organisms, as recorded in the Psalms. "Your (Lord's) eyes saw my unformed body. All the days ordained for me were written in your book before one of them came to be" (Ps 139:16).

6. SPONTANEOUS GENERATION AND BIOGENESIS

God created all things (Gen 1). "And God said, Let the earth bring forth grass, the herb yielding seed, and the fruit tree yielding fruit after his kind, whose seed is in itself, upon the earth: and it was so" (Gen 1:11). As such, the Bible records that God created various living things. Based on these biblical accounts, humans have believed in spontaneous generation, the idea that life arises spontaneously through God's creation. Until the Middle Ages, Christian clergy and laypeople alike believed that living things were created by God and spontaneously generated.

In the late 17th century, Dutch Antony van Leeuwenhoek (1632–1723) built the first microscope to view cells and microbes. Leeuwenhoek's discovery of microbes under the microscope led scientists at the time to believe that higher organisms could not arise naturally but that microbes could. John Needham (1713–81), an English Catholic priest and biologist, claimed that microorganisms could spontaneously form and grow in lamb gravy, even if it was boiled for a long time in a flask and sealed with a cotton stopper. Based on this research, people believed that microorganisms are spontaneously created from organic matter. This supported the theory of spontaneous generation of microorganisms. However, a number of scientists have conducted experiments that deny the spontaneous generation of microorganisms. As a representative example, Frenchman Louis Pasteur (1822–95) used elaborate and creative experimental methods to provide convincing experimental evidence that disease arises from pre-existing microorganisms. He and others demonstrated that cultures in sterilized flasks remain sterile even when they come into direct contact with the air depleted of microorganisms. Pasteur also showed that many different microorganisms can cause disease. After Pasteur, the theory of spontaneous generation was denied, and the germ theory of disease was established. The fact that living things (microorganisms) did not occur spontaneously was recognized by the general public. After Pasteur, the theory of biogenesis, which states that "life comes from life," that is, there is no life without parents, gained general support. Since then, the theory of biogenesis has been established as one of the most important fundamental principles of biology. In nature, a germ is the source of life for microorganisms, plants, and animals, and all living things are organisms. Living things are made of organic compounds. The Bible says that man was formed from the dust (fine fragments of organic matter) of the ground. "The Lord God formed the man from the dust of the ground and breathed into his nostrils the breath of life, and the man became a living being" (Gen 2:7).

5

Guidelines for the Christian Life

CHRISTIANS RECEIVE AND BELIEVE in the Lord Jesus Christ and enjoy a life of joy, grace, and gratitude in fellowship with him. Jesus Christ receives us in this way: "Here I am. I stand at the door and knock. If anyone hears my voice and opens the door, I will come in and eat with him, and he with me" (Rev 3:20). The Christian life should be about receiving God's grace in Jesus Christ and fulfilling God's will. A true Christian lives according to the will of God and in God and Jesus Christ for the glory of God. God's will is treasured up in God's mercy and grace. Grace comes through Jesus Christ (John 1:17), and in Christ we see the will of God. The Christian who has received grace is at peace and always with God (Luke 1:28). The apostle Paul says, "Grace, mercy and peace from God the Father and Christ Jesus our Lord" (2 Tim 1:2).

What we can gain from the Christian faith is our own comfort and peace. God is a God of mercy and comfort, who comforts us in all our troubles (2 Cor 1:3–4). God is a God of peace (1 Thess 5:23). Jesus emphasized "peace" to his disciples after his resurrection. "All hail" (Matt 28:9); "Peace be with you" (Luke 24:36; John 20:19, 21, 26); "Surely I am with you always" (Matt 28:20). The apostle Paul also told the churches, "Grace to you and peace from God our Father and the Lord Jesus Christ" (Rom 1:7; 1 Cor 1:3; Gal 1:3; Eph 1:2). The Christian life is a good, righteous, and godly life that does God's will. The life of faith is about living in a right relationship with God and enjoying God's grace forever. Christians are to be, first, honest and upright. Second, we are to be righteous and do good. Third, to share and give to others. Fourth, to be humble. Fifth, to rejoice and be thankful. In particular, Christians should always be humble and thankful in all things. This is because nothing in this world is done by our own will or power but by the sovereignty and grace of God. Christians who believe in and obey Jesus Christ and live a life of grace are comforted and freed from anxiety and worry. The life of a true Christian is always peaceful and full of joy and thanksgiving. Also, the God of hope fills us with all joy and peace in our faith life, so that we may abound in hope by the power of the Holy Spirit (Rom 15:13).

DOING GOD'S WILL WITH TRUE FAITH CHANGES YOUR LIFE

1. Christians must be born again. Those who believe in Jesus Christ are born of God (1 John 5:1) and are born again (John 3:3). "Just as Christ was raised from the dead through the glory of the Father, we too may live a new life" (Rom 6:4). We became a new creation with a new heart that God gave us (Ezek 36:26; 2 Cor 5:17).

2. We must make God's will (Word) the standard for your life. We must live righteously and godly by God's standards (Luke 2:25). "Train yourself to be godly, for godliness is profitable for all things" (1 Tim 4:7–8).

3. We must fear God (Deut 10:12–13). It is the duty of believers to fear God, to live according to his will, and to glorify him (Eccl 12:13). God is a God of justice (Ps 89:14). If you sin, you will be punished. God judges every secret work, both good and evil (Eccl 12:14).

4. Those who live in the fear of God live righteously, even without the law. All other fears disappear from those who fear God (Ps 27:1). God gives great grace to those who fear him (Ps 33:12). Those who have a right relationship with God have no fear.

5. The Holy Spirit (God) is in Christians (John 14:16–20). "God with us" (Matt 1:23). God is in Christians to protect them, and God is always watching over everything, so we should not live a false life. We have the Holy Spirit and conscience in our hearts. Therefore, if we do something bad (sinful), God is always watching within us like a

Guidelines for the Christian Life

CCTV camera, so we should not sin. Christians live by faith and conscience. "Hold on to faith and a good conscience" (1 Tim 1:19). Faith is dependent on God's law, and conscience is dependent on the moral law. Conscience is God's gift to humans.

6. If anyone lives in God, he must walk as Jesus did (1 John 2:6). We are to be imitators of Jesus Christ (1 Cor 11:1; Eph 5:1).

7. We Christians are always at peace, because God (the Holy Spirit [Comforter]; John 14:16] is with us and keeps us from sin. God has given us the Holy Spirit, so that we may be in God and God in us (1 John 4:13, 16). Today is the age of the Holy Spirit. We receive grace and guidance from the Comforter, the Holy Spirit of Truth sent by God (Jesus) (John 16:13). Jesus gave peace to those who believed, so he told them not to be troubled and not to be afraid (John 14:27).

8. We must live according to God's will (Word). Live the life God wants you to live. You must not commit sins (not working hard, criticizing others, committing crimes, etc.). Ask God before doing anything. God knows everything. God is sovereign and perfect. God accurately judges what is righteous and what is good.

9. We must live in repentance "Repent, for the kingdom of heaven is near" (Matt 4:17). We should throw away the thought that if we do something wrong (sin) and repent, God will forgive our sins, and that God will always help us even if we live according to our own will (greed and desire). True repentance is when you honestly confess your wrongdoing (sin), sincerely repent for it, and never do it again (see David's prayer of repentance: "I know my transgressions, and my sin is always before me. Against you, you only, have I sinned and done what is evil in your sight, so that you are proved right when you speak and justified when you judge" [Ps 51:3–4]).

10. Love the Lord, love your neighbor in the Lord, and love your enemies. We should live by the agape (selfless) love of God, not the eros (selfish) love of self. Christians are to love their neighbors (others) (Matt 22:39). God is love. Since God so loved us, we are to love one another (1 John 4:11). Those who love God must also love their brothers (1 John 4:21). Let us not love one another in word nor in tongue but in deed and in truth (1 John 3:18).

Part II: Understanding Christianity

11. "Not everyone who says to me, 'Lord, Lord,' will enter the kingdom of heaven, but only he who does the will of my Father who is in heaven" (Matt 7:21). Not every Christian or pastor (minister) goes to heaven (the kingdom of God). It is only through the true faith in God and Jesus Christ and the true practice of keeping his commandments (his Word) that one can be saved and have eternal life. God sovereignly judges who is saved and who goes to the kingdom of heaven.

12. God is light. Christians are to walk in the light (1 John 1:5–7). "The Lord knows those who are his" (2 Tim 2:19). Be honest. Avoid lies and evil deeds. "I say the truth in Christ, I lie not" (Rom 9:1). God in us is always watching our every action like a CCTV camera.

13. We must believe in God (Jesus) and put his word into action. Live righteously and do good. "As the body without the spirit is dead, so faith without deeds is dead" (Jas 2:26).

14. Christians should be faithful in their practice of the faith (reading the Bible, praying, and doing what it says). Live a godly life of practical, true faith at home and in society according to God's will.

15. Live in harmony with those around you (family, relatives) and with others (strangers). We are blessed when we bless others. "If it is showing mercy, let him do it cheerfully" (Rom 12:8). The one who gives freely gets more, but the one who spares excessively leads himself into poverty (Prov 11:24). Those who love to give to others prosper (Prov 11:25).

16. "Keep your lives free from the love of money and be content with what you have" (Heb 13:5). "The love of money is the root of all evil" (1 Tim 6:10).

17. "You cannot serve both God and Money" (Matt 6:24).

18. Act for the good of others and the common good rather than for personal gain. "Nobody should seek his own good, but the good of others" (1 Cor 10:24).

19. You should do your work (job) to the best of your ability and enjoy it. Work (job) is God's vocation. Labor is sacred. "You will eat the fruit of your labor; blessings and prosperity will be yours" (Ps 128:2). "A man reaps what he sows" (Gal 6:7). Think of it as God's vocation to you, and do all your work cheerfully. It is also a sin not to work or not to do it faithfully. This is how the Lord God punished Adam, who sinned

Guidelines for the Christian Life

by eating from the fruit of the knowledge of good and evil. "Through painful toil you will eat of it all the days of your life" (Gen 3:17). "By the sweat of your brow you will eat your food until you return to the ground" (Gen 3:19). Therefore, humans must work in sweat until they die. Not working in sweat is also a sin.

20. "He that is faithful in that which is least is faithful also in much: and he that is unjust in the least is unjust also in much" (Luke 16:10). There is righteousness in even the little things.

21. Since life itself is a blessing from God, we should be thankful in all things. Gratitude makes others happy and brings joy to the heart as well. Gratitude is manifested in love, and love finds joy in giving unconditionally. "For every creature of God is good, and nothing to be refused, if it be received with thanksgiving. For it is sanctified by the word of God and prayer" (1 Tim 4:4–5).

22. You must not live by comparing yourself to others. Do not compare yourself to others. It is in everyone's nature to compare. "Do not judge, or you too will be judged" (Matt 7:1). "If we have food and clothing, we will be content with that" (1 Tim 6:8). Those who are humble and concerned for others do not compare themselves to others (Phil 2:3–4).

23. Do not be conceited against one another (1 Cor 4:6). "God opposes the proud but gives grace to the humble" (Jas 4:6).

24. "Believers in our glorious Lord Jesus Christ must not show favoritism" (Jas 2:1).

25. "Do to others as you would have them do to you" (Luke 6:31).

26. "Everyone should be quick to listen, slow to speak and slow to become angry, for man's anger does not bring about the righteous life that God desires" (Jas 1:19–20).

27. We must fear God by reading and practicing the biblical book of Proverbs, and live according to God's word, doing what is wise, right, just, fair, and upright (Prov 1:3). The way of the just is uprightness (Isa 26:7).

28. If you covet unjustified gain, you will eventually lose your life (Prov 1:19).

29. "He who puts up security for another will surely suffer, but whoever refuses to strike hands in pledge is safe" (Prov 11:15).

Part II: Understanding Christianity

30. All days are unhappy for those who suffer, but for those whose hearts are glad, every day is a feast (Prov 15:15).

31. A joyful heart heals the sick, but a sorrowful spirit dries up the bones (Prov 17:22).

32. A man of knowledge spares his words, and an insightful man is not impatient (Prov 17:27).

33. A man's heart has many plans, but only the will of Jehovah God is done (Prov 18:21).

34. The humble and God-fearing man finds wealth, honor, and life (Prov 22:4).

35. Let others praise you, but don't do it yourself. Praise is for others to give, not for yourself (Prov 27:2).

36. To wives and husbands: "Wives, submit to your husbands as to the Lord" (Eph 5:22). To obey your husband is to obey the Lord. "Husbands ought to love their wives as their own bodies. He who loves his wife loves himself" (Eph 5:28).

37. Love your brother, giving friendship and respect to one another first (Rom 12:10). To the brother: "Leave your gift there in front of the altar. First go and be reconciled to your brother; then come and offer your gift" (Matt 5:24). Brothers are born to help in times of need (Prov 17:17).

38. If a brother or sister is naked and without daily food, and you say to him, "Go in peace, I wish you well; keep warm and well fed," but do nothing about his physical needs, you do not have a faith of works (Jas 2:15–17).

39. To children and parents: "Children, obey your parents in the Lord, for this is right" (Eph 6:1). "Honor your father and mother, which is the first commandment with a promise" (Eph 6:2). "Fathers, do not exasperate your children; instead, bring them up in the training and instruction of the Lord" (Eph 6:4).

40. To servants (subordinates) and masters (superiors): "Servants, obey your masters, just as to Christ, with sincerity of heart" (Eph 6:5–7). "Masters, do good to your servants, do not threaten them, and there is no favoritism with Him" (Eph 6:8–9).

41. "Rejoice with those who rejoice; mourn with those who mourn" (Rom 12:15).

42. "Encourage the timid, help the weak, be patient with everyone" (1 Thess 5:14).

43. "Bless those who persecute you; bless and do not curse" (Rom 12:14).

44. "Do not repay anyone evil for evil. Be careful to do what is right in the eyes of everybody" (Rom 12:17).

45. "Live at peace with everyone" (Rom 12:18).

46. "Be strong and courageous. Do not be terrified; do not be discouraged, for the Lord your God will be with you" (Josh 1:9).

47. "Ask and it will be given to you; seek and you will find; knock and the door will be opened to you" (Matt 7:7; Luke 11:9).

48. Have hope. "When the plowman plows and the thresher threshes, they ought to do so in the hope of sharing in the harvest" (1 Cor 9:10).

49. "Lead a quiet life, mind your own business and work with your hands" (1 Thess 4:11).

50. "Do good, be rich in good deeds, and be generous and willing to share" (1 Tim 6:18).

51. "Let us not become weary in doing good, for at the proper time we will reap a harvest if we do not give up" (Gal 6:9).

52. "Always follow the good; be joyful always; pray continually; give thanks in all circumstances, for this is God's will for you in Christ Jesus" (1 Thess 5:15–18).

53. Pray. God will make things happen in the right direction, according to his will, in his time.

54. We must live in gratitude for God's grace. "Always give thanks to God the Father for everything, in the name of our Lord Jesus Christ" (Eph 5:20).

55. "Blessed are the poor in spirit, those who mourn, the meek, those who hunger and thirst for righteousness, the merciful, the pure in heart, and the peacemakers" (Matt 5:3–9).

Epilogue

The Bible and Christianity Make Our Lives Peaceful and Prosperous

THE BIBLE IS THE testimony of Jesus Christ, and in the Bible we can have eternal life (John 5:39). All Scripture is God-breathed and is useful for teaching, rebuking, correcting and training in righteousness, so that the man of God may be thoroughly equipped for every good work (2 Tim 3:16–17). Based on the Bible, Christianity is a religion of practice. At the heart of the Christian faith is true faith in God and Jesus Christ. If a Christian finds comfort and peace through his faith in God, there is nothing more he can hope for. A true Christian believes sincerely in God (Jesus) and lives righteously with his conscience. "Hold on to faith and a good conscience" (1 Tim 1:19). Faith is our relationship with God, and conscience is our relationship with our lives. We have a good conscience to do good in all things (Heb 13:18). With true faith and a good conscience, Christians live according to God's will, giving thanks for God's grace and love.

The name of Jesus Christ, who is referred to as God the Son in Christianity's Trinitarian God, contains all of the main ideas of Christianity. The meaning of the name Jesus and his other name, Immanuel, is the whole idea of Christianity. The name Jesus means "He will save his people from their sins" (Matt 1:21). Immanuel means "God with us" (Matt 1:23). The core of Christian thought is that God is with his people (Christians), who

The Bible and Christianity Make Our Lives Peaceful and Prosperous

live in a sinful world by true faith, and that Jesus Christ frees them from their sins, protects them, and saves them to live in God forever.

Christians are baptized with water to become believers. Water is life. Baptism is a ritual that puts God's spirit of life into the heart of a Christian believer. Even the sinless Jesus was baptized by John the Baptist (Matt 3:13–17; Mark 1:9). God is present in the hearts of Christians and is always protecting them, so Christians are full of God's grace and at peace. On the other hand, Christians are not tempted to do evil things or live a false life because God who dwells in their heart is always watching. We humans have both good and evil natures. The conscience is our nature toward good. We have a good conscience (Heb 13:18). However, our evil nature is more readily manifested in the world than our good nature. This is because there is a wickedness (evil) in the human heart that falls short of goodness. Sin in the flesh of man does not do good but does evil (Rom 7:19). God and Jesus Christ are good. A good nature is a heart that has compassion for one's neighbor, a heart that is compassionate. Jehovah God is good to all and has compassion (mercy) on all he has made (Ps 145:9). The nature of sin is greed and desire (lust). The greed and desires of the human heart are the source of evil and sin. Humans commit sins and go to ruin when their greed and desire, or selfish self-love, become excessive. Greed (covetousness) gives birth to lies, and lies deceive and harm others. Christians obey God by faith and live righteous and good lives according to God's Word. True Christians turn away from physical pleasures and "the works of the flesh" (Gal 5:19), which stem from the greed and desire (lust) of the heart, in favor of God's truth and love.

Knowing who God is and how to treat him makes a difference in the lives of Christians. Christians believe that God (Jesus) will fulfill all their desires. Will God really make all our human desires come true? God does not address and solve what we want according to worldly standards. God is a God of justice and love. God is just and merciful. God is perfect and judges the world according to God's standards (principles). God judges every secret work, both good and evil (Eccl 12:14). Humans are selfish and self-loving. The faith that prays for personal blessings puts the focus on people's greed and desires rather than God's will, and they hope that their desires will be fulfilled. In Christianity, however, we cannot fulfill our greed and desires by praying for blessings. Christianity is not a religion that prays for personal blessings and happiness. Many fanatical Christians spend a lot of time seeking God and asking him to do many worldly things for them. Pastors say that if you pray in church, God will hear you and solve your problems someday. However, this is only human, self-centered, and arbitrary thinking. It must meet God's standard (will). We must do our best in practice with true faith with works to meet God's standards. "As the body without the spirit is dead, so faith without deeds is dead" (Jas 2:26). God gives what he desires to those who fulfill the work (vocation) he has entrusted to them by faith with works. We need to get away from the life of faith that asks for the blessing that "everything will come true if we pray." However, this does not mean that prayer is not necessary in the life of faith. "Ask and it will be given to you" (Matt 7:7). If you pray, God will hear you and make it happen in the right way. However, we should refrain from praying out of selfish self-love, that is, self-centered prayers to fulfill worldly human greed and desire. Godly prayer for the glory of God is an urgent need for Christians. Prayer is the link between Almighty God and sinful human beings, uniting them in personal conversation and fellowship with God. Prayer removes anxiety and worry, gives peace, and energizes life. In prayer, Christians do not fulfill their own will but God's will. Jesus prayed to God like this: "Yet not as I will, but as you will" (Matt 26:39). Korean Christianity needs to move away from being a religion of self-love. Korean Christians also need to be reborn into a life of doing and practicing God's will.

Christians in Germany and other European countries are lazy in the church life of attending and serving churches. Many Christians would rather not go to church. They are lazy about going to prayer centers and retreats, and they are not diligent about praying at meals and praying every hour of every day. They are also lazy about spiritual disciplines such as vigils, fasts, and early morning prayers. However, they are Christians who pay church taxes (offerings) and live a Christian life by practicing God's will. German Christians are honest and do not do bad (evil) things when others are not looking. They know that God is always watching their hearts and what they do in their daily lives. They live according to the Bible, according to God's Word, doing their best at what they have been given, sharing with others out of the agape (selfless) love of God, and living in humility, putting the common good above their own interests. The Bible and Christianity are deeply embedded in their daily lives. Christianity is their life. The German word "Beruf" (job) comes from the word "berufen" (to receive a divine call). Germans have a job they love, fulfill their responsibilities, work hard, and live happily. Work (jobs) are our lives. A true Christian in God's eyes

The Bible and Christianity Make Our Lives Peaceful and Prosperous

is one who does his best at what God has called them to do and lives righteously and good. God is always with the Christian in his daily actions of a Christian's life. The ordinary life (work) of a layman who lives according to the Bible is just as sacred as the ministry of a pastor. A person who goes to church, becomes a minister's servant, and seeks God only in words is not a true Christian. A true Christian is one who practices God's will in love. The Bible says, "Let us not love with words or tongue but with actions and in truth" (1 John 3:18).

Christianity entered the Korean Peninsula in the late 18th century and became the main religion of Korea. Over the past 250 years, Christianity has become embedded in Korean traditional culture. However, Korean Christianity does not grow into the original Western Christianity and is largely degenerating into a religion that prays for self-love and worldly blessings and well-being. Korean Christianity is thriving in quantity with a huge increase in the number of churches and believers. However, Korean society is still a Confucian culture that has not yet established a true Christian culture and is mixed with various indigenous traditional religions. Korean Christians are very active in church, attending worship services, praying, singing hymns, and serving. However, they neglect to read the Bible and practice the Christian life by doing righteous and good deeds according to the Word of God. Outside of the church, Korean Christians live a life of traditional Korean culture. They prefer to recite and act according to Chinese ancient events and Confucian idioms, instead of acting according to the words of God and Jesus Christ in the Bible. There is no Christian culture and life in Korea outside of the church. And Korean Christianity remains a religion similar to the Korean indigenous religion that prays for worldly blessings. Christianity is a religion of practice. The practice of Christianity is not a big practice that loudly brags about one's deeds. A small action that brings joy to God in the little things of our daily lives is a good Christian practice in the eyes of God. Jesus says, "Be careful not to do your 'acts of righteousness' before men, to be seen by them. When you give to the needy, do not let your left hand know what your right hand is doing" (Matt 6:1–3). We need righteous and good deeds that are invisibly practiced, not talked about.

Christians live their religious lives based on the New and Old Testaments. However, the New Testament should be more fundamental to our Christian faith. Pastors in Korean churches often emphasize laws and disciplines in their sermons rather than grace and love. Sermons should focus on the New Testament. Pastors encourage their congregations to donate to the church in God's name. This is because the Korean Christian Church (Protestant) is funded by the offerings of Christian believers. Church pastors ask laypeople to come to church and serve and dedicate themselves to the church in the name of God (Jesus). They want every layperson to become a priest (child) of God who serves diligently in the church. They still hold to the "all-priesthood" concept of the early church in the 1st century and the Reformer Martin Luther in the 16th century. Pastors emphasize the service and evangelism of the church more than the works and daily lives of laypeople. However, this is not what God truly wants, nor is it appropriate for the lives of laypeople living in the modern era of diversified globalization and the Fourth Industrial Revolution. The Bible says, "For those who are called in the Lord are Christ's slaves; do not become slaves of men, but you should remain with God as you have been called" (1 Cor 7:22–24). The Lord said that he will punish the prophets and priests who say, 'Peace, peace,' to those who believe in God but are not at peace, and who practice greed and falsehood (Jer 6:13–15). Jesus also said to his disciples, "Do not do what the scribes and Pharisees do; for they say things, and do not do them" (Matt 23:3). "Beware of false prophets, which come to you in sheep's clothing, but inwardly they are ravenous wolves" (Matt 7:15). Pastors of churches should be reminded of those words of God and Jesus Christ in the Bible. You are not true Christians just because you attend church diligently every day. A Christian who fulfills his vocation in his worldly workplace and lives in God's love according to God's will is a person of true faith that God really wants. True Christians should not be servants of churches and pastors but servants of God (Jesus), who lives according to the God's word and is with God. In Korea, there are many blind believers who devotedly serve their church pastors. However, there are very few Christians who live a life of true faith, serving God and Jesus Christ according to God's will. God is pleased to give grace and blessings to those who do their work honestly and faithfully. A Christian of true faith, whether he lives in Korea, the United States, or Europe, lives a life that becomes more like Jesus Christ by practicing God's word in a righteous and good manner according to the Bible.

"Where the Spirit of the Lord is, there is freedom" (2 Cor 3:17). Walking with the Lord sets Christians free. "It is for freedom that Christ has set us free. Stand firm, then, and do not let yourselves be burdened again by a yoke of slavery" (Gal 5:1). Jesus Christ, the God of grace, love, and life, is the founder of a democracy based on human dignity, freedom, and equality. Jesus Christ has given us freedom. Jesus said, "You will know the

The Bible and Christianity Make Our Lives Peaceful and Prosperous

truth, and the truth will set you free" (John 8:32). The apostle Paul also spoke of Christian freedom and love: "You were called to be free. But do not use your freedom to indulge the sinful nature; rather, serve one another in love" (Gal 5:13). Freedom in Christianity means freedom in truth, freedom from sin, and freedom to fulfill God's will. By the Holy Spirit, called by God and Jesus Christ, humans are set free from the yoke of sin. However, true Christian freedom is not the freedom of self-indulgence, which craves human greed and desire out of selfish self-love. The freedom to live in love and peace with our neighbors according to God's will, rather than seeking physical comfort or pleasure, is the true freedom of truth that Jesus wants.

Today's liberal democracies around the world are founded on Christian cultures. Many European countries and the world's most developed nations, such as the United States, United Kingdom, France, Germany, Italy, Canada, Australia, and New Zealand, have Christian cultures. The United States was founded by immigrants from all over the world. Therefore, it is difficult to explain the social phenomenon affected by Christianity in the United States in the same simplified way as in Europe. Korean Christianity is heavily influenced by American Christianity. However, it is now more desirable for Korean Christians to learn European Christianity, especially German Christianity, than American Christianity. This is because there are many similarities between Korea and Germany. Korea and Germany share many similarities in terms of mono-ethnic homogeneity, population, land area, climate (temperate), etc. In particular, they are composed of a single ethnic group, the Han and Germanic peoples respectively. Christian culture has been rooted in Germany for more than two thousand years. German rationality, honesty, reliability, accuracy, and diligence are based on the Bible and Christian culture. Germans neglect their religious life (going to church, worship, prayer, etc.); however, they live a biblical life by faith with practical actions at home and in society according to the Bible and the will of God. German life and all its norms are based on Christian culture. German life is a Christian life. For example, in the Munich region of Bavaria, where traditional German culture is well preserved, people greet each other every day by saying "Grüss Gott" (greetings to God; Guten Tag; good day) and "Gott sei Dank" (thank God; I'm glad). In this way, many everyday terms used by Germans include the word "God." Germans speak and look for "God" in their daily lives. However, Korean Christians seek "God" only in church and forget about "God" in their daily lives outside of church. In Germany, churches are funded by church taxes paid by Christians to

Part II: Understanding Christianity

the government. Priests, pastors, and other clergy are highly respected in German society. Most German universities have a theology department. Students who want to study theology need a letter of recommendation from a priest, professor, or teacher to get into a theology school. In seminary, students learn classical languages such as Latin, Hebrew, and Greek, receive a high-quality theological education, and must pass a state exam (Staatsexamen) to become priests. The church in Germany is a state organization, meaning that pastors and individuals are not allowed to establish their own churches. Most public holidays in Germany are based on major events recorded in the Bible. For example, Good Friday, Easter, Ascension Day, Pentecost, and Christmas are national legal holidays. German political parties, social organization and institutions, festivals, family events (weddings, funerals, etc.), and the names of German people are closely linked to the Bible and Christianity. As such, German life is embedded in a biblically based Christian culture. Churches in Germany are not only used for worship but also as community spaces for citizens.

Those who do the will of God enter the kingdom of God (Matt 7:21). God's will is to do what is right and good in our daily lives of faith. Jesus said, "He that is faithful in that which is least is faithful also in much: and he that is unjust in the least is unjust also in much" (Luke 16:10). There is righteousness in small things. True Christians do seemingly mundane, everyday tasks with sincerity and sweat. God's true will is obeying God and doing the little things we must do every day righteously and faithfully, but not the big things we long to do. The Bible says, "Whatever you do, work at it with all your heart, as working for the Lord, not for men" (Col 3:23). "Whether you eat or drink or whatever you do, do it all for the glory of God" (1 Cor 10:31). Christians do their part in their respective positions for the glory of God. They do not work for their own glory and honor but for the glory of God. Jesus said, "Whoever wants to become great among you must be your servant, and whoever wants to be first must be slave of all" (Mark 10:43–44). Furthermore, we fulfill God's will when we live a life of faith and serve others, selflessly sharing God's love for the common good.

Christians live by God's grace (Acts 13:43). God's Word gives us wisdom for salvation through faith in Jesus (2 Tim 3:15). We are to hear and do what God says in the Bible. Those who live a life of faith according to God's Word are saved by grace and have eternal life. We hear God's voice in every word of God. God's voice is heard by us humans through Jesus, the Son of God. True Christians discern what the good, pleasing, and perfect

The Bible and Christianity Make Our Lives Peaceful and Prosperous

will of God is (Rom 12:2). God's will is treasured up in God's mercy (Rom 12:2). God's will must always be seen in light of God's grace. By coming into contact with Jesus Christ through the Bible, we find God's perfect will in his grace. Grace reigns through righteousness and leads to eternal life by the Lord Jesus Christ (Rom 5:21). This is the age of the Holy Spirit. The Holy Spirit, the Comforter, is God, the Spirit of Truth (John 14:17; 16:13). The Spirit of Truth comes and guides us into all truth (John 16:13). The "Holy Spirit of grace" (Heb 10:29) breathes into us not only living and breathing life but also God's love and grace. By being filled with the Holy Spirit, we are set free from the desires of the flesh, walk by the Spirit, and live in peace and spiritual abundance by faith.

God is a God of love. "Whoever does not love does not know God, because God is love" (1 John 4:8). God's love is poured out into our hearts by the Holy Spirit (Rom 5:5). Grace came through Jesus Christ (John 1:17). While it is important to bring offerings to God, it is more pleasing to God to have compassion for the poor and needy outside of the church and help them with love. God will have mercy on those whom God will have mercy, and God will have compassion on those whom God will have compassion (Rom 9:15). "Blessed are the merciful, for they will be shown mercy" (Matt 5:7). Christians reach out to people with love and mercy in Christ (Phil 2:1–2). They do not do anything out of selfishness or vanity, but in humility, they consider others higher than themselves (Phil 2:3). The Bible says, "Love the Lord your God with all your heart and with all your soul and with all your mind. This is the first and greatest commandment. The second commandment is to love your neighbor as yourself" (Matt 22:37–39). We are not to love one another in word or in tongue but in deeds and truth (1 John 3:18). "These three remain: faith, hope and love. But the greatest of these is love" (1 Cor 13:13). Christianity is a religion of love. "Love is patient, love is kind. It does not envy, it does not boast, it is not proud. It is not rude, it is not self-seeking, it is not easily angered, it keeps no record of wrongs. Love does not delight in evil but rejoices with the truth. It always protects, always trusts, always hopes, always perseveres" (1 Cor 13:4–7). Without love, we are nothing (1 Cor 13:2).

Christians live according to God's will in God (Jesus) for God's glory. Christians who live according to the Bible and God's will have peace and abundance in their lives. This is because when we live according to God's will and word as written in the Bible, we receive God's grace and love in Jesus. Those who have received grace are at peace with God (Luke 1:28).

Part II: Understanding Christianity

God is a God of peace (1 Thess 5:23). "Do not be anxious about anything, but in everything, by prayer and petition, with thanksgiving, present your requests to God. And the peace of God, which transcends all understanding, will guard your hearts and your minds in Christ Jesus" (Phil 4:6–7). When you cast your worries and anxieties on God, peace of mind comes to you. God is a God of mercy and comfort, who comforts us in all our tribulations (2 Cor 1:3–4). God wipes away all tears (Rev 21:4). We receive Jesus Christ to live in him and enjoy a life of joy and grace. Jesus says, "I stand at the door and knock. If anyone hears my voice and opens the door, I will come in and eat with him, and he with me" (Rev 3:20). Like an earthly mother, Jesus Christ is with us and always protects us. "My peace I give you. Do not let your hearts be troubled and do not be afraid" (John 14:27). Several times after his resurrection, Jesus told his disciples, "Peace be with you" (Luke 24:36; John 20:19). Peter and the apostle Paul continued to tell the churches. "Grace to you and peace from God our Father and the Lord Jesus Christ" (Rom 1:7; 1 Cor 1:3; Gal 1:3; Eph 1:2; 1 Pet 1:2).

To be saved, we must be born again from a life of fleshly desires to a life of spiritual faith that follows God's righteousness and truth. The vast majority of modern people do not unfortunately live mentally healthy lives because they are unable to break free from the evil "works of the flesh" (Mark 7:21–23; Gal 5:19–21), which by worldly standards are fornication, theft, murder, adultery, greed, lying, drunkenness, slander, and pride. Worldly people indulge their own desires for worldly pleasures, money, honor, power, and lust. They pursue worldly things, such as a good job, a nice house, a nice car, nice clothes, and good food. However, in the modern world, the outward approval of others, social status, and material abundance do not bring true spiritual peace and happiness to our lives. The Bible says, "Do not love the world or anything in the world. If anyone loves the world, the love of the Father is not in him" (1 John 2:15). Spiritual blessings are given to those of faith who love what is in heaven through God's grace and love. The Bible and Christianity bring spiritual peace and enrichment to our lives. The lives of true Christians who live by practicing love according to God's standards (will) are full of God's grace and blessings. Christians are justified by faith and have peace with God through the Lord Jesus Christ (Rom 5:1). We are at peace as we live in the Lord, and our righteousness and goodness are eternal. The God of hope fills us with joy and peace in faith, so that we may abound in hope by the power of the Holy Spirit (Rom 15:13). Christians work in hope and fulfill their assignments.

The Bible and Christianity Make Our Lives Peaceful and Prosperous

He who plows the field works in hope, and he who threshes the grain works in hope that he will get his share (1 Cor 9:10). Our hopes are fulfilled by grace in a loving God, and our daily life of faith will always be peaceful and spiritually enriched with gratitude and joy.